VICOMTE

To Nadine and Clio:
Thank you for a life rocket ride so far

To Bambou, our loyal Eurasian:
Thanks for keeping me Zen throughout the writing

Foreword

Marketing isn't rocket science. You do it every day in your connections with family, friends and business colleagues. It comes naturally in how you connect, communicate and influence others, every day.

Where it gets complicated is when you don't know the other person personally. When you're trying to influence, build trust, connect and communicate, simply and quickly, with more than one person, potentially across multiple cultures. To convince them to buy your product or service. This is where marketing gets really interesting—where it requires a lot more art, science and discipline to deliver sustainable pricing power.

Marketing should be fun, and not feared. CEOs and general managers should not treat marketing as a black hole, where you feel out of your depth with the verbal gymnastics of marketing speak. You have your CFO to explain the P&L balance sheet and cashflow to you in simple terms. You find it easy to understand, because it's all grounded in income, expense, assets and liabilities—all tangible items. You can actually do the same with your CMO. Marketing is common sense. Just like finance is. Both have rational and emotional components.

CEOs often miss the point that marketing drives the key part of your business that builds relationships and trust with others. Great marketing requires the right structure to think through this. This book really helps with a framework of 8 fundamentals to be discussed and considered with your leadership team when building brands. The checklists and models in the book are extremely useful as a self-analysis and conversation starter. It takes something that can be seen as subjective, to something that is built on principle, fact, insight and market realities. It helps to discuss on a very strategic level, internally and externally with investors and stakeholders. It also works on a more tactical level. You discuss a piece of work, but keep an eye on the broader brand business context. The idea is your marketing dialogue becomes a more structured discussion, versus a subjective *like or dislike* control game.

During my time together with Chris at The Coca-Cola Company in Europe, we successfully built brand businesses together. I proudly remember our design and launch of the original Coke Zero, first in the UK and then rapidly across Europe. It started a long-lasting transformation of the full Coke Trademark portfolio, and became a major success for the company worldwide. It is great to see his broader thinking and experience, clearly crystallized in this book, years later—provocatively painted against the galactic backdrop of Space Race 2.0.

This is a book that you will pick up, read and use more than once!

Michael A. Clarke
CEO, Treasury Wines Estates

TWE (tweglobal.com) is one of the world's largest wine companies, listed on the Australian Securities Exchange (ASX). Through world-class winemaking and brand marketing, TWE is focused on meeting evolving consumer interests across the globe, and on delivering sustainable growth. Everything we do is dedicated to realizing our vision of becoming the world's most celebrated wine company.

Table of Contents

α^{M}

Once you have tasted flight, you will forever walk the earth with your eyes turned skyward, for there you have been, and there you will always long to return.

Leonardo Da Vinci[1]

Why this book, and how to best navigate it?

CEOs of marketing-driven companies today need their teams to master an ever more complex consumer information and decision funnel, from awareness to final sale. They need to constantly rethink what customer service was/is/will be about, in a world where decisions are increasingly driven by bots and algorithms. The path and storyline from first contact to conversion is more challenging than ever. As things stand, it will only get even faster and more complex, until AI possibly takes over completely.

By virtue of my marketing consultancy, teaching, and continued active portfolio investing and operating roles in startups and scale-ups around the world, I remain reasonably in tune with most of the latest (digital) tool developments in the marketing field. However, what worries me deeply is that these new digital marketing tools are starting to reframe the beliefs of many CMOs and CEOs around the fundamentals of marketing. Even top marketers say they have *no more time* to do the right long-term things. Under the pretext of *social listening*, they are *busy* reacting to the next *tweet*, the next *post*, the next *like*. Many investors, boards, company leaders and their ever younger marketing teams start confusing the use of the fast-changing tools with mastery of the fundamentals of marketing discipline. Tools are tools. Marketing is much more than mastery of digital skills and m-e-commerce, especially as people increasingly lose trust in whatever lives on *fake* social media.

Silicon snake oil **starts to undermine CEOs' and boards'
deep understanding of marketing fundamentals.**

The above insight got me slightly frustrated. And curious. Why and how did we as marketers let things get this far out of hand? We can never forget what purpose great marketing truly serves. So, as a positive reaction, my ambition is to offer CEOs and their top teams a simple yet modernized set of blueprints to (re)discover the *fundamentals* of modern marketing, all while helping to progress their thinking beyond the frameworks of the last decades. Let's create what I will call *renaissance brands* for the new Galactic Age, balancing understanding of the latest digital tools with respect for all the fundamentals of the art, science and discipline of marketing.

The CMO leads the marketing function. The CFO leads the finance function. They both technically lead their respective functions. However, in the end, it is the CEO who sets the overall tone. The everyday priority of CEOs is creating sustainable business growth. Focus on the bottom line—*and* on the top line. To make that happen, structurally connecting marketing better with finance is proving one of the biggest challenges.

- How can I support my CMO and CFO to build a world-class marketing capability using scalable, repeatable models generating sustainable pricing power on my key brands?

- How to keep my brand (portfolio) and corporate brand relevant to ever new generations?

- Everybody tells me *be digital*. How can I avoid *Silicon snake oil tools* clouding my company's focus on the *fundamentals* of marketing art, science and discipline? What are those fundamentals anyway?

- Last but not least, how to sell my current and future level of marketing excellence to my board, to investors, and to stakeholders, while everything around me exponentially changes?

Success in marketing is often referred to as "*marketing miracles.*" I deliberately put miracles between inverted columns. Miracles are great. People want to believe in miracles. They crave them. However, there is much more rocket science behind marketing than CEOs and investors are aware of. If you follow the right marketing playbook, the probability to create *alpha*—miraculous extraordinary returns in finance speak—is much higher. Not guaranteed, but much higher. Think of marketing miracle*$, with a $ sign at the end.*

I am not a rocket scientist, nor an alchemist promising to turn lead into gold. I *am* an experienced consumer scientist with a passion for aviation, for space and for the future. As I found out, there is a fascinating world at the crossing of marketing, finance and space. A story not yet told, and relevant to help solve the dilemmas outlined above. I started to share and test new thinking in my post-corporate professional life over the last six years, and finally put it all together in this book. I owe a great deal to fellow senior marketers, business partners and consultancy clients, and especially to my (executive) students and fellow faculty at the TRIUM Global EMBA for having encouraged me to do so.

There are a handful of marketing core concepts, and a bit of jargon, that every protagonist touching brands should really understand, starting with the board and the CEO. They are necessary to truly appreciate the power of marketing, regardless of the times we live in. This book is all about helping business to (re)appreciate the core components of a powerful marketing capability, packaged in some simple, fresh and future-centric language. It will also introduce language and models that should help finance-oriented people and investors to make better bets on marketing or brand-driven companies. Capital will be more smartly used by the most deserving brands.

In July 2019, humankind celebrates 50 years since the first Moon landing. Driven by Branson, Bezos and Musk, and other new rock(et) star billionaires, Space Race 2.0 is generating a massive new investment and consumer change cycle no business marketer can afford to miss out on. To benefit from its transformative impact over the next 50 years, companies need to urgently upgrade all prevailing marketing and finance mindsets and models. Most date back 50+ years, to the Space Race 1.0 of the Sixties.

The models and blueprints contained in this book will help all protagonists in the business of building brands today *and* tomorrow:

- CEOs, their boards, and their CXO colleagues, regardless whether they run *Main Street* brands interested in becoming galactic, or *Space Brands* interested to connect better with main street.

- Wall Street and investors at large, including government agencies investing our tax dollars, on how to successfully pick the sustainable brand winners of the galactic age.

- Business students of all ages, from undergrad to grad school to EMBAs, interested in a galactic career (and ditto life).

Strap yourself in, as you will go for a rocket ride, organized in 4 stages:

Stage 1
Look Up: Adopt a New Galactic Mindset

Marketing and Finance are *both* Mars and Venus. Understand the impact and transformative power of the last 50 and next 50 years of Space. Start thinking beyond the historical *think local, act local* and *think global, act global*, towards a new unifying mindset that raises the bar: *Think Galactic, Act Galactic.*

Stage 2
Launch Preparation: Secure Basics Before You Fly

In flight, safety always comes first. Get your business marketing wings before you skyrocket. A crash course in the key marketing models for the CEO and CFO. A quick study of the one finance model each CMO should know. Also, understand the limits of models, and why people in the end crave miracles.

Stage 3
Lift-off: Successful Marketing in a Galactic Age

Discover Burggraeve's 8 fundamental drivers of world class marketing capability (MC), expressed in a simple and memorable rocket metaphor: the **MC-Rocket©**. Build a sustainable brand business for the new Space Age.

As a CEO, how can I better assess and explain my level of marketing excellence internally and externally? How can investors pick the best marketing-driven companies? Discover an advanced concept for a new-to-the-world marketing excellence and rating model: **Alpha M™**. Complete with its **(downloadable) checklist audit,** it will help investors assess and compare marketing capability excellence between companies to pick galactic winners. Over time, the model can even help *predict* top-line growth.

This book is not for people with a fear of heights, for people afraid of testing new limits, or for those just not interested at all in anything related to space discovery. For all you bold people, may this book become your hitchhiker guide through a new marketing and finance galaxy. I will not talk about the marketing *jungle* or *black box* here. I will use space language. I will try to help light escape from the *black hole* of marketing finance (thank you, Stephen Hawking).

The MC-Rocket© and Alpha M ™,
will increase the *probability*
of more marketing miracle$
in the new galactic age.

Miracle$ as such are never guaranteed. The thinking in this book helped yield results both at big global companies and at some new scale-ups. The blueprints are built on a mix of personal practice and theory (see *About the Author*).

The writing of this book is not intended to win awards for brilliant prose. The narrative is kept simple, presented in snackable formats, with tables and side bars, and spiced up with a touch of edutainment. To accommodate how you prefer to read, there will be a print and an e-book version. Where possible, broadly accessible English-language sources have been used. The key visuals and schematics are copyrighted and trademarked, yet downloadable for free on your mobile or laptop from my website. You are welcome to play with them. We intended to service the busy experiential mind in search of some new learning and practical, customizable, personal application. I share both general as well as personal stories and examples. I apologize in advance if you think I am losing myself in a few musings and personal opinions. In true renaissance spirit, you are welcome to wholeheartedly (dis)agree with them, and reach out to me for a constructive debate (see below how).

Last, as a marketer, I believe in the emotional appeal and beauty of a product. This book has been craftily designed by "chef" Christian Loos from KitchenNYC (see: *About the designer*). Also, learning can be multisensorial. If you want to get in the right mood while you read this book, connect on **Spotify** to my specially curated *free* list covering **Rockets, Space and the Universe.**

Welcome aboard the incredible business and societal opportunities generated by the new Galactic Age. A big thank you for being here. Fasten your seatbelts, please. Let's make marketing miracle$ happen.

Chris R. Burggraeve
New York, Q4 2018

vicomte.com/galactic
@ChrisBurggraeve

Stage 1
LOOK UP: ADOPT A NEW GALACTIC MINDSET

Jargon seems to be the place where left and right brain meet.

Wendy Kaminer

Chapter 1
Marketing and Finance are both Mars and Venus.

The roles of the CEO and CFO are generally well understood. When it comes to the CMO, many investors and business leaders tend to be much more vague. Finance tends to be perceived as rational, and marketing as emotional. If a CEO wants to succeed in the galactic age, start with debunking the old perceptions. Marketing and finance are both Mars and Venus.

What is marketing? What do marketers do? What should they do? These days, anybody can just ask: Siri or Alexa.

Alexa's answer: Marketing is the study and management of exchanged relationships.

Siri's answer: The same first sentence as Alexa. However, on the mobile she elaborates on the definition, and refers you to Wikipedia. Hmmmm. Time to update Wikipedia?

I always ask students in class, or participants in a workshop, that same basic question. Based on the typical answers, and based on who is in the room, two groups always emerge: those that are in marketing, and those who would identify as non-marketers (almost everybody else).

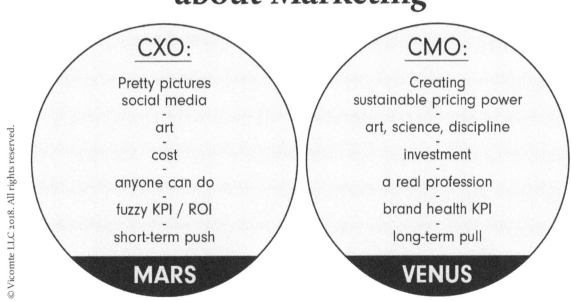

The wrong perception
about Marketing

CXO:

Pretty pictures
social media
-
art
-
cost
-
anyone can do
-
fuzzy KPI / ROI
-
short-term push

MARS

CMO:

Creating
sustainable pricing power
-
art, science, discipline
-
investment
-
a real profession
-
brand health KPI
-
long-term pull

VENUS

© Vicomte LLC 2018. All rights reserved.

Marketing people tend to place themselves on Venus, the planet that stands for emotional connections. The other group places themselves on Mars, the planet for people that drive a cool and fact-based bargain. They tend to see marketing as a black box, a jungle. In planetary terms, marketing is perceived as a black hole, a place in space, according to NASA, where gravity pulls so strong even light cannot get out. In CFO language, a place where people or things, like money, disappear without a trace.

As this book will demonstrate, nothing is further from the truth. It is high time to debunk this persistent myth. Marketing is both Venus and Mars. Vice versa, the ugly truth is there is as much emotion in finance as there is in marketing, if not more. Finance is both Mars and Venus too, while marketing can be much more fact- and process-driven than finance leaders know or believe. There is plenty of method in the best marketer's perceived madness. And as we will see later in the book, some madness is actually strategically necessary to make miracle$ possible.

As a proof point of how emotional Finance can be, just look how mergers & acquisitions tend to play out. If there ever was an emotional game of chicken, this is it. The practice is covered in a veil of constantly changing numbers and charts. It is a drama in secret offices, led by high-powered world of investment bankers and corporate lawyers. There are press leaks and boardroom brawls. Analysts who smell blood have a shark fest. The eventual financial decisions get wrapped up in a mythical aura of fact-based, rational decision making, superbly spun towards stakeholders on why it all makes so much strategic sense. The seller will celebrate why the price was the best one ever. The buyer will show why the deal made supreme sense: how the sum of the parts works so magically—and *look at these synergies…* Yet here is the sobering and well proven statistic every finance major gets taught at university:

> **>80% of M&A fails to create lasting value[1].**
> **So who is emotional, and who is rational?**

The facts are indisputable. M&A is a financial minefield. Still, the M&A train rolls on. Why? Because the CEO and CFO love this area naturally. It is their comfort zone. It can build careers faster. It is tempting as a shortcut to success, under intense pressure. Investors value and reward the behavior—until the party ends and they move on. It is usually much easier for CEOs and for CFOs to buy a brand and show some form of ROI, than for the CMO to show the value of building a real brand organically over time. The people who truly build brands over time are often referred to as *a 10- to 20-year overnight sensation.* Few people have stamina and patience for that. Just ask founders and entrepreneurs. They know how hard it is to Finish Big[2]. A sale transforms their lives. They deserve the premium—if they can get it.

Don't get me wrong. I actually believe, and have lived many times, how selective M&A *has* its place in the CEO toolbox. It *can* transform a company or industry. Still, no major company can rely on M&A only to be successful over a long time. Organic growth capabilities matter over time. Yes, it is much harder, but it is doable, if done in the right way. Organic growth is so much harder than inorganic growth. However, despite the evidence on the corporate side, *hunting* is still perceived as easier and more effective and efficient than *farming*, and rewarded more short term.

Hunters versus Farmers

The above planet table shows an issue I would like to explore a little further. Korn Ferry's CMO Pulse (2018) illustrates the disconnect between CMO and CXO, stating *nearly 30% of CEOs don't understand the CMO role*[3]. If one does the same exercise for other functions, asking about the role of leaders in finance or manufacturing or sales, the answers are much closer. The planets seem to be aligned much more. Whoever or whatever is to blame for this discrepancy does not matter. What matters is to understand where the perception gap in marketing comes from, and how we might close it again. If marketers claim their role is to impact brand health (behavior and perception) to create ever stronger pricing power, it is time to bridge the perception gap for the function overall.

Marketing *has* to acknowledge that as a function, it may have lost a clear definition and positioning itself. I started to see it during my later years as a senior corporate marketer. It really became apparent after I started my consultancy, serving mostly non-CPG firms, and during my teaching to both marketers and non-marketers. Marketers deserve a lot of the responsibility for having let this disconnect happen. Especially since the advent of everything digital, and since the rise of social media, there seems to be collective confusion as to what marketing is really about. We allowed marketing to be reframed and narrowed to a programmatic social media black box, filled with jargon nobody understands anymore. *Silicon snake oil* pushed out (marketing) leadership's understanding and focus on marketing fundamentals.

The anecdotal and survey evidence above seems to translate in tenure. The most popular proxy for the issue may be the average **CMO** career longevity. Mind you, longer tenure does not necessarily automatically equate to adding more value, nor to real legacy creation. But it is a good starting point. In senior marketing roles, little structural work can be done if you are only 2 years in the role. You can score some campaign hits and start big capability moves, yet 3-4 years is a minimum to start anchoring real potential legacy moves. In my view, one can see a CMO's true track record appear only after 4-5 years, especially if we are talking bigger companies. That is where you can start to see the tangible impact of marketing excellence driving sustainable pricing power.

Few CMOs get this far. Since 2004, executive search consultant Spencer Stuart has been tracking CMO tenure[4]. It went up from just shy of 2 years (23.6 months) in 2004, to a peak of 4 years (48 months, 2014), to the end of 44 months in 2017. The survey covers only about 100 of the top US most advertised brands as the of end December 2017. Despite being a narrow sample, it created a clear perception around the role. And perception is reality, rule number one in marketing.

Oscar Wilde already taught us *beauty is in the eye of the beholder*. The survey results are always amplified and exacerbated in the business press, not in the least by the advertising industry. They hope to either defend their incumbent role, or to break in with the new CMO. With each passing year, this tiny US sample cemented the perception that CMO roles are only for dare-devils with a kamikaze-like tolerance for pressure. Given the expectations to perform in no time, this surely must be a role only for super heroes. Only Supermen and Wonder Women should apply.

In contrast, **CEO** tenure is getting longer, according to Equilar Inc., another executive search firm. Based on their 2016 study for CNN among S&P 500 companies, average CEO tenure grew from 6.6 years in 2004 to 8.1 years in 2015. More CEOs than ever even seem to pass the 10-year hurdle. So, simplifying, CEOs last on average easily more than twice as long as their CMOs.

And what about the **CFO**? According to Korn Ferry Institute's latest tracking (2017), the CFO is the longest-tenured C-suite member behind the CEO at an average of 5.1 years. Their numbers show the CMO average at 4.1 years, with a range from 3.1 years (life sciences) to 5.1 years (financial services). In their sample, CMOs tenure at CPG (Consumer Packaged Goods) is on average 36 months, 6 months below the 42 months of Spencer Stuart's top 100 sample.

The average CEO outlasts their CMO more than twice

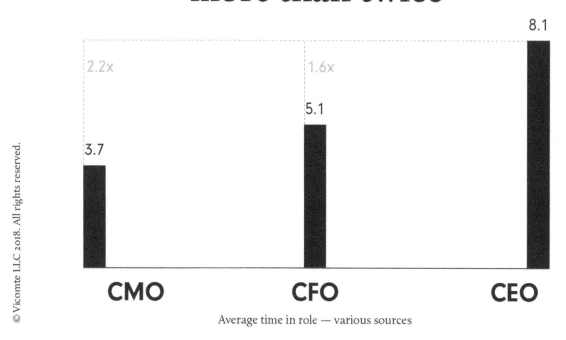

Average time in role — various sources

I started to look for a rationale behind these relative differences in tenure. There are number of plausible ones. A 2017 HBR article attributed it to poor job design in the first place: CEOs are not clear about what they expect from their CMO[5], but the issue may be deeper than that. Do CEOs even know what to expect from their CMO in the first place, to ensure a decent job design is possible? Here is a mid-2012 study among 1200 companies by the UK-based The Fournaise Marketing Group. It stated boldly: *80% of CEOs do not really trust marketers and are not impressed by the work they do*. And even better (or worse): *in comparison, 90% of the same CEOs do trust and value the opinion and work of CFOs and CIOs*.

Obviously the Fournaise research group was just stirring the pot to get some awareness for their own marketing performance consulting services. Nothing wrong with that as such. Congrats on a clever campaign. Except that the line that lived on in the broader press was the one above, and not the rest of the report headline that added: *...except if they are ROIMarketers(R)*[6]. The last word was a made up and copyrighted one by Fournaise. We will come back to that.

There are counterexamples defying these rather depressing observations and statistics, but indeed they may be more of the exception than the rule. Jim Stengel was CMO at the world's largest advertiser P&G from 01 to 08, succeeded by Chief Brand Officer Marc Pritchard since then. Keith Weed leads Unilever since 2010. I was CMO for nearly 5 years at AB InBev (07-12). My successor at AB InBev, Miguel Patricio, was there for about 6 years before his successor Pedro Earp started.

It would actually be great to meet the CEOs that were interviewed by Fournaise. It would help to understand better what they were expecting from their CMO and from marketing in general in the first place. There is an old Chinese saying: *the fish rots from the head*. If CEOs would indeed make such bold claims, what does it say about *their* ability to clearly state what they really wanted from their CMO in the first place, and how they helped him or her to be successful at delivering on that brief?

To that end, there is no shortage of advice on the profile of *The CMO of the Future*, handily written up by leading executive search companies. I invite all of you to google and compare. As an example, Caren Fleit from Korn Ferry will take you on a practical time travel from 1950 to 2010+, highlighting the changing needs per decade[7]. She ends her observations with the provocative statement "*Most CMOs now sit on executive committees and report directly to the CEO. But there is confusion about the role, leading some to question the title and explore alternatives like chief customer officer, chief customer experience officer, and chief growth officer.*"

Her sentiment is echoed in CMO circles. LinkedIn has an active CMO Network, sharing all kinds of best practices. In an October 2017 article *The CMO mess and how we can clean it up*, fellow CMO Jennifer Korn argued similar points on the mismatch between CEO expectations and CMO real authority, on technology resulting in a mind-boggling range of expected new duties for this poor CMO, and on unclear short-term (lead-generation) versus long-term (branding) priorities[8]. Many colleagues chimed in. My friend *agent provocateur* Joe Jaffe called it the *Chief Muddled Officer* at some point. It felt like a self-help shrink couch for CMOs. My conclusion was twofold:

- There is no standard expectation list for a CMO, as opposed to for the CEO or for the CFO.

- CMOs need to be rocket scientists creating marketing miracle$, preferably in two years or less.

This book will address both of these issues, and proactively deal with the key takeaway of the Fournaise report. The thinking and models presented should help close the disconnect between marketers and the business model they are supposed to serve.

Two Planets?

It is hard to admit, but this incredible disconnect has existed for a long time, even in the best companies. Rudy Moenaert is a distinguished professor of strategic marketing at Tias School of Business & Society in the Netherlands. We both received our Master Marketer award in 2011 from the Belgian Association of Marketing, and have occasionally been comparing notes on marketing (and on soccer)[9]. In his latest book on the personal leadership traits of senior marketers, he shared a telling anecdote. Asking a room of presumably high-level marketers if they knew what the *EBIT* abbreviation stood for, there was only... silence[10].

My own realization of this shocking marketing-finance disconnect came early in my career. A few years into brand management roles at P&G back in the early Nineties. As one of the top schools in marketing, P&G was (is?) known to have lots of its senior management come up thru the marketing ranks. To attract talent, the company would tell its new brand managers they always needed to act as the general managers of their brand. They were responsible for their *Brand P&L*. Whilst that may have been true as an idea, I found out that mindset was not really alive in practice (see the special sidebar below). The idea to write this book one day may have been born then.

Marketing is Finance is Business

The first P&G brand I worked on as *assistant brand manager* in the early Nineties was top global brand **Pampers**. Upon promotion to *brand manager*, I got two areas to take care of. My main responsibility was running Belgium's leading new liquid detergent, a brand called **Vizir**. The second project was to run the core laundry and cleaning innovation pipeline. Then, in a weird twist, P&G added a third area: to turn around a juice drink called **Punica**.

Punica was a storied German juice drink brand in returnable glass bottles. P&G Europe had bought it as part of a global strategy to become a major global player in the *healthy drinks* category. P&G wanted to double in size every 10 years, which meant generating growth at +7% annually. Healthy soft drinks had been a category identified to fit P&G's

corporate growth plans. In the US, similar ambitions existed for a brand called **Sunny Delight**.

In classic P&G detergent *shock and awe* style, the launch team in Belgium had sampled one in three households, and designed an intense TV campaign inviting kids (and moms) to join *The Punica Oasis*. A vintage P&G launch playbook at that time. Punica quickly achieved a high double-digit share in the juice (drink) category, rocking **Minute Maid's** world. However, market leader Coke was not about to let P&G enter one of its core categories without a fight. It realized full well that if this door would open in juice drinks, they could face a new deep-pocketed CPG enemy, beside the classic PepsiCo nemesis.

The gloves came off. Coke started to fight back on all fronts, focusing on Punica's health claims as a possible Achilles heel. The drink faced sudden (unfounded) claims that it was actually bad for kids, and that the sweeteners could cause cancer. A reputation battle ensued, and the consumer watchdogs and media smelled blood. After its meteoric rise, caught in this unexpected crossfire, Punica took an equally meteoric nosedive. And there it was: *Chris, can you please turn around this brand?*

Of course, in our youthful hubris, as brand and finance teams we thought we were invincible. Clever marketing and smart financial re-engineering would fix this, indeed. As a team we went ahead: new consumer work, new concept testing, changing parameters (like packaging from returnable to consumer-preferred tetra packs), new campaigns to regain trust (in pre-internet age, mind you). We started to regain share. There was hope again.

A brand manager is the general manager of his brand

However, even as we started to regain momentum, it increasingly became clear that, in mathematical finance terms, we were trying to solve a linear program model with too many constraints. After running about 75 scenarios over many long pizza nights, my finance counterpart and I concluded there was no way this brand would ever make economic sense in Belgium. With trepidation, I finally decided to recommend my then General Manager close the business. P&G had always told us since day one of being hired: *you are the GM of the brands we entrust to you.* As a responsible brand manager feeling accountable for its P&L, I recommended we move scarce investment money to more financially rewarding brands in detergents and cleaners.

The GM categorically refused. He was probably not eager to displease the P&G European president at that time. His boss had been the one to buy that business, and championed its European expansion. I learned an important lesson then: country managers don't like to bring a region president bad news. I will never forget his direct answer though: *you are not in the business of killing brands.* I was stunned. I thought we were in the business of delighting consumers and making money for shareholders. Not much later, I left P&G for a pioneering finance-driven brand role with The Coca-Cola Company in Eastern Europe. Punica Belgium muddled on, wasting more investment. The brand was withdrawn a few years later.

If you flip the image to the other side, and ask marketers to describe finance people, other extreme images emerge. During the exuberant Eighties, the term *yuppies* was invented: *young urban professionals* with a rather flashy lifestyle. David Mamet created the play *Glengarry Glen Ross* (1983), dramatizing how far a group of Chicago-based real estate brokers would go to survive. Tom Wolfe wrote his satirical *Bonfire of the Vanities* (1987), masterfully depicting the fall of the self-declared Masters of the Universe on Wall Street.

More movies and TV shows kept coming: *Wall Street* (1987), *The Wolf of Wall Street* (2013), *Billions* (2015), all cementing the cynical image of not only Wall Street, but also of the people who supposedly should regulate it. They all are depicted as ready to get rich at whatever cost, with disdain for retail clients and their financial well-being. "Greed is good" became legend. And whilst Wall Street is getting more regulated and a bit more careful, the Master of the Universe excesses seem to have moved east. Chinese sell-side analysts seem to be willing to go very far to win the analyst of the year award, including unacceptable gifting, inappropriate use of social media, etc. Wall Street, the Asian sequel?[11]

Mars is Venus

As fascinated as we all seem to be with the dark side of haute finance, it is a rather well working money allocation market in the first place. One that marketers ignore at their peril, just as CXOs ignore the consumer at their peril. Aside being obsessed with consumers and branding, business marketers need to be obsessed with the current and future business model of the company they work for. They need to intimately understand how successful the external world perceives that business model to be. Analyst reports should be required reading for any marketer at any level of seniority.

In *Arrival* (2016), the critically acclaimed movie, actress Amy Adams plays an expert linguist who patiently deciphers the symbols and language of the aliens that seem to threaten world peace. The movie is a bit of a mind bender, but she finds a clever way to bridge the left and right brains involved, to make Mars meet Venus. The foundational theory behind the split brain was developed in the early space age Sixties by Caltech cognitive neuroscientists Richard Sperry (Nobel Prize

1981) and Michael Gazzaniga. For years since, you have heard about fights between *the head* and *the heart*. People were easily classified as either/or. Marketers were the heart, the creatives, the right-brain people. Finance people became the head, the analytical nerds, the left-brain people. As it turns out, these easy classifications are just part of our desire to create shortcuts that serve our mental models or arguments.

Over recent years, more and more academic evidence debunked the myth of people being either/or[12]. We are all both Mars and Venus. If we chose to be. Unless the marketer chooses to learn about the difference between a P&L, a balance sheet, and a cashflow statement, they should never become a senior marketing leader, let alone CMO or CEO[13]. Any marketer who has never heard of DCF, or thinks of alpha and beta as just old Greek alphabet letters or fraternities/sororities, can never be a business marketer. Investors should not bet on their companies. Vice versa for CFOs. Learn the fundamentals of marketing before you aspire to become CEO. Just being an M&A and treasury or accounting wiz should not cut it. Any CEO/CFO will seriously benefit from further perusing this book. Your current CMO will appreciate the frank conversation after. For CEOs, your next CMO hire will be a much better one.

Marketing is not brand management for the sake of brand management. I passionately love brands, but as I said before: they are a means to an end, not an end it itself. Marketing was, and is, all about creating sustainable pricing power on the brand or brand portfolio you are entrusted, so you can grow the franchise profitably over time. In Chapter 15 (Business Marketers) we will explore the CMO role much more in depth. As a starter, here is my simple definition for a successful CMO:

The (galactic) CMO inspires all internal and external stakeholders,
to deliver *sustainable pricing power* across the brand portfolio over time

That requires art, science and discipline. A relentless focus on what I will refer to as *Burggraeve's 8 Fundamentals*, is the focus of stage 3 of this book. Marketing is much more about finance than most marketers know, or even want to believe. Vice versa, finance is much more about marketing than many finance leaders know, or want to believe. Both CMO and CFO should be like a crab with two very developed claws, not just with one.

CMOs are (and should act as) the GMs of the brands and categories they lead. CFOs finance the brands. Galactic CEOs are business marketers themselves, bringing the best out of CMOs and CFOs. They know jargon matters: Marketing *is* Finance *is* Business. Marketing and finance are both Mars and Venus.

The hardest part is leaving Earth behind.

Kim Stanley Robinson

Chapter 2
Mars is the new Moon

Apollo 11 landed on the Moon in that iconic Summer of '69. The 12th and last man set foot on the Moon in 1972. The key marketing and finance concepts we use today were mostly developed in that *Space Race 1.0* era. Then we witnessed an exponential rise of urbanization and globalization, defining marketing and finance today. With *Space Race 2.0* a new reality, why can business marketers and investors not afford to miss out?

From October 2018 through December 2022, NASA will mark the 50th anniversary of the Apollo Program that landed a dozen Americans on the moon between July 1969 and December 1972. Around 400,000 people helped make 33 spaceflights happen, including the six that reached the lunar surface. Neil Armstrong declared his first step on the Moon from the ladder of the Eagle lander on July 20, 1969, to be *one small step for a man, one giant leap for mankind. First Man* (2018), starring Ryan Gosling, celebrates one of humankind's most daring achievements.

Depending on whose definition you follow, to date, the number of people have been in space or in an orbit around Earth is between 553 and 562[1]. Only 12 of them walked on the Moon, and the last Moon landing was in 1972. They collectively spent over 29,000 days or about 77 years space. Eugene Cernan (died January 2017), the last man to walk on the Moon, famously said that *We will be back.* Unlike Schwarzenegger's *Terminator* (1984), who already made good on a similar promise, humankind has not been back yet. In a later interview, Cernan would go further:

> *"It was the press who was saying we've been to the Moon,*
> *so what are we going to do now?*
> *We've done that, and that was pretty easy.*
> *So, where to now, Columbus?*[2]*"*

The original Apollo emblem, adopted by the program in 1965, used renderings of the Moon and Earth linked by a double trajectory to reflect President John F. Kennedy's lofty ambition of *putting a man on the Moon and returning him safely to the earth* by the end of the 1960s.

In June 2018, NASA unveiled its official logo to celebrate these milestone anniversaries. The Apollo 50th anniversary logo aims to bridge the past 50 years with the new NASA mission, sometimes referred to as *Space 2.0*. It depicts NASA's vision for the next half-century of deep space exploration. NASA is working to return astronauts to the Moon to test technologies and techniques for the next giant leaps: Mars and beyond.

The arc through the word Apollo represents Earth's horizon, as seen from a spacecraft[3]. It serves as a reminder of how the first views of Earth from the Moon forever transformed the way we see ourselves as human beings. It affirms NASA's intention to continue pushing the boundaries of knowledge. And it delivers on the promise of American ingenuity and leadership in deep space.

The advancement of cutting edge space innovation relies on more people having access to the Moon. As will be discussed in Chapter 3, this increased access is made possible by private sector investment on top of renewed government commitment. Space is following the development of the modern airline industry. Following pioneers like Lindbergh and the Wright Brothers, commercial space travel unlocked its real potential. According to the new breed of *astropreneurs*[4], the American government had been too slow. President Obama shared this sentiment during his one major speech on space back on April 15, 2010. In that keynote, he diplomatically suggested that while going back to the Moon would be valuable, it could be only be a milestone of a much larger ambition[5]:

"I just have to say pretty bluntly here:
we've been there before...
There's a lot more space to explore,
and a lot more to learn when we do."

Urbanization

As we will see in detail in part 2, many of the most critical concepts and frameworks developed in marketing and finance stem from this Space 1.0 time. Over the last 40+ years, two major drivers shaped the world of marketing and finance even more: urbanization and globalization.

Planet Earth is preparing to deal with many more people. They live in more and ever bigger cities, as urbanization continues to increase. By 2025, McKinsey Global Institute expects two billion people, 25% of a 10Bn+ global population, to live in the 600 biggest cities, accounting for US$ 64 trillion or 60+% of global GDP[6]. All mayors of megacities are regularly coming together to share best practice and ideas on how to keep megacities vibrant and livable. Big cities keep iterating new greener and greater visions for the future, like New York's PlaNYC 2030[7]. Megacities may even de facto replace nations in our lifetime[8].

New companies like Sidewalk Labs, an Alphabet subsidiary, are not only helping cities to reinvent themselves today (like Toronto), but are intent to build and test new ones[9]. Not to be outdone, Bill Gates, via his Cascade Investment Group, acquired a stake in a 24,800-acre of desert land development 45 minutes outside Phoenix, called Belmont, for about US$ 80 million[10] in 2017. The plan is to build a new smart city and tech-driven forward-thinking community from scratch, consisting of 80,000 homes, 3,800 acres of industrial, office, retail space, and 470 acres for public schools, leaving about 3,400 acres of open land. It sounds like Henry David Thoreau's Walden Pond mixed with a modern Thomas More Tech Utopia.

As the population grows, doom prophets predict that food shortages and other calamities will threaten humanity's existence. These prophets famously include people like the English political economist Robert Malthus (1798), and the influential Club of Rome think tank (1968). Armageddon has been predicted time and time again, but has never truly materialized. In *Factfulness* (2018) and TED talks, the late Swedish physician and statistician Hans Rosling taught us all to go back to the *facts*, to (re)shape our true perceptions about the miracle of progress and the true state of the world[11].

Somehow, at least to date, humankind has always found a way to break through Earth's limitations. The drivers were survival instinct, ingenuity, a sense of urgency, and an *abundance* mindset, advocated by the likes of Peter Diamandis[12]. People can and do learn to live differently. Vertical farming solutions from new companies like Aerofarms are tackling fresh food supplies in ingenious ways[13]. In 2012, the economic and social *Doughnut model* was launched, aiming to solve humanity's 21st-century challenge to meet the needs of all within the means of the planet. It is designed to help us think how to best balance *individual needs* to never fall short on life's essentials (food, housing, healthcare, political voice, etc.), with our *collective responsibility* to avoid we overdoing our pressure on Earth's life-supporting fundamental systems (e.g. a stable climate, fertile soils and a protective ozone layer)[14].

Globalization

While cities became megacities, a number of local brands became global brands. In terms of marketing and branding, modern marketers evolved their mindset from *no/limited marketing*, to *Think local, Act local*, to *Think global, Act global*. The idea of *globalization* took the world by storm over the last 30 – 40 years, impacting all aspects of our lives. As with all major disruptions and movements, like the digital change, globalization came with many benefits at first. The downsides materialized slowly over time. There have been many perceived winners, but there have also increasingly been perceived losers.

Think Global, Act Global: 40+ years of Global Branding

These are must reads (still) relevant for anybody developing world-class brands today, albeit in a more complex and less flat world than in the last decades or centuries. Globalization has been a concept around since at least 1000 years. If you are brave enough, browse this excellent historical review:

2009 - Power and Plenty: Trade, War, and the World Economy in the Second Millennium (Ronald Findlay & Kevin O'Rourke)

The recent globalization phase we refer to in this book is the marketing-related one that started in the early Eighties. During the first 10 years of the wave, everybody was focused more on its *what* and *how*. In the last 3 decades since then however, there is more existential discussion on the deeper *why*, and on the *who* (benefits) of globalization. It redefined the *what* & the *how* as a result.

Focus: What & How

1983 - The Globalization of Markets (Theodore Levitt)

1983 - Big Business Blunders: Mistakes in Multinational Marketing (David Ricks)

1985 - Triad Power: The Coming Shape of Global Competition (Kenichi Ohmae)

1989 - Managing Across Borders: The Transnational Solution (Christopher Bartlett & Samantha Ghoshal)

1991 - International Dimensions of Organizational Behavior (Nancy Adler)

Focus: Why & Who - impacting What & How

1997 - Has Globalization Gone Too Far? (Dani Rodrik)

2004 - Why Globalization Works (Martin Wolf)

2005 - The World is Flat (Thomas Friedman)

2007 - Redefining Global Strategy: Crossing Borders In a World Where Differences Still Matter (Pankaj Ghemawat)

2010 - The Global Brand CEO: Building the Ultimate Marketing Machine (Marc de Swaan Arons)

2016 - Global Inequality: A New Approach for the Age of Globalization (Branko Milanovic)

2016 - Global Vision: How Companies Can Overcome the Pitfalls of Globalization (Robert Salomon)

2017 - Global Brand Strategy: World-wise Marketing in the Age of Branding (Jan-Benedict Steenkamp)

2018 - Us vs. Them: The Failure of Globalism (Ian Bremmer)

I graduated from university in 1986. Most of my professional career has been colored by this local to global shift. I naturally thrived on it. I started out running smaller brands in one country. Then my responsibility systematically expanded to overseeing larger brand portfolios on regional and continental level. Finally, as global CMO, I took on oversight of a 300+ brand portfolio, composed of global, regional and local brands. Global brands were, and still are, my favorite complex type of brand to work with.

I see globalization still as a net positive for the world. I don't believe that *going back to local* will be the panacea. Nor will it be possible in the interconnected world of today. I *can* see the counter argument though. As a marketer you need to forget about your own biases and world view. Like it or not, a new protectionist wave is hitting the world. Perception is reality. At the moment, globalization is going out of geo-political fashion. Protectionist policies like Trump's *America First* and trade wars are back in the news. At the same time, in a number of categories, fickle consumers seem to turn away from bigger global brands toward local ones they perceive to be healthier and more natural. They appreciate their transparent and perceived more-responsible sourcing. In a selfie world that creates even more of a *one tribe feel* and even more *sameness*, they crave sharing perceived *unique and authentic experiences*. In the beer category for example, so called *craft* breweries have capitalized on that trend. Bigger breweries have responded by acquiring the best of them, or marketed their own small brews.

But inevitably this pendulum will swing back, if it hasn't already. Many smaller players are cute but unprofitable. I predict fickle consumers will go back to now re-invigorated big brands. Protectionism may feel warm for a few constituents, yet economic history has shown it is unlikely to be the long-term inspiring answer for society at large. Innovation stalls, competitiveness declines. Still, one cannot reliably predict how this new local mindset will impact society in a few years.

Back to the Future

Back in the Sixties, under JFK's presidential impulse, NASA got serious about space discovery. The Cold War competition with Russia was on. To help justify all the tax dollars that were flowing to these ventures, TV programming was not far behind to help the American people embrace the wonders of the future. A new era of brand journalism was born, an unprecedented public relations partnership between NASA and its stakeholders[15].

"We choose to go to the moon in this decade and do the other things, not because they are easy, but because they are hard, because the goal will serve to organize and measure the best of our energies and skills."

John F. Kennedy

As a result, the July '69 Apollo 11 launch to the Moon was followed by the biggest mass audience ever: 94% of American televisions tuned in. And many more in the world. Space interest beat the Super Bowl and the soccer World Cup, and may do it again. By the ingenuity of the tech at that time, it made the whole event a shared and inclusionary one. Every humble TV set became a personal window to outer space. Imagine what the broadcast tech today and tomorrow could do (see further: Mars One).

Where there is mass emotion, there is Hollywood. Hanna-Barbera studios invented two iconic cartoon families that have delighted entire generations since: the Flintstones (stone age), and the Jetsons (space age). Building off earlier visions by French science fiction writer Jules Verne and many others, the recognizable stories featured *people like us* and their flying cars, their life in the clouds and between planets. It all helped society at large to get accustomed to the idea that there can and will indeed be more than life on this planet alone. Since then, many movies have tried to make us more both comfortable (and uncomfortable) with the idea of *life out there*.

(Still) in search of...

Here is a list of must see space-related movies or TV series. It is interesting to see how the tonality and content evolved over the years, from fear to fascination. Still, most questions remain unanswered. So, *don't panic*[16], the saga is bound to continue for a long time....

1950 - Destination Moon

1951 - The Day the Earth Stood Still

1953 - The War of the Worlds

1953 - Invaders from Mars

1953 - It Came from Outer Space

1954 - Them

1956 - Forbidden Planet

1956 - Invasion of the Body Snatchers

1960 - The Time Machine

1965 - Lost In Space

1966 - Star Trek (+ sequels)

1968 - 2001, a Space Odyssey

1968 - Planet of the Apes (+ sequels)

1972 - Solaris

1976 - The Man Who Fell to Earth

1977 - Star Wars (+ sequels)

1977 - Close Encounters of the Third Kind

1978 - Battlestar Galactica

1978 - Superman

1979 - Alien (+ sequels)

1980 - Flash Gordon

1981 - The Hitchhiker's Guide to the Galaxy

1982 - E.T.: The Extra-Terrestrial

1982 - Blade Runner (+ sequels)

1982 - Tron (+ sequels)

1983 - The Right Stuff

1984 - The Terminator

1987 - Predator

1990 - Total Recall

1991 - Tintin: Destination Moon

1994 - Stargate

1995 - Apollo 13

1996 - Independence Day

1997 - Contact

2000 - Mission to Mars

2000 - Space Cowboys

2000 - Buzz Lightyear of Star Command

2009 - Moon

2009 - Avatar

2013 - Gravity

2014 - Interstellar

2015 - The Martian

2016 - Hidden Figures

2016 - Arrival

2016 - Voyage of Time: Life's Journey

2017 - Mission Control: The Unsung Heroes of Apollo

2018 - Lost in Space (Netflix remake of the 1965 TV series)

2018 - First Man (beginning of 50 years since Moon landing celebration)

New Space 2.0 discoveries fuel the age-old existential idea that we are not alone in the universe. Somewhere in the billions of galaxies beyond our own Milky Way possibly lies the answer of how life on Earth was created, and where it may migrate to once we feel too overpopulated. The writer and futurist Yuval Noah Harari provoked as follows: *What are the projects that will replace famine, plague and war at the top of the human agenda in the twenty-first century?*[17] I leave you to discover his answer yourself. I for one share Elon Musk's viewpoint that society's biggest opportunity to rally around together lies in the ambition to become a spacefaring, multiplanetary civilization. To keep giving meaning to our existence, with exciting prospects for future generations, as well as to hedge possible catastrophic risk on Earth. Elon Musk became "Mr. Mars" ever since he unveiled his vision for establishing a colony there. Back in 2013 he famously said *he intends to die on Mars, just not on impact*[18].

Mars is the new Moon

To date, only an average of six people per year go to space. Their destination is usually the International Space Station (ISS). This US$ 150 Billion project is still humankind's single biggest outpost in space since the last 20 years[19]. As NASA prepares for Mars, it continues to reinvent its pre-launch, on-board and follow-on training[20]. During the Shuttle program, which followed the Apollo program and ended in 2011 after 135 flights, astronauts trained 5 to 8 years for a 10- to 14-day mission scripted to the minute. Now they train 2+ years for 4- to 6-month missions. Astronauts like Scott Kelly are already staying at the ISS for one year.

The number of people in space remained rather modest so far. But something is fundamentally changing. Space is getting cool again. The masses are tuning in again. Many wannabe astronauts are stepping forward again. Since July 2015, eight new astronauts have completed their training at NASA's Johnson Space Center in Houston[21]. In 2017, NASA picked 12 new astronaut candidates, from a record 18,300 applicants. These new generations can be followed on social media. They will continue to leverage their new skills to do scientific research aboard the ISS. More importantly however, they will start to prepare America's new space launch capabilities and planned journeys to Mars. The longer humans have to stay in space, the more it deeply effects the body, mind and spirit. A trip to Mars may last up to three years. The effects of microgravity, radiation, and loneliness are yet to be truly experienced. Not to mention people may simply forget certain skills after 2 1/2 years in space. Every agency and private company intent sending people to Mars is already experimenting with how to deal with these new challenges.

Many authors already envisaged Mars colonies, and increasingly described the grueling process and training to get there. In *Red Mars* (1992), author Kim Stanley Robinson already described in vivid and plausible detail how this could really happen. Twenty years later, the Netherlands based Mars One Foundation aimed to establish a Mars colony by 2022. That ambition has been delayed multiple times since to 2030+. Nearly eight years after its set-up, Mars One is considered from utopian to very controversial by the serious space community[22]. Some consider it even a full scam[23]. But what has been interesting about Mars One from a marketing engagement point of view is its initial success in creating a truly globally shared social media spectacle[24].

When they opened a call for the *first true Mars colonists*, de facto *a one-way ticket to death*, they claimed over 200,000 people from all over the world sent in their candidacy. The organization then narrowed the selection in a second round to 660 hopefuls. Round three culled the pack to the *Mars 100* based on interviews and testing to assess risk understanding, team spirit, motivation and grit[25]. Reminiscent of the *Red Mars* book, the criterion for the fourth and final round: *In the final selection round, international groups of four candidates will be placed in isolation to face multiple challenges. An individual in-depth Mars Settler Suitability Interview (MSSI) is also part of the final selection round.* Mars One hopes to make its last selection round to find *the last 40* as dramatic as *Survivor* TV. Mars is clearly the inspiring next frontier of space.

The public is getting increasingly involved and responsive. Bruno Mars, the pop star, has smartly perfected Michael Jackson's iconic Moonwalk into a Mars Walk. With every new major discovery suggesting life on Mars, like the existence of underwater lakes, more people are tuning in[26]. Here is an example of how the global *vox populi* decided to rename an important planet. NASA's New Horizons satellite made it past Pluto, the farthest of deep space discovery journeys. By New Year's Day of 2019, the satellite is expected to fly past the planet-like mass called 486958 2014 MU69. In classic *The Voice*, or *Dancing with the Stars* style, NASA appealed to its many social media followers to help find a more inspirational name for MU69. Over 115,000 people from 193 countries already submitted over 34,000 nicknames for this new distant world on frontiersworld.org. Space is definitely not any more just about black holes. It simply is *the new Black*.

Space Race 2.0

What does this all mean for the CEO/CFO/CMO, and for investors? They need to capitalize on the gigantic Space Race 2.0 business momentum. We chased the Moon over the last 50 years. Many current products, services and solutions on Earth derive from the substantial investments in space research and exploration. From the simple calculator, to carbon bikes and microdosing pills, all the way to the internet itself. With a new electrifying destination like Mars, a new cycle has already started and will continue for the next 50+ years. The space industry is about to generate trillions of dollars for the global economy again. No true business marketer or investor can afford to miss out on the Space Race 2.0.

It *will* require adjusting underlying mental models though. It *will* require a significant upgrade of the old mindsets, and of commonly used marketing and investment frameworks. It is time to think beyond the Moon. Welcome to doing business in the new Galactic Age.

Space is hard, but worth it. We will persevere and move forward together.

Richard Branson

Chapter 3
The new Galactic Age: open for business

The government invested your tax money during the first 50+ years of space discovery. The next 50+ years has started, driven _both_ by government and by private entrepreneurship. The new rock(et) stars may be billionaires, yet frugal smarts are already making a difference. Space 2.0 offers truly galactic opportunities, but also forces us to think what we can do differently versus the globalization era, to ensure more people benefit this time?

In 2016, two billionaires, Facebook CEO Mark Zuckerberg and Russian entrepreneur Yuri Milner, and physicist Stephen Hawking (1942 – 2018) announced _Breakthrough Listen_[1]. Hoping to be the first to find alien life, over US$ 100 million was invested in the world's most powerful telescopes at the Australian Parkes Observatory, the area used back in 1969 to receive live televised pictures of the Apollo 11 moon landing. Astronomers will now be listening for signals of life on Proxima b, a planet _only_ four light years away from earth (still >25 trillion miles), and believed to have the right basic conditions for biochemical cycles and earth-like life (e.g., water, carbon dioxide, rock).

Early 2017, two Belgian astronomers, Michael Gillon and Emmanuel Jehin, discovered seven Earth-like exoplanets like Proxima b, circling around a star only 39 light years away[2]. As a nod to Belgium's high-quality monk beer, they called the star TRAPPIST-1. As a demonstration that money cannot always buy the most interesting discoveries, the Belgians did so on a shoestring budget of only US$ 320K.

Humankind has shown agility and aptitude to adjust to life in all corners of the earth, from the most sophisticated urban jungles to the highest mountains, on and under water, in deserts, and deep into the darkest forests. Medical progress will allow us to increasingly manage the travel with hibernation, to move around and live in zero gravity, to adapt muscles and skin tissue to radiation and different forms of aging[3]. Here is how Lee Morin, NASA astronaut, describes that the way humans might explore and colonize space is not anymore the subject of _science fiction_, but of _science reality_[4].

> _Everything that humans do starts with a fantasy and with an idea._
> _Back in 1996, I never thought that I would actually be in a shuttle-like vehicle,_
> _docking into a space station under construction during the year 2002._
> _I would have never have believed that._

Instead of dull astronaut food pills, future colonists will enjoy their customary Budweiser and pizza, galactic style. Where there is beer and pizza, much to the chagrin of some, there will be advertising. In 2017, the Tokyo-based lunar advertising agency Ispace raised a whopping US$ 90 million to start moon ads by 2020, in support of an expected booming lunar economy[5]. Its backers include Japan Airlines and television network Tokyo Broadcasting System Holdings. New Zealand is eying the set up of SpaceBase, a new venture aiming to help make space more accessible to more people in a perfect geographic setting (open skies, minimal overhead flights....)[6].

A galactic playground for all?

Founded only in 2006, the Commercial Spaceflight Federation (CSF) is the new leading voice in the U.S. for the fast-growing *commercial* spaceflight industry[7]. Together with its 70+ members, it wants to nurture a sustainable space economy, and to democratize space access for scientists, students, businesses and people like you and me. Through the promotion of technology innovation, according to its mission statement, CSF is *guiding the expansion of Earth's economic sphere, bolstering U.S. leadership in aerospace, and inspiring America's next generation of engineers and explorers*. In the process, thousands of high-tech jobs will be created, driven by billions of dollars in investment. Smart kids today may be mining bitcoins and cryptocurrencies. Smart kids tomorrow may be working in new roles for new companies:

- Engineers turning water into hydrogen and oxygen on the Moon colony for **Moon Express**, whose flamboyant founder and chairman Naveen Jain wants, among other things, to bring Moon rocks back to Earth to fully replace diamonds as a sign of true love: *In future, don't give her a diamond, give her the actual Moon*[8]

- Asteroid miners at **Planetary Resources**

- Payload masters for **Astrobotics**

- Microgravity manufacturing supervisors in the International Space Station for **Made in Space**

- Satellite navigators for the likes of **Kymeta** or **OneWeb**

- …

Space is already big business again, and poised to become much bigger in the coming decades. According to **Crunchbase** data on 56 companies around mid-2017, venture capital accelerated in funding of space deals[9]. As the cost of capital investment drops, in line with Moore's law, it dramatically lowers the cost to launch many tiny satellites simultaneously. Based on further data from CB Insights, analysts detected a similar increase in private space-tech investments following NASA's embrace of private spaceflight since 2012, with 4 Bn US$ investments just over the 16-17 period across eight sectors: natural resources, consumer tourism, interplanetary robotics, research and development, satellite constellation operations, communication and tracking, data analytics and spacecraft design and launch providers[10].

Another report is possibly even broader. Investment firm **Space Angels**, which counted 303 companies in the space sector globally, claimed investors poured a record $3.9 billion into commercial space companies in 2017, a year that included 51 government launches and 37 commercial launches. The report adds that over the last eight years, investors and founders have made $25 billion in exits following acquisitions and public offerings[11].

Predictions are always to be taken with the appropriate grains of salt, but they give you a first sense of the opportunity. Because of falling input and operations costs, a Morgan Stanley Q4 2017 prediction sees the space industry to be worth US$ 1.1 trillion by 2040, up from US$ 350 billion today[12]. Expect space related mutual funds to be growing equally exponentially.

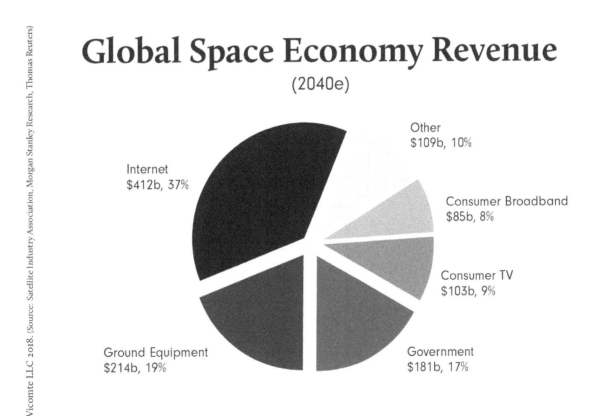

Vicomte LLC 2018. (Source: Satellite Industry Association, Morgan Stanley Research, Thomas Reuters)

Global Space Economy Revenue
(2040e)

- Other $109b, 10%
- Internet $412b, 37%
- Consumer Broadband $85b, 8%
- Consumer TV $103b, 9%
- Ground Equipment $214b, 19%
- Government $181b, 17%

National governments are the key actors in space since the beginning, and they are still a major player in the game. Professor Mariana Mazzucato demonstrated governments are much-maligned when it comes to leading innovation[13]. In actual fact, tax money invested by governments is often behind the biggest breakthroughs and the boldest societal risks. For example, in 1958, the US not only created NASA (1958), but also **DARPA**, the Defense Advanced Research Projects Agency.

DARPA created many innovations that led to spin-offs in the commercial area that changed all of our lives forever. One of the best known ones is ARPANET, which laid the technical foundation for the internet as we know it. The second best known is GPS, the Global Positioning System. While space is tax-free at the moment, surely governments will be devising ways to get some form of payback for all their earlier tax front spending.

The United Nations has had a dedicated Committee on the Peaceful Uses of Outer Space (COPUOS), since 1959, right after the Sputnik launched and the Cold War threat appeared. Supported out of Vienna by its UN Office for Outer Space Affairs (UNOOSA), the COPUOS mission has been to foster international cooperation and preserve a sense of law and order in the Universe[14]. More people are expected to live there, and more nations have and will stake claims. The new multipolar political power game, and the arms race that goes with, already sees space as the next battle frontier. With its authority and budgets being challenged, the UN, and therefore UNOOSA, will be tested like never before. President Trump already floated the idea to create a *space force*, besides the army, navy and airforce[15].

Wherever humans go, environmental concerns inevitably follow. A new challenge is emerging: how can we keep near space clean and safe? More and more satellites are being launched, on top of an estimated 7000 tons of space trash already orbiting around us. They may endanger future astronauts, or simply cause damage by falling back on earth, like the 8.5 ton Tiangong Chinese space station launched in space back in 2011. For the oceans, gritty Dutch teenager Boyan Slat was able to mobilize the world to help him set up **Ocean Cleanup**[16]. He is pioneering a historical new way to pick up over 5 trillion pieces of plastic currently littering our precious waters. Similarly, new *vacuum cleaners* are starting to be designed by Europe's Clean Space program[17]. And there is much more to come.

Last but not least, as we embark on a new galactic period, we should carefully reflect on the lessons from the last 40+ years of globalization. What can governments, companies and brands do to ensure the galactic age will be more inclusive than globalization from the outset? A critical question for political scientists. Without a smarter approach, there are likely to be (perceived) winners and (perceived) losers again.

A possible answer lies in completely rethinking our education approach for the galactic age. As an example: in 2000, the TRIUM EMBA program was *the* pioneer of the *Global* EMBA, a very successful education format copied by many other universities afterwards. As an alumnus and faculty in the program, we always focused on the triple bottom line: profit, people and planet (Earth). May this book inspires TRIUM to design the first ever *Galactic* EMBA, whatever that curriculum will look and feel like. The triple bottom line should evolve to *profit, people and the Universe.*

Branson, Bezos and Musk:
The new rock(et) stars

Elon Musk's SpaceX team successfully launched their Falcon Heavy launch in Q1 2018, including the trackable red Tesla[18]. Following the iconic footprint on the Moon, this orbiting Tesla will become a new defining space picture in the minds of many future generations. It clearly said: we are in Space 2.0. Still, in my slightly biased view, sir Richard Branson deserves to be talked about first. For a true homage to *Ballooning, Birdmen and Blasting into space*, or *how a handful of pioneers risked it all to make dreams a reality*, Branson's *Reach for the Skies* (2010) is a must read.

Richard Branson is the soul of the Virgin Group[19]. Currently in his 60s, he is a grandfather of four, still lives a fast life, and remains as inspiring as ever. True to his DNA, he continues to defy age and conventional wisdom[20]. He remains a role model not only for all active baby boomers, but for many generations after that. Rock & roll, adventure and space: it seems a powerful cocktail for staying eternally young. Pass that cup please.

Starting in 1970, he built Virgin up from Virgin Records to a GBP 19.5 Bn holding by end 2016. It now includes space ventures wholly or partially owned like Virgin Galactic (2010, co-owned with Aabar from the United Arab Emirates), The Spaceship Company (2005, started with Burt Rutan from Scaled Composites), and the newest creation to help launch small satellites called Virgin Orbit (2017). Branson has been or is in everything from drinks to mobiles to trains to cruise ships to Hyperloop to space. But he can't wait to go up in the inaugural commercial space flight in the world's first reusable, air launched, winged, piloted space vehicle, flying from the world's first purpose-built commercial spaceport, with a run way landing.

Some billionaires have the urge to own soccer teams. It is rather unlikely we will see *Virgin City* or *Virgin United* anytime soon. Real Madrid, *Los Galacticos*, could be the only fitting soccer team defying laws of soccer gravity so far, but as far as I know it is not for sale, and Branson's passion lies elsewhere anyway. He is one of the defining rock(et) stars of the new space race. His latest space collaboration focused on supersonic transportation (faster than the speed of sound), partnering with Denver-based **BOOM** Technologies and with Japan Airlines[21]. BOOM aims to bring back a modern-day and affordable version of the iconic Concorde. *Same price as business today*, claims Boom's CEO Blake Scholl, a pilot and former Amazon executive, adding his vision is *for anybody to get anywhere in the world in less than five hours for under US$ 100*. Until that bigger vision is reality, if BOOM is delivering by 2025 or earlier, we should be crossing oceans again from London to NY in less than 3.5 hours (instead of 5-6), and in about five hours from Japan to the US West Coast (instead of 10-11 hours).

BOOM is not alone. Other players, like **Aerion Supersonic**, **Lockheed Martin** and **EADS**, are equally eyeing what is a technically challenging and possibly commercially risky market. But the potential size of the prize is huge. Just consider the number of Chinese in the middle class looking to start to discover the world[22]. In 2016, 83 million Chines traveled outside of their country, eight times more than in 2000. They bought US$ 102 Bn worth of goods and services. Germans were well-known tourist champions in Europe. Now imagine *all* of Germany on the road each year. According to the China Tourism Academy, by 2020 around 200 million Chinese will be on the road, good for around US$ 250 Bn in spending.

Meanwhile, Scholl's former boss Jeff Bezos keeps selling regularly US$ 1 Bn of his invaluable Amazon stock to silently fund *his* space passion: Blue Origin, founded back in 2000[23]. Depending on the day, Bezos is the richest man on the planet, worth around US$ 100 Bn. He is reclusive, and avoids the media wherever possible. That does not mean he is less active or making less progress. If Elon Musk is considered the hare in the Space Race, then Bezos is the deliberate *step-by-step* tortoise[24]. Not unlike what happened on Amazon, Bezos may be surprising everybody (again) in the end.

His reusable New Shepard booster and capsules used for brief suborbital flights are fully automated. If all goes well, Blue Origin may even become the first at flying paying customers on suborbital rides, beating Virgin Galactic to the punch. It opened its own second chapter with the launch of New Glenn, a much bigger rocket to take people and payloads into orbit. Bezos is building a world-class facility to produce and launch New Glenns on Florida's Space Coast. Bezos loves to name his rockets after the first group of Apollo astronauts. He is really intent on going back to the Moon, but this time, to stay[25].

The race is definitely on between Bezos and Branson for space tourism, spurred on further by a third space disruptor: Elon Musk. *Musk is the new Steve Jobs*, according to Silicon Valley. The world seems to agree, at least so far. Musk founded Space Exploration Technologies Corp, or SpaceX, in 2002[26]. Although he may not come across as thoughtful as his peers, he certainly acts with galactic swagger. In doing so, he gained a bit of a mixed reputation—boldly overpromising and often un-derdelivering. Yet equally he keeps baffling his naysayers with stunning achievements in record times, earning a global cult following ready to forgive any slip of the roadmap.

While Tesla keeps missing deadlines and is under investor pressure, SpaceX *did* indeed achieve some historic milestones. In 2002, Space X was formed with US$ 12 M in funding for a US$ 27 M valuation. In Q2 2018, following a US $ 507 M raise, it is now valued at US$ 25 Bn. In September 2018 he announced his first client for a trip around the Moon[27]. As a private company, not a government, it returned a spacecraft from low-Earth orbit in 2010, and delivered cargo to and from the ISS on its Dragon spacecraft multiple times since 2012[28]. Unlike anybody before, he achieved the first re-flight of an orbital class rocket, and major progress towards full and rapid rocket reusability (2017). Early 2018 the FCC approved SpaceX's application to launch its Starlink 4,425 high-altitude satellite constellation, which will deliver a fast internet network serving rural areas everywhere[29]. Musk intends to eventually launch 11,000 of them, on top of the roughly 1,400 that currently orbit around us. The first two were launched in February 2018, and named after the iconic Belgian cartoon star reporter: Tintin, a and b. I mentioned it before: when capital expenditure starts to drop, many more business cases start to make sense, and the satellite business is one of the potentially biggest new space businesses. His latest bold plans for SpaceX: sending BFRs, *Big Fucking Rockets*, to Mars by 2022.

On top of what would already be more than a day's work for any CEO, Musk finds a seemingly inhuman way to invest considerable managerial time and money for other equally massively disruptive ventures[30]: Tesla and Solar City (electric cars and batteries, maybe flying cars or driving drones tomorrow), Hyperloop and The Boring Company (connecting cities via tunnels with bullet trains), Neurolink (healthcare, augmenting our brains with chips), and a number of other visionary projects in AI. To understand what drives Elon Musk, refer to Chapter 15 on the new galactic business marketers.

The Great Man Theory

These three billionaires receive quite a bit of media attention, and deservedly so. They are defining Space Age 2.0. Some people call them the *alt.space barons*. Musk wants to retire on Mars, and as well he might. Their ventures are major ones, with financing needs few can bankroll, and with risk levels only few have stamina for. Branson (born in 1950) is the definite baby boomer. Bezos (born in 1964) is the very last of the baby boomers (like me). Musk is the youngest (born in 1971), a Gen X/Y. Each is a child of his time, and each has his own idiosyncratic style. They share the unbridled ambition, the drive, the huge appetite for a risk, and the desire to make a real difference for humankind.

Tim Fernholz, author of *Rocket Billionaires: Elon Musk, Jeff Bezos, and the new Space Race* (2018), wondered if we may be witnessing again the theory of a great man. Capturing the *Zeitgeist* in a similar way, another writer, Christian Davenport, also deconstructed Musk and Bezos in *The Space Barons: Elon Musk, Jeff Bezos, and the Quest to Colonize the Cosmos* (2018). In 1840, Scottish writer Thomas Carlyle boldly claimed that *the history of the world is but the biography of great men*. He was rebuffed 20 years later by sociologist Herbert Spencer: *before a man can remake his society, his society must make him.*

Regardless of the fascination we have for these three rock(et) stars, even the greatest of men remain human. Virgin Galactic suffered a major setback on October 31st 2014, when SpaceShip Two broke up during a test flight, killing the co-pilot, Mike Alsbury. His colleague, pilot Pete Siebold, miraculously survived, for which we are all grateful. *Pete was one of the first people to live after a supersonic accident, an in-air vehicle break at top speed and on a height leaving almost no chance for survival* (Branson in his latest autobiography)[31].

Both SpaceX and Blue Origin had a number of setbacks as rockets crashed on landing, before they succeeded in recovery and reuse. It is part of progress. They take personal risks too. Just like daredevil Branson survived balloon crashes a few times, Jeff Bezos narrowly escaped a deadly 2003 helicopter crash while scouting for his new launch test site in Texas in adverse weather conditions[32]. His response later: it would have been *a silly way to die.*

For every one of these big ventures, there are other big ones that collapse, like the relatively high profile California-based **XCOR**. The XCOR's Lynx also proposed a suborbital rocket-powered spaceplane. In design since 2003, it was intended to carry one pilot (versus two on Virgin Galactic), one ticketed passenger (versus six on VG) and/or equivalent payload, targeting above 100 km altitude. By mid 2016, XCOR put activities on ice[33].

The next Space Heroes

There is plenty happening in the world of transport and aeronautics. The world expects an increasing numbers of true electric cars and the emergence of self-driving cars. **Nissan** committed to be the first car company to produce mass models by 2022 at the latest[34]. Soon, we will hop in flying drone/cars/taxis in cities like Dubai for its World Expo 2020[35]. In the world of planes and rockets, distances will get shorter and shorter faster, with possible incredible economic and societal impact. Besides the examples shared before, here are a few more projects to watch out for over the coming years and decades.

Airbus

Airbus, in partnership with Rolls-Royce and Siemens, is betting the future belongs to hybrid-electric aircrafts, called the E-Fan X[36]. Target fly date is 2020. The project is part of the European Commission's vision for sustainable transport, called Flightpath 2050.

UAE

The United Arab Emirates (UAE) officially plans to build a first city on Mars by 2021[37]. The plan for its *Hope* spacecraft is to arrive on Mars by 2021, to coincide with the 50th anniversary of the founding of the UAE. The launch is scheduled for July 2020, when Earth and Mars are again aligned at their closest point to each other given their different orbits around the sun. Such a moment only arrives every two years.

EasyJet

Together with Wright Electric, low-cost carrier EasyJet targets one fifth of its fleet to be 100% electric planes by 2027[38]. The planes can cover distances top to 530 km in less than 2 hours. It intends to use them primarily on short-haul flights in Europe.

Ultra Long Haul Flights

The best flight is straight and does not stop. That was the best line in John Gapper's FT comment as he experienced the newly opened Quantas connection between London and Australia[39]. Next up is Singapore Airlines, reopening its 19+ hours direct flight to New York in Q4 2018. More *Ultra Long Haul flights* will follow, as people prefer to fly direct if the cost is acceptable.

...and Much More

While airlines continue to make the world smaller, there is an ever growing list of incredible initiatives on the intergalactic calendar in the coming years. Here are just a few great ones:

• The next steps on Paul Allen's Stratolaunch—the largest airplane ever flown, capable to air launch rockets

• The Slovenian Alpha Electro II full electric planes tested by the Norwegian airport operator Avinor. Norway is a global leader in trying to reduce dependency on fossil fuels, and wants to crack the code to airplane batteries

• Progress on the Lilium Jet, the world's first electric vertical take-off and landing jet

• The BepiColombo Euro-Japanese rocket to Mercurius

• The Parker Solar Probe (to study solar wind)

• The Boeing Starliner transporting astronauts to the ISS

• NASA's Insight probe to Mars (studying Mars geology)

• The Villanova University Martian biology experiment

• Rocket Lab launches in New Zealand, launching satellites in orbit cost effectively

• Russia launching new unmanned moon missions

- Draper University hosted the most disruptive event for space innovators end of January 2018: the first annual Space Tech Summit in Silicon Valley

- Relativity Space is a US-based rocket company, claiming it can 3D print rockets for *only* USD $ 10 Mn, on what they claim is the world's largest metal 3D printer

- Space Decentral, founded by the international Space Cooperative, uses blockchain technology to launch a social space network. It is an international group of scientists, engineers, architects, futurists, artists and software developers that works collaboratively to share the latest scientific research, and plans to crowdfund projects that lack government funding. They may be offering a Faster Than Light coin (FTLcoin), an ICO to raise at least $10 million with a maximum goal of $35 million

- Belgium-based Antwerp Space will help ESA's ExoMars 2020 mission with LaRA, a communication device the size of a *milk box* to better connect Mars with Earth

- Space Tango, research and manufacturing in microgravity—the basis for so-called exo-medicine—they already did the first tests with Budweiser yeast

- …

Many of the new initiatives will fizzle or fail spectacularly, the inevitable price of progress. The Google-supported Lunar X Prize (to land a robot on the moon) was canceled after the organizers did not see any team making it[40]. But each of these initiatives will contribute to the collective body of knowledge, and to the grander goal of a peaceful interplanetary civilization.

The Galactic Age is here

Branson, Bezos and Musk are on the vanguard of space discovery today, challenging all our rocket scientist paradigms. Many are following. Zuckerberg and Milner may define the next heroic wave of space pioneering in more ways than one. Next to *Breakthrough Listen*, it may be worth your time to keep track of their other space project called *Breakthrough Starshot*[41]. To avoid the limits of legacy learning, the Starshot project intends to jettison *all* previous learning on spaceships, including their size. Their latest idea is to laser shoot many tiny little one-gram nano ships called *Starchips*, all the way to Proxima Centauri, the nearest star to us after the sun, 10000 times further away than any satellite has ever been (Pluto).

Clearly, we are at the dawning of Space Age 2.0, the start of a real galactic period. New ideas and projects will keep popping up, one possibly bolder and more visionary than the other. Space 2.0 may actually yield the first *trillionaires*. So, what new mental model should underpin how will we do marketing and investments in this impending galactic age?

We will go back to the Moon by not learning anything new.

Burt Rutan

Chapter 4
Think Galactic, Act Galactic

How do the best brands stay young and relevant forever? Will so-called *disruptors* really replace them? Who were the first major brands in space? Why do both local and global brands need to evolve *ASAP* from a *think local/global* mindset to a *think and act galactic* mindset?

In early 2018 an independent study challenged NASA's internal ways of working, particularly in how the organization approached manned missions to the moon and beyond. The key conclusion: NASA could save 300 Bn USD by jettisoning its tradition to do everything in-house, and by embracing collaboration with emerging commercial alternatives like Blue Origin and SpaceX[1]. It was, to paraphrase the saying, a small step for mankind, but a very big step for NASA. A fundamental mindset switch. The first step to reinvent itself as a brand to stay relevant in the galactic age.

There are many examples of iconic brands that failed to timely evolve their mindset. Remember **PanAm**, the airline? It stopped existing in 1992, despite its pioneer DNA, celebrating many firsts in the airline business. Between 1969 and 1971, following the Apollo Moon landing, it had even signed up a stunning 93,000 people for its *First Moon Flights Club*[2]. Pan Am was already dreaming to fly commercially to the Moon, well before the idea of Virgin Galactic suborbital flights was born.

The PanAm brand still exists, with latent equity to leverage. Maybe one day it reincarnates as *Pan Am Galactic*. Chances are it may be relaunched not in the US, but from Bengaluru by the ISRO, the Indian Space Research Organization famous for setting world records on shoestring budgets[3]. As we speak, a modern day version of the 1912 **Titanic**, the **Titanic II**, is being built in China by Australian billionaire Clive Palmer. The maiden voyage is planned for 2019. Not on its old route, but between China and Dubai - another piece of evidence of a new world order? As the world order changes, brands need to change their mindset.

Only the paranoid survive

Classic forms of distribution are fundamentally changing, both in B2C and B2B environments. Iconic industrial brand leaders like **GE** (1892) or **Siemens** (1847) are struggling to evolve their legacy systems. GE and Siemens risk going the way of **Kodak**. They have to completely rethink the fundamentals of their business model. What are the retail consumer and business renewable energy needs in a galactic age?[4] If everybody can afford **Tesla** Power Walls, or cuts the cord and goes off-grid somehow with solar and other sources of energy, new value propositions are needed to remain relevant. Mid-2018, after 111 years, GE already lost its coveted spot from the blue chip index Dow Jones[5]. Andy Grove, the former **Intel** CEO, kept repeating: *only the paranoid survive.*

Consider the urgency for brands like **Walmart** who have existed since 1962. **Amazon,** created in 1994 is in the process of eclipsing Walmart. Yet Amazon is not invincible either. **Ali Baba** (1999) shows China's scale already exposes the vulnerability of every US-based 800-pound gorilla, including Amazon. Technology has completely upended the competitive advantages of longtime local brick and mortar distribution companies and is being rewritten by global e-commerce. China's *11.11 Singles Day* is now the world's biggest online shopping festival, bigger than the two major shopping days post Thanksgiving in the US combined (Black Friday and Cyber Monday): US $25 Bn sold within 24 hours (+41% vs. 2016), of which $1 Bn in just two minutes[6]. Walmart proved it can turn itself around if it wants to, yet it will have to sustain the action. After the 2016 purchase of Jet.com it started to successfully play the game of e-commerce at scale. In 2017, its stock was back up over 40%, but let's see if it sticks[7].

Nothing and nobody is sacred. Even the champion of disruption can be disrupted. **Silicon Valley**'s hegemony as the world's top tech hub is being challenged by other cities, led by the **Zhongguancun** tech district in Beijing[8]. Silicon Valley detractors argue it more than deserves the challenge. Instead of focusing on meaningful disruption, addressing real world challenges and advancing society at large, they feel too much money is chasing frivolous causes that only add limited to zero value to people's lives. Who needs a **Juiceroo** juicer costing US$ 700?

Silicon Valley, historically a name with a positive association, is being replaced by a more negative name: *Big Tech*, like Big Oil or Big Tobacco. In *Move Fast and Break Things* (2017), Los Angeles – based professor Jonathan Taplin effectively accused the top Big Tech players of undermining democracy itself. His message is being heard by governments. Not only in Europe, always a bit more skeptical about Big Tech's clout, but equally in the US home market. It seems there is a renewed sense of urgency for Silicon Valley to reinvent and repurpose itself.

Can Silicon Valley evolve its mindset, and become a galactic brand? There is no short-term solution to create a true renaissance for any brand in a galactic age. It is difficult when the media does not stop raving about the FAANG stocks (**Apple, Alphabet/Google, Netflix, Amazon** and **Facebook**), as the greatest brand examples combining scale and innovation. Some of these tech brands now do top the global brand value lists, and they deserve to be there. Who knows what will happen in a few years?[9] Many of these current brands are all still young in terms of brand longevity. Apple has only been around since 1984. Where will it be in 2084? Steve Jobs himself cautioned for hubris, warning that every great brand, even Apple, needs constant reinvention[10].

A renaissance mindset

I love brands. I had the honor to work with some of the biggest, best and most iconic ones around the world for decades. I equally had the good fortune to work with many new startup brands. I like to help create brands from scratch, or to nurture their health back to glory. Together with clients, my consultancy (Vicomte LLC, see inset) is not afraid to radically reinvent brands when needed. Nor are we afraid to sell them, or even to kill them. We always remind companies that brands are a means to an end, not the end by themselves. Brands are at the heart of a brand-based business model that should deliver sustainable results.

According to the self-declared *disruptors*, Big Brands have no future. They belong to a bygone Baby Boomer era. Millennials only want local brands. Many newspapers are sold on these headlines, and they certainly cause a lot of anxiety in boardrooms. Jorge Paulo Lemann, the highly respected soul of 3G, publicly admitted end April 2018 for the first time that *the era of disruption in consumer brands caught 3G Capital by surprise*[11]. The dinosaur theme is echoed for all classic big-brand CPG. It is very fashionable these days to claim *traditional stalwarts aren't keeping pace with younger, perhaps scrappier competitors, despite what their reputation suggests*[12].

These articles have a point, yet I only agree partly these statements. I have lived that pressure. It is good pressure, not every day, but still. It makes CEOs *wake up and smell the coffee*. However, the pundits should never dismiss the big giants. They have some unassailable sources of competitive advantage if they play their cards right. Nobody dislodges an incumbent just like that, unless the top leadership choses to remain myopic over a long time. Not all companies are Kodak. Most will figure it out faster than you think in one way or another.

For starters, I have never been a fan of a company owning just one brand, big or small. I am a big proponent of smart *portfolio* plays, meeting different consumer needs with different branded solutions that reinforce each other. Being a *branded house* is a natural start for many brands, but tends to evolve to become a *house of brands*. A brand like Apple can only stretch its equity so much, and started to amass smaller brands like **Beats**. **Facebook** started as a branded house, but it became fast a house of brands upon buying **WhatsApp**, **Instagram** and other distinct brands. **Google** morphed to become **Alphabet**. Just like most successful CPGs. The shift from one model to another is a big mindset shift.

Second, *Big* and *Small* brands need each other more than ever. In summer 2015 I had the pleasure and honor to become an investor and board member of premium condiment maker **Kensington & Sons**. **Sir Kensington's**, created by founders Mark Ramadan and Scott Norton, is a brand that pretty much *wrote the Millenial playbook*, at least according to the *Financial Times*[13]. From a garage, it slowly grew to create a cult following. It became a cool scale-up. In the end, the best course of action for Sir K's long-term future was to accept to be bought by Unilever. Based on deeply shared values, the brand continues to thrive as part of Unilever's phenomenal condiment portfolio, along with big brands like Hellmann's. Both Sir K and Unilever were thinking bigger. They both changed their worldview. The sum of the parts is bigger.

Third, if I learned anything at the biggest global CPG companies, it is all a matter of mindset. I deeply believe in the power of *Creating Renaissance Brands (TM)*. That became the selling line of Vicomte LLC, the marketing strategy consultancy I set up mid-2012 in NYC. Vicomte defines *renaissance brands* as *brands that are at the heart of a sustainable branded business model, with pricing power and with icon potential*. They have a point of view on society and are relevant in people's lives. In Stage 3 we will go deeper into the concepts of pricing and purpose, the real *why* of marketing. Vicomte's approach always brings marketing and business together. On my website vicomte.com/insights you can find my 2x3 core beliefs related to business and marketing, distilled over years of life in the CMO trenches. Let's explore the power of mindset change deeper.

Homage to Da Vinci

No image better represents the idea of constant mindset shifts than **Da Vinci's polymath Vitruvian Man**. It is one of the most iconic and celebrated hallmarks of the Renaissance. The drawing is the embodiment of a cultural movement, taking people out of their darkness during the Middle Ages. Art and science cross-fertilized like never before, resulting in more than one Copernican revolution. Humankind was set free again to express their own truth and humanity at a level unseen since the Roman empire. Exactly that euphoric feeling —having successfully created something big—is what a renaissance marketing mindset should recreate. Especially in the new galactic age. Vicomte's logo subtly pays tribute to the maestro.

Forever young

Marketing has evolved substantially since Kotler's famous 4P model (see Chapter 7). The world is entering a galactic age, with plenty of growth room for *both* the current local and global brands. We need to tackle 21st-century marketing and investment challenges with concepts, frameworks and tools fitting for the 21st-century challenges, which is what stage 3 will be all about. But the first thing is to look up and start to evolve our mindset, beyond the current ones.

Time to upgrade?

Upgrade our old Marketing and Finance Mindset for the New Space Age?

- **Local brands: become hyper local, but at least *think* galactic from the outset.** Many of the 8 fundamentals I will share in this book equally apply to smaller brands. They may start from a smaller base in terms of means and reach. Barring a few exceptions, their path will probably lead to an acquisition, part of the portfolio plays of larger companies. But the best guarantee for a long-term future is to think galactic from the outset. Surprise the big brands with breakthrough thinking. That is how you get on an M&A wishlist.

- **Global brands: move squarely *beyond* global, and start thinking and acting truly galactic.** The global brands need the most significant reset. The galactic brands of tomorrow will be the ones able to continuously reinvent themselves for a very long time. It is the single toughest challenge for any marketer: to keep an icon Brand topical for every new generation—over more than 100 years. Baby boomers love to say: 60 is the new 40, or 70 is the new 50. For galactic brands, the challenge is even more radical—to stay forever young: 100 should be the new 20. Actually, *every* year is the new 20. For the next upcoming decades, adopting a galactic mindset will help. Jeff Bezos has his mantra of Day 1[14]. He obsessively wants all the people in his massive empire to stay as sharp and hungry as if it was their first day of conquering the Universe.

When you think of successful marketing across generations and centuries of drama, it is worth studying the continuous reinventions of brands like **Louis Vuitton**, a luxury travel brand desired since 1854[15]. Close your eyes and think of another discovery brand, captured in a magazine with a yellow frame cover. **National Geographic**, has been inspiring us to understand our universe in all its colors since 1888. The iconic look was created in 1910, but its content can be consumed in all digital forms imaginable. Observe the recent moves from **Ermenegildo Zegna**, now also well over 100 years young, also created in 1910. Under impulse from the 4th generation Edoardo Zegna, the group is now covering *from sheep to shop to screen* to reinvent themselves again in the casualisation world[16]. In beverages, it remains an absolute must for business marketers and for investors to study **Coca-Cola**'s enduring brand power, which started in 1886. Likewise it is critical to understand the incredible resilience of **Budweiser**, born in 1887, just one year after Coke.

There are incumbent and challenger analogies to be found in every area of life: business, culture, politics, systems, education, publishing, etc. Life is full of renaissance brands. *The Economist* (1843) is a remarkable example of staying relevant throughout the ages—surviving various ownerships, and in the last years successfully scaling across many digital platforms all while keeping its idiosyncratic view on the world. Editor-in-chief Zanny Minto Beddoes is very clear on who should read the *Economist: the globally curious*. She estimates her market to be around 70 million people, and she seems determined to keep providing them her content in whatever ways modern times dictate. You can read Zany Minto Beddoes in classic print, as well as in a more *snackable* form on Snapchat for the new generations (leading them to the magazine afterwards).

Why do education brands like **Harvard** top many education rankings so long? What is behind the magic pull *and* ever-growing pricing power of the US top schools to attract so many students from around the world? They invest in their reputation on a constant basis, through faculty pressure on relevant publications, technology use in teaching, facility upgrades, core curriculum renovation and innovation, alumni fundraising and recognition.

BelCham: 100 = the new 20

BelCham is short for the Belgian American Chamber of Commerce. A nonprofit designed to help unleash the American Dream for young Belgian students, interns, trainees and, most importantly, for scale-ups. It was born in 1919 as a classic Chamber of Commerce. Nearly defunct by 2009, it went through its first major reinvention in 2010. Under the leadership of its dynamic young MD, Bieke Claes, and driven by a rejuvenated board and new governance system, BelCham 2.0 has completely overhauled itself since 2012. After six years of hard work, it became one of the most pioneering and respected European country chambers in NYC. Back in Belgium, BelCham is now firmly established as one of *the* gateways to a successful US expansion. In 2019, it turns 100 under the motto *100 is the new 20.*

Galactic pressure

A great brand is always the result of hard work over many years. Reaching the #1 spot of any category is a major achievement. Staying there for decades, or even centuries, deserves a lot of respect for the owners and managers of the brand. They can never stop pushing, not for one day. Big Brands will always have tough battles ahead. The bigger the brand, the bigger the battleground. The higher you fly, the thinner the air. What makes them win time and again despite all odds is the right winning mindset. That mindset will have to evolve to be galactic.

When you play for a top club, or compete as a top athlete, you cannot crack under the pressure of the biggest stages. Similarly, when you lead big brands, you cannot crack under the pressure. The mindset *must* be a galactic one. *Getting* to number one requires one form of adrenaline, grit, tactics and skill. *Staying* number one, as long as you can, requires a very different kind of mindset and set of competencies. It needs a relentless reconfiguration of the assets at the disposal of the brand owner, without sacrificing the essence of the brand. Imagine you are **Roger Federer** when he became number one in tennis. What did he do to stay number one in the ATP rankings longer than anybody else (over 300 weeks)? If you think individual athletes have a more limited life span as a brand (for now), try to decode the secret behind successful teams that transcend generations: the **Patriots** and the **Dallas Cowboys** in the NFL (the latter being the most valuable sports franchise in the world); the fearsome **All Blacks** in rugby; soccer teams like the German *Rekordmeister* **FC Bayern Munich**.

One of the most inspiring cases from the last few years is **Real Madrid**, the world's most successful soccer club. Ever since the magistral **Figo/Zidane/Ronaldo/Roberto Carlos** generation, fans expect the Real Madrid *Los Blancos* players to play on a *galactic* level. Nothing less will do. In May 2018, Zinedine Zidane, Real's trainer for only the last three years, delivered on that galactic expectation. With a mix of skill, grit, tactics and some luck, Real Madrid won the most coveted soccer club title, the UEFA Champions League, *for the third time in a row.* No trainer ever did that, let alone a new trainer. No club ever did that. The win was unprecedented, historic, *badass*—Big Fucking Galactic (BFG) indeed. A new *Galacticos* dynasty may be born. With the bar raised again for everybody, it will put a turbo under Real Madrid's world domination plans as it moves forward, in a soccer world that equally starts to think BFG (see Chapter 23). At the heart of Real Madrid's success: a *BFG*-winning mindset.

Jetsons 2.0

Branson, Bezos and Musk are space visionaries, but Coca-Cola and Budweiser were there before them. Coke was the first soft drink to be consumed in outer space[17]. Back on July 12, 1985, astronauts tested the *Coca-Cola Space Can* aboard the Space Shuttle Challenger. On August 26, 1991, the space can was tested again on board the Soviet space station Mir. In February 1995, diet Coke became the first diet soft drink in space, and the Space Shuttle Discovery's mission marked the first use of soft-drink fountain equipment in space (the *Coca-Cola Space Dispenser/Monitor*). Just one year later, on May 19, 1996, another fountain dispenser innovation (Coke, diet Coke and Powerade) was tested aboard the Space Shuttle Endeavor.

Not to be outdone, **Budweiser** wants to be first to serve a cold one on Mars[18]. Right before Thanksgiving in 2017, the brand announced it will start testing barley, one of its four key ingredients, in the ISS. The idea is to experiment with how barley seeds germinate in and react to low or zero gravity. Yes, Budweiser may still have some reconsideration challenges in the US, which it is addressing systematically. However, it starts to think galactic. There is no time for complacency. There is always a small brewing upstart somewhere at the fringes ready to steal its thunder, also in the space area. Check the website of the joint venture between the **4 Pines microbrewery** and a space company called **Saber Astronautics**[19]. They started the VOSTOK Space Beer project in Manly, Australia, raising US$ 1 M via IndieGogo. As I said, if they think galactic, small brands can outsmart big brands anytime.

Bud and Coke remain true renaissance brands, at least so far. Both brands are still there, despite all the naysayers. In the **Interbrand** 2017 list of Best Global Brands, Coke is still in the top 10 and Budweiser was still ranked 31, valued at US$ 15 Bn. They know they can never take that status for granted. Their historical brand strength, marketing capability and superior distribution and commercial power gives them time to stay relevant for the next generation. However, the forward-looking pressure on the public capital markets keeps any big-brand manager from slacking.

Many brands would benefit from just looking up and dreaming a little bigger, without necessarily aiming for deep space as a first step. Dunkin' Donuts has been running a consistent and brilliant campaign since 2006: *America runs on Dunkin'*. In Q2 2018, the brand launched a summer drinks promotional extension called *The Universe runs on Dunkin'*. There is a great nugget of an idea here. If its owner Dunkin' Brands would truly embrace a galactic mindset, and inspire its people and agencies, imagine what could happen?

To really unlock the promise of the galactic age, we need modern versions of how the Jetsons made the future accessible and acceptable for people in the 1960s. Big moves made by big brands are great and impactful, but rare. In real life we usually progress fastest with practical baby steps adopted by many. Truly democratizing access to the galactic world presents a massive opportunity for forward-thinking creatives in the marketing and agency world. By building new bridges between three worlds—every day brands, space brands, and the regulated world of space—they will truly help to unlock the promise of the galactic age in our daily lives. When global brand managers start to operate in a new galactic context, the whole ecosystem will follow suit.

More importantly, as *Main Street* brands are becoming galactic, real space brands should be interested in connecting with them. Many new space brands in the fast-growing commercial space industry (the CSF members) would benefit a lot from working closer with the bigger nonspace brands, to bring the promise of space in an accessible and democratized format in our daily lives. Paradigms are being challenged in the most unusual places: Under its new administrator Jim Bridenstine, NASA is carefully exploring if/how it should work closer with big brands, to the point of allowing advertising on its rockets to finance more launches.

Not an evident move of course, and many astronauts have their rightful reservations[20]. But life moves on. Perceptions change with new generations. Whatever assumptions made a great spaceship and launch yesterday, will not make a great spaceship today. A spaceship is more than just a flying car. While smart engineers make cars that can fly, true rocket scientists think differently, and make drones that can drive[21]. The very best global brands already started thinking truly differently in the last few years. They start thinking and acting galactic. Many should follow soon.

In terms of our journey in this book, we are a big step closer to liftoff (Stage 3). For those readers who feel they can use a refresher before jumping to Stage 3, Stage 2 allows you to quickly get your business marketing wings. In the business of flying, safety is always first. Take the test. For the impatient ones among you, jump straight into the new rocket that awaits you—at your own risk.

Stage 2

LAUNCH PREPARATION: BASICS BEFORE YOU FLY

We could definitely make a flying, car – but that's not the hard part. The hard part is, how do you make a flying car that is super safe and quiet?

Elon Musk

Chapter 5
The Daedalus Paradox:
why preparation matters

Safety first. Understanding where the fundamentals come from matters. The business of flying and rocket science learned the hard way why pre-flight training is a must. Darwinian survival is at stake. If Daedalus had met Darwin earlier, Icarus might actually have made it. How high can people fly without training? As you plan to think galactic, better prepare.

January 28, 1986. I was looking forward to graduating end of June from my university alma mater, the KU Leuven in Belgium. My friends and I felt ready to take over the world. However, on that cold January day, our world would be shaken. Along with millions around the world, we saw in horror how the magnificent Space Shuttle *Challenger* exploded 73 seconds after liftoff[1]. All seven American crew members perished either instantly in the breakup, or latest when the cockpit crashed in the sea. There was disbelief everywhere. I've never forgotten that shocking visual.

It was not the first major Space Shuttle incident, and it would not be the last. After another deadly crash in 2003[2], NASA ended the whole program in 2011. Since the start of serious space campaigns across the world, at least 31 astronauts, test pilots and space personnel have paid the highest possible price for their courage. Yuri Gagarin was the first man in space: an orbit around the earth on April 12, 1961. He died 7 years later in an MIG jet trainer crash. For every major mission, many (expensive) test rockets and some fatalities seem to be the price of progress. However, the learning curve is exponential, and slowly but surely engineers are able to reduce that price.

I have no doubt people will land on Mars in the coming decades, but it will come at a price. Yes, the design thinking and assumptions that got us to the moon and beyond will be successfully challenged. Elon Musk has plans to get people on Mars by 2022, using BFRs (*Big Fucking Rockets*)[3]. But I doubt the bold language will be enough, and the timing is more than doubtful. Musk's credibility in delivery management is mixed. Tesla has significant electric car rollout delays. But he *did* surprise on SpaceX in a big way, and Tesla *did* deliver the world's biggest lithium-ion battery plant in South Australia in 100 days after contract signing, or would have given it for free[4]. The new battery plant already served its purpose a few times to alleviate sudden blackouts of the normal grid. Musk should never be underestimated. What is most relevant at this stage is not who will be right. One thing is sure though: we will see both triumph and tragedy.

In the leadership literature, the *Icarus Paradox* is a well established concept[5]. The term refers to the curious phenomenon of businesses (and its *heroic* leadership) failing suddenly after a period of apparent success. Critically, this failure is brought about by the very elements or drivers that led to the initial success. Any company once revered and idolized, is at risk to eat Icarus humble pie one day, unless they can completely reinvent themselves before that happens. Think of the various companies that became a *School of X*, whether of management (e.g. GE), marketing (e.g. P&G), money making (e.g. Goldman Sachs), cost-efficiency (e.g. 3G), or social media (e.g. Facebook). The same may happen to any and all companies and brands getting involved in Space Race 2.0.

Icarus

The background story on Icarus is found in Greek mythology (Diodorus, about 30-60 BC). After building the (in)famous labyrinth on the isle of Crete that would later house the Tauros of Minos (the Minotaur), the relationship between the craftsmen builders' father and son Daedalus and Icarus, and their client King Minos had soured. The King had them simply locked them up in the very maze they built. Their only escape route was via air (although there seems to exist a less sexy boat version of the story). The inventive architect Daedalus built two pairs of wings, attaching feathers to a wooden frame using wax.

He cautioned Icarus not to fly too low, or the sea damp would deny them the lift, nor to fly too high, or the wax would melt if he flew too close to the sun. However, in his youthful exuberance, feeling the adrenaline rush in his newfound flying abilities, the son ignored the father's warning and flew too high too fast. Wax melted, the makeshift wings fell apart, poor Icarus plunged and drowned in the sea below. The failure of the very wings that allowed him to escape imprisonment and soar through the skies was what ultimately led to his demise, hence the paradox.

How high can people fly without training? How can you know the boundaries of your knowledge, to get smart enough before hubris kicks in? How much risk is enough for a mere mortal, before he or she defies the Gods? Many people contributed to the progress of flying throughout history, setting new records. The Wright brothers took flight in 1903 across the Atlantic and survived. What is very risky for one, a definite *no go*, is just the start of normal for others. The concept of risk is very personal.

People love to hear about the records, but seldom look deeper to understand what it really took to get there. Space movies like *Hidden Figures* (2016), or *Mission Control: The Unsung Heroes of Apollo* (2017), show the incredible amount of people, processes and systems it took to deliver the level of excellence at the time of the first space missions. The careful planning, testing, failing, celebrating milestones, retesting, etc. The crushing personal weight on the leadership of the unknown, of ambiguity, of uncertainty and defeat, as assumptions are proven or disproven. The societal dogmas and paradigms that needed to be broken: a black female engineer, a black female *computer*, a black IBM mainframe supervisor.

Could Daedalus have saved his son?

As Branson, Bezos and Musk are demonstrating with Virgin Galactic, Blue Origin and SpaceX, for space economics to work at scale in the future, it is as important to prove that new spacecraft can get as high as we intend them to go, as well as to come back safely, to be reused and recycled again and again. No more nail-biting capsule crashes in the ocean resulting in complete write-offs. That new capability requires a different type of thinking, a new set of paradigms, a new approach to problem solving. Progress in flight and space will continue to require Darwinian revolution in thinking and process[6].

If Icarus had met Darwin earlier, he might have listened to his father more. However, if Daedalus had met Darwin earlier, he would probably have planned a series of test flights with his son before making their final escape. As an architect-builder, he would have tinkered with the wings, the feathers, and the wax, to find the best combination. Time permitting, he would have had a test flight plan. Equally critical, if not more important, he would have experimented with what flying high could do to the *psychology* of his inexperienced son. Understanding fundamentals matter.

> The *Daedalus Paradox* happens
> when even the wisest of men
> thinks he can skip
> even the most basic rules of evolution science.

The realization was never as profound to me as when Mike Alsbury, one of the Scaled Composites test pilots, died during a critical milestone test flight on October 31st, 2014. A terrible moment for the whole project. I lived thru this as a member of the growing Virgin Galactic Future Astronaut family. The subsequent media onslaught was creating a lot of confusion and doubt for what was, and still is, a very risky project. We had all been secretly starting to mark our calendars for flights in the years to come. Until that point the test flights were progressing well. Milestones were being met. Branson had learned to manage our expectations much better in the last years. Learning from previous unmet deadlines, he had stopped making promises about when he would go up first. Our mood was good, hopes had been high, and spirits were up—until that late October morning.

The setback was unexpected and really tough on everybody. Not because of any delays and questions about the future of Virgin Galactic, but in the first place because it was more personal. Many of us had met Mike and Pete. To us, they were not anonymous names in a newspaper article. In the end, staying on the moral high ground, Branson and the team at Virgin Galactic did a masterful job at helping us all move on. New safety processes and redesigns were put in place, to never make the same mistake. We were all offered a chance to get out of our earlier commitments, if we wanted to. Interestingly, virtually nobody did. Over time, the contrary happened. The VG community keeps growing, honoring Mike and everybody that has given so much already. Because it is worth it. This project has purpose. And the test flight program is back on track, with the team achieving three successful powered test flights in 2018.

Breaking Barriers

Test pilots are incredible. They risk their lives for the benefit of progress for humankind. They defy the Gods. But their breakthroughs are the result of careful preparation, iteration, reinvention and teamwork. Here are two great historical examples illustrating how meticulous preparation and thinking differently helped move frontiers of what humans could achieve:

Chuck Yeager
Breaking the sound barrier *inside* a vehicle (1947)

On October 14, 1947, US Air Force pilot Charles Elwood "Chuck" Yeager first broke the sound barrier, flying level in the Bell X-1, an experimental rocket-powered airplane[7]. Chuck was not a rookie test pilot. Before he hit Mach 1, he had built up a whole career and expertise in unusual flying, during and after the war. He also had the physical ability, analytical skills, and, last but not least as we have seen from the Icarus debacle, the psychological strength needed for such undertakings.

He listened to feedback from the engineers, and especially from fellow pilots around him. They inspired him, amongst others, to try out new tail movements at certain speeds. All this allowed them as a group to get closer to their goals in a systematic way, without major crashes. On first tests they achieved 0.83, then 0.88, 0.92, and ultimately, on that special day, first 0.98... and then he did break through the magical Mach 1, faster than 758 mph (1,220 kph) at sea level.

Felix Baumgartner
Breaking the sound barrier *outside* a vehicle (2012)

If you want to see another example of the full opposite of an Icarus flight: watch the YouTube video of Felix Baumgartner's hallucinative record-breaking jump in October 2012 from a helium-filled balloon. He jumped from an altitude of 39,045 meters (128,100 feet) over New Mexico in the US. He set the record for fastest speed of free fall at 1,357.64 km/h (843.6 mph). He is the first human to break Mach 1 *outside* a vehicle.

What Felix Baumgartner did outside the comfort of a machine still baffles me each time I watch that video. It took years of meticulous preparation and iteration to get to that moment. Team Stratos learned from previous experience, but ultimately completely jettisoned accepted wisdom from base jumping and other forms of high altitude jumping. They learned stratosphere jumping required a whole new way of thinking and test protocol to get there[8]. Their secret in summary: it was *one test jump at a time*. Learn on the fly. This capacity to let go of old wisdom, and to rethink from the ground up, is what helps fundamental progress. Just as SpaceX and Musk's software engineers are proving to NASA today.

How can companies or organizations, and the people that make them up, avoid succumbing to the Daedalus Paradox? How can we keep reinventing our own rockets to fly higher and faster, yet safer than ever?

The answer: get your business marketing wings before you fly higher. Invest some time to understand the fundamentals, and where they come from. When you start to think galactic, the air gets real thin fast. Better be prepared. Do the quick test on the next page.

Test:
Get your business marketing wings

Before a major sports effort, you warm up. Before you fly, you want to get your wings. Especially before you fly to galactic new levels.

We already covered how our space knowledge evolved over the last 50+ years. Interestingly, a lot of marketing and finance theory also evolved significantly over the same last 50+ years since these Golden Sixties. Before we discuss new marketing and investment models in a galactic age in stages 3 and 4, quickly (re)discover historic essentials about marketing and finance models (and miracles). Some of these fundamentals will continue to be true, even as we need to rethink a lot at the same time.

Take this fun 10-question test. Let's agree we apply Pareto's 80/20 rule. If you score at least eight out of 10 (>80%), you deserve your business marketing wings and can skip directly to stage 3.

1. Who invented *Miracle Whip*, and when?

2. Can you explain each of *Kotler's 4 Ps* invented in 1967?

3. What does the *AIDA model* stands for?

4. Why is the *CAPM model* important for marketers?

5. Why do investors care about *positive alpha*?

6. What are the *6Ds of Exponential Change*?

7. Why should you care about *black swans and grey rhinos*?

8. Why does the *5' shower challenge* matter to business?

9. Who spoke the immortal words *Eureka, Eureka*?

10. Where does the notion *Devil's Advocate* come from?

How did you do? If you did not make 8/10, no worries. You will certainly benefit from browsing this part before moving to stage 3. Before you fly a more sophisticated vessel like the new Marketing Capability Rocket, it is helpful to have your wings.

Welcome to flight training. Enjoy the ride!

Marketing makes selling unnecessary.

Peter Drucker

Chapter 6
Key marketing models the CEO/CFO should know

Marketing, finance and space: many of its core theories and breakthroughs developed in the Golden Sixties in the US. Philip Kotler developed the *4P* marketing model in 1967. Every self-respecting student of marketing should study this model, as should every leader and investor. Despite being challenged and amplified numerous times, many of its fundamentals still hold up 50+ years later. A miracle, or a curse for the profession? What other marketing models should any CEO and CFO have heard about?

Miracle Whip salad dressings were invented and launched by venerable Kraft Foods at the Chicago 1933 World Fair (the Century of Progress Exposition), as a healthier alternative to *fat* mayonnaise. It was designed to be slightly sweeter and a tad more spicy and tangy. For Belgians, such imitation white *dressing* wannabe mayo was probably sacrilege. Belgians worship their tasty homemade and great commercial mayo to go with their world-famous fries. But as much as the Belgians claim global mayo fame, Russia and the Baltics are the champions of mayo per capita consumption in the world[1]. Here in the US, the only *non home made* versions I would recommend is Sir Kensington's delicious avocado mayo or innovative Fabanaise[2]. But then I am biased.

We are not here to belabor culinary tastes and cross-cultural consumer preferences. Miracle Whip became fast a much bigger idea than the actual food it stood for. In those days, after World War 1, it reflected the dawning of the age of modern food. It was another symbol of progressive new thinking for the households. Its value proposition was *more for less*: whip things up faster, enjoy a same or better taste, and save time for more important things. It became shorthand for smart easy ideas that replace old complex ideas[3].

Marketing Miracles were first celebrated in New York, in Irving Levy's publication called *Miracles of Marketing* (1962)[4]. It was part of a series including *Miracles of Science*, *Miracles of Healing*, etc. He equated marketing to advertising. His was also actually the first plea for frugality in advertising efforts, listing a number of cases where smart, insight-driven copywriting combined with direct mail for great products got better results than mega campaigns supporting mediocre products. *Any promotion is most effective in its simplest, quickest, boldest, most direct, (and as a result) least expensive form.* To be effective and efficient, nothing beats going as direct as possible from brand to consumers. A lesson I applied thought my entire marketing career: cut out the middleman where possible.

Marketing Miracle Whip was invented soon after, in 1967, 50+ years ago, when Philip Kotler released his seminal textbook *Marketing Management*. He immortalized what is known now, or should still be known today by every student of marketing, as *The Marketing Mix, and its famous 4Ps: Product, Price, Place, Promotion.* These four are *the set of controllable variables that the firm can use to influence the buyer's response.*

The Kotler 4P Model
Summary of the original definitions

Product

Defines the product or services mix, and covers everything from the physical product (functional benefits, features, aesthetics, lifespan...) to the extensive product (packaging, brand name, ancillary services like guarantees...) to the total product (emotional and immaterial benefits, values...).

Price

As defined by supply and demand, adjustable as needed to reflect elasticity per different channel of distribution (place). Optimized over time for the firm depending of its objectives (volume, share, profit...).

Place

Wherever the product or service is offered. Covers not only the various distribution outlets, but also the specific place inside each outlet (eg shelf space). Attention goes to the pros and cons and economics of direct and indirect forms of distribution.

Promotion

Really all forms of communication, above- and below-the-line advertising, stimulating sales.

Interestingly, the base idea behind the 4P conceptual framework seems to have been proposed earlier in 1960 by another academic, Jeremy McCarthy, in his book *Basic Marketing: a Management Approach.* It was the first book to define marketing as a true management science, clinically defining the challenges of the marketing manager in the 4P typology. McCarthy was an American marketing professor teaching at different top universities in the Midwest (Michigan State, University of Notre Dame).

Up until his death in 2015, McCarthy had been very active in the world of marketing teaching and publishing. And though he never achieved Kotler's notoriety, the American Marketing Association awarded him the Trailblazer Award in 1987. It remains a bit of a mystery how the 4P typology may have traveled between these two men. But whatever happened, the 4Ps became a massive success, a secret formula to market anything successfully. It became *the* way to deliver on Drucker's famous quote on marketing (see opening of this chapter).

AIDA

Historically speaking, AIDA is likely the oldest marketing model[5]. The model apparently goes back to the 19th century. However, it was not as comprehensive in its contribution to the breadth of the marketing science. If you were to apply the 4Ps, AIDA would fit more in the last P of Promotion—the P we would call advertising and/or connections today.

AIDA is built on the theory that an individual prospective buyer will go through four distinct cognitive stages in a buying process. Marketers need to capture their target consumer in a purchasing funnel that starts by creating *Awareness*, converting that into *Interest*, creating *Desire*, and finally closing the sale with *Action*. Later on, some people added an *R* to the model, representing the important role of *Retention* (repeat sales).

Since 2000, the advent of internet and social media has completely turned this model on its head. Other consumers and communities now interlope this process on all levels. To this end, explore my dear friend and master provocateur Joe Jaffe's breakthrough challenge to the AIDA model in his marketing bestseller *Flip the Funnel: How to use Existing Customers to Gain New Ones* (2010). His key thesis in our hyperconnected world today: retention is the new acquisition. Leverage your best fans as brand ambassadors to close new sales.

The 4P Challengers

Since 1967, many things happened in the world of marketing thinking. Impactful new marketing concepts were launched that would inspire marketers forever. One of the names every student of marketing should study is *Theodore Levitt*, an American professor at Harvard. He rose to global fame in 1983 with a Harvard Business Review (HBR) article on *The Globalization of Markets*, arguing the emergence of similar consumer tastes around the world for companies to organize around. Later, in HBR of summer 2004, he pushed the idea of consumer-centricity in *Marketing Myopia*, criticizing business for too narrowly defining what they were doing, and persuasively arguing the case for marketing to work hand in hand with sales and other functions to create sustainable growth based on consumer needs and desires.

Levitt was the one to provoke amongst others that existential question any business leader should ask from his team: *what business are we in?* For example, if you are in the railroad industry, are you in the business of running trains, or instead providing transportation. Hence, you could offer multiple forms of transportation. Or, pushing the thinking even further, are you in the business of connecting people? In that case, why would you let a telecom company build telegraph capability for free on *your* tracks and outgrow you, instead of offering this new type of service yourself?

Since then, many others started to issue their own models, frameworks or secret recipes for successful marketing: observant authors, management consultancies, and yes, CMOs. There is lots for marketers to google/read. You will find a curated list on vicomte.com/insights. But here are some key ones worth knowing now:

- The 1994 classic bestseller *The 22 Immutable Laws of Marketing* by **Al Ries and Jack Trout.**

- **McKinsey**'s systematic BrandMatics® brand management approach explained in *Power Brands* (3 editions since 2006 by Jesko Perry and colleagues).

- The science-based works by **Byron Sharpe** since he wrote *How Brands Grow: What Marketers Don't Know* (2010). Sharpe is a must read[6]. He challenges convention and replaces it with empirical facts. In a nutshell, he argues that for most brands, growth will primarily come from gaining new users (penetration) rather than from driving increased loyalty. Most of a brand's users will be light users. He therefore will urge brands to build physical availability (distribution) and mental availability (saliency). He also forces brand owners to be active portfolio players, accepting that users will always have a repertoire of partly interchangeable brands. So being as distinctive as possible is a must, rather than accepting mere differentiation. Advertising can help this saliency. As most users will be light users, the more reach you can get as a brand, the better.

- **Jobs to Be Done Theory – Customer Journeys (2016)** I could equally have placed this theory already in 1990[7]. Since that time, **Anthony Ulwick** has been on the core idea of brands (products/services/solutions) to essentially solve a specific job for the consumer: *Consumers don't buy drills. They want to fill a hole.* The practice of mapping every step of an ever evolving consumer decision journey's starting from their needs got extra attention in the technology-enhanced world of the last decade. It inspired changing business models from marketing products to delivering solutions. For example: Volvo's newest cars are sold based on the new *from car to care* principle[8].

- Back in 2013 – 2014, the most comprehensive global marketing study ever was undertaken, called **Marketing 2020.** Nicknamed M2020 – Organizing for Growth, it was the brainchild of **Marc de Swaan Arons**, himself an accomplished marketer with Unilever training, author of *The Global Brand CEO* (2010). Marc also co-founded Effective Brands (now Kantar Consulting), one of the first consultancies focused on global brands. In partnership with the ANA, the leading Association of National Advertisers in the US, Spencer Stuart and Adobe, M2020 focused on how to best align marketing strategy, structure, and capabilities for business growth.

The M2020 fieldwork included vision interviews with more than 250 leading CMOs and an in-depth online survey of an unprecedented 10,491 contributors from 92 countries. I became part of the M2020 Steering Committee, presided by Keith Weed, Global Marketing and Communications Officer for Unilever. By Summer 2014, exactly 10 years after Levitt's last groundbreaking article, Keith, Marc and fellow Kantar leader Frank van den Driest published the key M2020 findings in what would become one of Harvard Business Reviews best selling articles: *The Ultimate Marketing Machine*.

CMOs and CEOs have always been looking for silver bullets, but the HBR article argued there was no one size fits all structure to support great marketing. It outlined a model to better understand what values and goals would guide brand strategy, what capabilities drive marketing excellence, and what structures and ways of working would best support them. In 2016, building on these M2020 insights, Keith released his own internal *5C* framework to help inspire Unilever marketers to deliver on its *Brands for Life* mantra. The 5C's stood for focus on Consumer, Connections, Content, Commerce and Community.

All these models have their value. Better a half decent playbook to operate with than having no playbook at all. If you want to dig deeper, and read the greatest marketing books of all time, just google exactly those words. Some books are more groundbreaking or provocative than others. Each of them has pushed the thinking further, challenged and reinvented, sometimes building on previous findings. One that influenced me more than others at the time was former Coke CMO Sergio Zyman's *The End of Marketing as We Know It* (1999). More about him later in the key chapter on pricing.

CEOs also entered the marketing discussion. If you have never done so, watch the late Steve Jobs, YouTube talk on Apple marketing. Some other CEO's perspective on marketing was not yet what I would hope it to be. Here is Jeff Bezos, Amazon CEO, quoted on value creation versus advertising on Google:

The balance of power is shifting toward consumers and away from companies… The right way to respond to this if you are a company is to put the vast majority of your energy, attention and dollars into building a great product or service and put a smaller amount into shouting about it, marketing it.

Like many senior business executives, he equates *marketing* again too much to one-way old school *advertising*. Amazon, love or hate them, is actually doing brilliant consumer-centric work. I will discuss the Amazon Prime case in Chapter 9 on pricing power. Marketing, as we will see, is so much more than advertising. Advertising is part of marketing. What is true however is that the concept of (paid) advertising existed much earlier than the broader field of marketing. In *The Attention Merchants: The Epic Scramble to Get Inside Our Heads* (2016), Columbia Law professor Tim Wu magnificently describes the evolution through time of all forms of attention-seeking. And then takes us through the fast evolution from the invention of the first paid advertising in the 19th century penny press in New York, to all forms of digital connections to date. He makes you reflect deeply on how our attention has become the product monetized at our expense. Still, I repeat, advertising is not marketing. Just a part of it.

Kotler's Curse?

In true Darwinian spirit, the 4P model was challenged numerous times. Yet somehow his Miracle Whip marketing model stuck, like a curse. Kotler's curse. A good curse. The 4P model has endured. Something is there. Something immutable indeed. While Kotler also expanded his own thinking over the years, he never wavered from his basic model. Many additional Ps have been suggested by various sources. Examples include:

- **Personnel:** the role of your own employees to help market and sell

- **Periphery:** the societal context in which one operates

- **Partners:** the role of all sorts of partnerships, even with competitors

The fundamentals in his 4P marketing model are sound, and we should respect and honor Kotler for it. After 50+ years, he can truly claim the mantle as the godfather of fundamental marketing thinking. Marketing Management is still among the most sold and used marketing books, with over 15 editions since 1967.

However, for everything there is a time and a place. I do agree the 4P model format, and its packaging, may have grown a bit stale and dusty after 50+ years. More importantly, since the digital revolution, and since the advent of a more science-based approached evangelized by authors like Byron Sharpe, there is truly new thinking that merits to be highlighted in its own right in a refreshed model. It *is* time to repackage and amplify the core ideas behind the 4Ps in a metaphor or model that students and business executives will *want* to study and can more easily remember in a galactic age. Marketing needs to eat its own dog food of reinvention, without dismissing the fundamental thinking that remains valid.

That is what stage 3 of this book will be all about. I will refresh and upgrade Kotler's fundamentals, all with the deepest respect for the maestro. Before we go there, let's discover the next chapter of stage 2: the one finance model all marketers ought to know before they fly.

In investing, what is comfortable is rarely profitable.

Robert Arnott

Chapter 7

The one finance model the CMO really needs to know

Nobody should ever become a CEO, CMO or a senior marketing leader without understanding the core theories behind risk and financial capital allocation decision-making. Like marketing, finance is a wide arena with many subcomponents. Galactic business marketers understand the greek letters *alpha* and *beta* in the *CAPM* model, and why investors are on an eternal hunt for *positive alpha*.

Some of the concepts you learn at university only sink in many years later. My undergraduate studies were in International Business at the Catholic University of Leuven (KU Leuven), Belgium's oldest university (1425). I graduated in 1986 from its Faculty of Economics and Business. I always liked economics. But looking back, I must admit that I only understood much later how impactful some of its concepts were in real life. I am not talking about the basics of supply and demand. But about the real power of ideas like utility curves, price elasticity, consumer and producer surplus, scarcity, and especially risk and opportunity cost. *Risk is the core driver of human progress,* a great quote from Peter Bernstein's magistral *Against the Gods: the Story of Risk* (1996).

Closely linked with that notion of risk is the idea of *capital ownership*. Employees in a company always moan that their company should take more risk. They will claim it should be more open to experimentation and make bolder moves. Wall Street analysts will write scathing reviews of companies or CEOs that don't move fast enough to deliver on their share predictions. Consultants will come tell you what you need to do better. Bankers will encourage you to invest in higher yield products and be open for more risk in your investment portfolio.

Most people talk about risk with the benefit of hindsight. As they say in German: *Der Historiker Ist ein rückwärts gekehrter Prophet,* the historian always beats the prophet. In plain English: *hindsight is 20/20.* There is limited to no risk looking at the past. Business school students will provide smart analysis based on elaborate case studies about why company X was so much smarter than company Y, after the facts. History has already been written. At best we can learn from the past to help us in the future. But a galactic future is full of galactic risk.

Many people love to *talk* about taking more risk, but they usually want *you* to take that risk. Most people don't want skin in the game. Or, at best, they manage OPM: *Other People's Money.* Our biases tend to be very different when it is not really about us, not about our own wallet, or not about our own life. The concept of risk only truly comes alive in full color when you bet your *own* money, when you stake your *own* reputation, when it is your own life. When, for some entrepreneurs, you go *all in*[1].

Alpha and omega are respectively the first and last letters of the Greek alphabet. In Christianity, the expression *being the Alpha and the Omega* is well known to position Jesus (or God) as *the beginning and the end of all*, the one and only. In rocket science, within an infinite universe, people now start to dream of reaching Alpha Centauri, the closest star system to our solar system where we will be sending ships to soon. The best known omega linked to space is actually a watch brand. The iconic *Omega Speedmaster* has been the astronauts' timepiece of choice and linked to space travel adventures since 1957[2]. It is nicknamed *The MoonWatch*, after Neil Armstrong wore it on July 21, 1969, during mankind's first moon landing.

In finance, to manage risk, only the first two letters of the Greek alphabet really matter: alpha, and beta. They are part of the basics of financial theory every galactic marketer worth his or her salary needs to know.

α, **Alpha**
the financial symbol representing exceptional returns
over and above the expected return from a risky asset.

β, **Beta**
the financial symbol representing individual risk profile
of an investment.

Financial markets help modern market economies by allocating scarce capital resources. As we will also see further in part 4, savings from various sides of the economy are transferred to companies to deploy in their growth plans. Investors expect to be compensated for the investment risks they take. To optimize the risk/return equation, they collect as much information in advance as they can before allocating capital. There are *two* key financial theories every marketer should be aware of, developed in the Fifties and Sixties in the US.

1. The Theory of Portfolio Choice (Harry Markowitz – 1958)

His primary contribution consisted of developing a clear operational theory for portfolio selection under uncertainty. To reduce risk, investors should diversify. They should spread their risk carefully over multiple investments in function of their respective return potential. In simple terms, this is the idea of *not putting all eggs in one basket*. By putting together various investments with different risk profiles, risk cannot be completely eliminated, but the portfolio risk tends to become lower than the sum of its parts.

2. The Theory of Price Formation of Financial Assets (William Sharpe – 1964)

Sharpe (and others) built on Markowitz'ideas to develop the Capital Asset Pricing Model (*CAPM*)[3]. It is predicated on the idea that investors need to be compensated both by the time value of money as well as by the risk they assume. Successful investing is all about seeking and unlocking what is called *positive alpha*: the *additional* return above the *expected* return, which is the beta adjusted return of the market.

CAPM has constantly been challenged on its empirical robustness and underlying assumptions. For example, the model assumes all market actors behave rationally all the time, all information is available to all in the same way at the same time, etc. The reality has proven to be more complex and ambiguous, but still virtually every self-respecting business school teaches CAPM. Every analyst will use its base principles, along with techniques to determine a company's weighted cost of capital, and valuation techniques like Discounted Cash Flow.

CAPM in a nutshell

In *A Brief History of Time* (1988), eminent Cambridge cosmologist Stephen Hawking warned that for every formula you put on a page, you may lose half of your readership. So I put it in a separate frame, for those who are curious to know more.

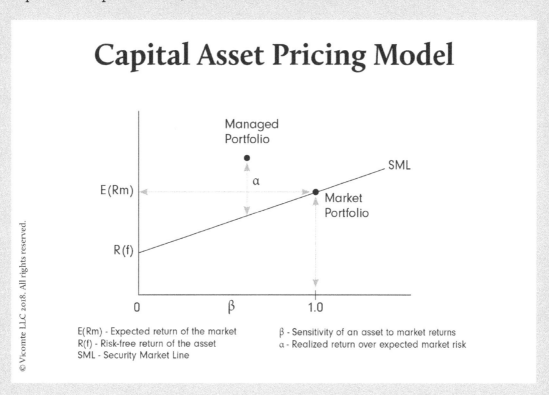

Capital Asset Pricing Model

E(Rm) - Expected return of the market
R(f) - Risk-free return of the asset
SML - Security Market Line

β - Sensitivity of an asset to market returns
α - Realized return over expected market risk

The formula to calculate an expected return of an asset given its risk profile is as follows

$$\overline{r_a} = r_{f} + \beta_a(\overline{r_m} - r_f)$$

Where:

r_f = Risk-free rate

β_a = Beta of the security

$\overline{r_m}$ = Expected market return

The **risk-free rate (Rf)** is the market's reflection of the base time value of money, usually the yield of the safest type of investments, like US treasuries or government bonds.

The **beta** of any security is a measure of its volatility, or systematic risk, in comparison to the market as a whole. A beta is typically bigger or smaller than 1.0. Above 1.0, the asset is seen as more volatile than the market, so a higher risk, and therefore possible higher reward choice versus market average. Below 1.0, the asset is perceived as being lower risk, and therefore possible lower return versus market average. If the beta is zero, the asset makes the risk-free return.

Lastly, there are **3 potential outcomes of your investment in terms of alpha**. Any good manager will always strive for positive alpha through asset allocation, diversification, valuation, stock picking, and leveraging information asymmetries. But there are no guarantees. Alpha can turn out to be positive, zero or negative (see table).

- $\alpha < 0$: the investment has earned too little for its risk
      (or, was too risky for the return)

- $\alpha = 0$: the investment has earned a return adequate for the risk taken

- $\alpha > 0$: the investment has a return in excess of the reward for the assumed risk

To increase their chance to create positive alpha, analysts and investors will do everything in their power to get accuracy and predictability of the numbers they base their capital allocation decisions on. That is an area where this book will try to help. In Part 4 we will offer a new methodology to help unlock alpha hidden inside the marketing black hole.

In the end, investors will make calls. They will play different degrees of volatility, and will make short- and/or long-term bets. They they will start to pray they will come out on the good side of the position they ultimately took. For all the phenomenal number-crunching behind the decision, they are humans like the rest of us. As we will see in the next chapters, nobody controls the future. No model offers 100% control. Not in finance, not in marketing, nowhere. Beating the market with exceptional returns is far from easy, as I learned (see inset: the facebook IPO).

The facebook IPO

Here is a personal learning of how difficult it is to create positive alpha: the *facebook* IPO (Initial Public Offering). An IPO is essentially the first time that the stock of a private company, typically a fast-growing scale-up, is offered to the public markets. Its objective is to raise capital to fuel expansion. It also offers loyal or former employees who were often paid a significant part of their salary in stock options an opportunity to finally exercise them, possibly after a six-month lock-up after the effective IPO date.

IPOs take time to happen, if they happen at all. So, to create some liquidity for its early-hour employees, many companies in Silicon Valley started to endorse a new practice: to selectively allow key current or former employees to cash in on options they had received. New secondary, unregulated markets emerged to connect this new class of sellers with many eager buyers who all wanted in before the IPO. Market actors included companies like Second Market and SharesPost.

Seeing the growing impact of social media in the brand landscape, I believed it was worth betting on the long-term potential of what this new company called Facebook was trying to do. Short term, there were a thousand open questions. It was a crap shoot. I was also curious about how these new investment mechanics worked. So, as a believer in experiential learning, I decided to try to buy a few of these Facebook options on the secondary market.

It was a very paper-heavy cumbersome process, definitely only worth the time if one sees real upside later. These options could not be traded anywhere until an IPO would eventually happen and a new primary market would be created. The theory was that, *if* an IPO or other exit would be done at a significantly higher price later on, the early risk-takers would create significant alpha. The *expected* risk (beta) was certainly already high. To generate any *additional* return (positive alpha) over the expected return, Facebook would have to be sold at a killer price. I rolled the dice.

As it turned out, Facebook did IPO much sooner than anybody had assumed. After a much hyped process, on May 18, 2012, it raised over $16 Bn as the largest tech IPO in US history. Uncharacteristically for an IPO however, the final $ 38 opening price was not only very close to what I had paid for on the secondary market months before, but there was no *first day pop* either. There was no first day premium for anybody who got their hands on IPO shares from the banks authorized to offer them. Actually worse, Facebook shares declined soon after from the $ 42 opening price, before coming climbing back months later, and ultimately growing to what it is now. The decline was due to two reasons: 1) because the IPO was already priced at the level which allowed Facebook, not investors, to capture most alpha for itself (great move for them), and 2) a technical issue during the NASDAQ opening session that caused a lot of market confusion.

In any case, this IPO upset a number of old beliefs on how to make alpha. Since Facebook's experience, a great deal of the alpha is being generated pre-IPO. Witness for example the frenzy in Uber shares. If and when they will IPO, most of the cream will likely be gone. Spotify also changed the rules in their latest IPO. I ultimately made some decent capital gains on the few Facebook shares I had been able to buy before the IPO, holding on long enough after the IPO. I should have kept them even longer, but I did not for other reasons. Hindsight is always 20/20. In summary: the investment paid back in absolute, but my alpha was negative. My learning ROI was very high. More than ever I realized how important these financial concepts are for marketers.

As a senior marketer you better know how your CFO thinks, and how public market or private investor analysts are incentivized. It is worth finding out why analysts do what they do, and how they are trained to do it. While good CFOs think both short and longer term, analysts typically focus on so-called critical inflection points over the next 90-180-360 days that may cause an asset's value to go up or down. These inflection points could be pricing news, markets share moves, product renovations or new product launches, key personnel changes, market regulation changes, etc. Anything that could possibly impact future earnings.

Buy. Hold. Sell.

After collecting whatever data they can get their hands on, they will develop a *base case* scenario. Then they will develop some form of *bull & bear* scenarios along with outcome *ranges* pending on a number of factors and assumptions about future performance. Next they will weave an impactful and provocative narrative around their numbers, with the hope to catch the attention of their bosses and the investor market, as well as of the asset owners. Their personal purpose is to build a reputation over time as a market mover. By correctly calling the trend more than they miss in the categories they specialized in, they can become rockstars in their own right. Yes, Masters of the Universe. The concept is as alive today as it was in the Tom Wolfe Eighties.

During my TRIUM Global MBA I had to write two analyst reports as part of a masterclass in corporate finance (on PepsiCo) and one in bankruptcy risk (on the European airline industry). I admit it was quite an exhilarating experience to try to predict the future of an asset. Since then, I appreciate the work of analysts more. If anybody wants to give it a try for his or her own company, download the excellent material from NYU Stern's *guru on valuation* Aswath Damodaran[4]. Once you go through that, you will better appreciate how your own CFO, and external analysts, will look at the key investment decisions (invest or not?), financing decisions (the role of all forms of debt and equity), and dividend decisions (how to pay investors back).

In conclusion: future galactic marketers who want to attract funds for their ideas need to learn to speak better Wall Street. Think positive alpha. In the new galactic age ahead of us, there is a lot of positive alpha to be had if you play your cards right. Equally, investors and CFOs need to develop empathy for Main Street, and learn to understand the key models that underpinned marketing through the ages.

There are a few more general business models to work through, as they all tend to impact Brands somehow. Business loves these models, even though they occasionally blindside us. Buyer beware.

When you view your world exclusively through the lens of science, your prescription will never be strong enough.

Jay Nichols

Chapter 8
Models work, but buyer beware

Besides CAPM (finance) and 4P (marketing), there are some other models that influenced business marketing decisions over the last 50+ years. As old ones fade or evolve, and new ones emerge, models will continue to influence our decisions, despite their built-in flaws and limitations. Luckily, black swans, grey rhinos and irrational human beings will keep life and business more unpredictable and fascinating than ever.

You know the *Eisenhower Matrix* (circa 1950). Maybe not exactly by that name, but most of you have seen the prioritization matrix invented by former US President Dwight Eisenhower: four quadrants resulting from the axes *urgent* and *important,* resulting in different decisions[1]: what to do first, what to schedule, what to delegate, and what not to do at all. As per the General: *what is important is seldom urgent, and what is urgent is seldom importan*t.

If you are or have been a business student, if you work or worked in a corporate environment, changes are high you ***did a SWOT*** at some point in time during case analysis, or during strategic review times. The ask: develop a matrix with four quadrants visualizing Strengths, Weaknesses, Opportunities and Threats, all relative to your current (and future) competition. The basis for many scenarios and decisions afterwards. The SWOT model is credited to Albert S. Humphrey, a business management consultant who worked in the Sixties and Seventies at the Stanford Research Institute.

Some of you may have been asked to go even deeper, and ***do a Five Forces.*** This was the brainchild of Michael Porter, Harvard professor and one of the world's most influential thinkers on management and competitiveness. *Porter's Five Forces Framework* (1979) is a tool for assessing the competitive strength and position of a business or organization. It invites you to deeply reflect on five forces that his research suggests determine the competitive intensity and, therefore, the attractiveness (or lack of it) of an industry in terms of its profitability (ROIC, Return on Invested Capital): threat of entry (1) and of substitution (2), bargaining power of suppliers (3) and of buyers (4), and the level of industry rivalry (5).

The most widely used models are perceived to be memorable, simple and useful. They provide a framework to organize thoughts in an organized way, putting order in chaos. Perfect for the left brain thinking that is typically dominant in a business setting, just like biologists love taxonomies.

Powerful Models

1 Are easy to <u>remember</u>

2 Are very simple to <u>apply</u>

3 Align the minds for <u>action</u>

There are a number of useful models that have broken through in the management and entrepreneurship literature over the last 50+ years. Here are five more models used widely in business, in chronological order.

1. The BCG Growth-Share Matrix (1970)

Every student of marketing has seen this iconic 2x2 matrix, invented by Bruce Henderson from the Boston Consulting Group to help companies with long-term strategic portfolio planning. The tool visualizes in a simple way the relative attractiveness of brands or business units in four quadrants: dogs, stars, cash cows and problem children. As a result, depending on their objectives, companies know where to allocate more or less resources over the years to come[2].

2. The CAGE Distance framework for semi-globalization (2001)

Created by Pankaj Ghemawat, currently professor at NYU Stern, the premise of CAGE is that perfect globalization (*a flat world*) never really existed despite all the hype[3]. To be successful on a global scale, and versus local competition, companies still need to address *Cultural, Administrative* (institutional and regulatory), *Geographic* and *Economic* differences, or distances, between countries. On his website you will find a practical CAGE Comparator online tool: covering 163 countries and 65 industries, allowing simulation of 16 CAGE distance types.

3. The Business Model Canvas: a handbook for visionaries, game changers, and challengers (2010)

The Canvas was written by Strategyzer consultants Alexander Osterwalder and Yves Pigneur, co-created by 470 practitioners from 45 countries, and delivered in a stunning visual format[4]. The model became a sensation in teaching, and among young founders, offering a practical blueprint to think through business model reinvention and starting a new company. Realizing over time that the central *value proposition* part of the canvas was definitely one of the most difficult parts to crack for anybody, a sequel followed: *the Value Proposition Canvas* (2015).

I have gone through many workshops using this model, or similar other ones. My personal experience remains that, despite the extra book, the value proposition area remains the toughest one for aspiring entrepreneurs. This is an area where mastery of the marketing fundamentals can be of immense value. If you don't get the value proposition right from the start, the risk is high that your entire business model will be flawed from the outset (see later in Part 3, Chapter 15).

4. The Lean Start Up (2011)

Eric Ries is an innovation evangelist. He made words like *Minimum Viable Product (MVP)*, iteration and continuous innovation buzzwords for the new generation of startups and scale-ups. Seeing its success, he released *The Startup Way* (2017), extending his thinking to shake large so called *dinosaur* organizations into applying the same methodology that made many scale-ups successfully disrupt their incumbent markets.

5. The Six Ds of Exponential Change (2015)

Peter Diamandis wears multiple hats. He is the Singularity University co-creator, inventor of the XPrize, and author of radically positive outlooks on the future, like *Bold* and *Abundance*. Along with co-author Steven Kotler they advocate the principles of Digitization, Deception, Disruption, Dematerialization, Demonetization, Democratization to drive exponential (1, 2, 4, 8, 16…), not linear change (1,2,3,4,5…).

I am in Control

CEOs, investors and boards all love models. They give a feeling one is control of one's destiny. You control your future. Models create comfort, alignment, decision clarity and a sense of predictability. The future is perceived easier to control by jargon. As we already learned: jargon matters. And while all models have built-in limitations, they tend to work. Johan Cruyff, the Dutch football legend, said it in his own idiosyncratic way: *every disadvantage has its advantage*.

Models provide the simplification of the multitude of potential options and scenarios out there. You will discuss what the model tells you to discuss, within the time you allocate for it. More often than not, due to time constraints and general impatience to get to a decision (*any* decision), we neglect to prepare for the real *what if* scenarios or for the real *events* that could derail the fundaments of the business. We usually don't have the willingness to see the deeper underlying shifts in consumer preference for our product, often only observable only at the very fringes of your industry (like what happened on the emergence of so called *craft* beer repositioning *mainstream* beer, or lately the emergence of cannabis versus alcohol).

TLAs

Every company has its own *TLAs*, Three Letter Acronyms. I spent countless hours in model related sessions at P&G, Coke and AB InBev.

For example, back in the early 2000s, when internet use started to proliferate, our Coca-Cola marketing mix models were built on historical data linking investments in classic forms of advertising (TV, print...) to market share and volume growth. However, soft drink users, like everybody, were moving to digital channels, social media, word of mouth and other difficult to quantify and measure model inputs. So what good was it to keep making decisions on bygone connection models? Still, we were animals of habit. And the law of inertia exists precisely because it is a law: habits die hard. Just witness the number of businesses that still have not come to grips with the promise and challenge of a digital world, more than 15 years later.

Later on, with AB InBev, our future was designed via *CCW* (Cost-Connect-Win), ABI's recipe for success that connected the externally well known and feared *ZBB* (Zero Based Budgeting), with the lesser known *VBB* (Connect – Values Based Brands), to Winning in the marketplace. In the marketing department we had a bunch of models: market growth projection models (1 to 10 years into the future), marketing mix models (to determine future marketing investment allocation), etc.

Decision clarity was usually achieved after a bunch of iterations and negotiation involving lots of pizza and beer nights. However, the comfort was often false, in both directions. One could be positively or negatively surprised, but business leaders usually hate surprises. They want to be right. They love predictability. They want to control the recipe of the playbook, and repeat it with certainty. If you did much better than anticipated, you could be accused of sandbagging, or not being ambitious enough. If you fell below, all hell broke lose in a different way.

Halfway through the year, for many companies the cycle starts again, with a vengeance. Everybody has to review all assumptions again, starting from a variance analysis. More quant and qual research is commissioned to underpin the new rationale. Blame or fame goes around, targets are renegotiated, new decisions made, etc. Again and again. This is the managerial grind, and in agile world it is probably to be expected and normal. This simply is the hard everyday task of *what management does*, and what keeps most people at companies busy on an ongoing basis. A perennial P&G favorite drilled into all its people is the use of the OGSM model to translate Vision into plans: Objectives, Goals, Strategies and Measures[5]. Another favorite is the *OKR* technique that promises to drive 10X growth: Objectives and Key Results. Companies like Intel and Google swear by it[6].

All these models and tracking techniques have value, as long as the they don't end up ruling the business. Here I risk to enter the more delicate debate on management versus leadership. I won't go there in this book, other than cautioning the reader to not let models define your course entirely. The tail should never wag the dog.

Black Swans, Gray Rhinos and Superforecasting

There are however never guarantees that when you apply any model, you can expect guaranteed miracles. Unpredictability and irrational behavior are and will remain part of business life, and luckily so. At least for now, consumers and stakeholders will never accept to be reduced to just being a convenient input in a model. The world would be a boring place without surprise. Prof. Nassim Nicholas Taleb, currently at NYU's Tandon School of Engineering, made this thought immortal following his book *The Black Swan: the impact of the highly improbable* (2007).

A black swan event is defined as a rare and unpredictable one that undermines everything you've known and assumed before. It can literally annihilate everything you've built your life or company on. Essentially, it is an unpredictable history-defining event. In soccer, it is the unfathomable 7-1 defeat by Brazil to Germany in the World Cup 2014 semi-final[7]. It was their biggest world cup defeat ever, and nobody would expect such a scenario. Certainly not a single gambler or bookmaker. Equally, four years later, nobody would ever have anticipated all the *unthinkable* moments making the 2018 Russia World Cup one of the most unpredictable and fascinating ones ever:

- Two football powerhouses eliminated early: reigning 2014 World Champion Germany, as last of their group[8]. Argentina, not making it out of the group stage after uninspiring showings

- Russia progressing to the quarterfinals after beating Spain, and proudly leaving the tournament after the narrowest of wins by Croatia after (on penalties)

- Brasil's Neymar-led *Yellow Canaries* eliminated in the quarterfinals, this time by the magistral Belgian *Red Devils*

For the movie business, its black swan could actually take the form of a *Black Panther*, the superhero movie with black talent only. It shattered all records, defying any stereotypes around predominantly white superheroes in a racially challenged Hollywood[9]. It may be a catalyst for a very different Hollywood in the future. And it seems it may have peacefully achieved what the original Black Panther Party political organization fought for in the United States from 1966 until 1982.

A second animal that you should avoid being run over by is the Gray Rhino. *Behind every Black Swan is a crash of Gray Rhinos. You'd think we don't need to wake up to obvious crises; aren't we dealing with them already? Yet quite the opposite is true. We are terrible at paying attention to what should be anticipated*[10]. Another expression is to timely recognize and deal with the proverbial *elephant in the room*: the highly probable, highly obvious, high-impact dangers that are—or at least ought to be—treated as clear and present, yet all too often are neglected. The weak signals were there, yet there is a reluctance to see and act on the warning signs despite being observed by many. Brexit comes to mind. The impact of aging societies. We all know it is coming, we see the Rhino charging, yet action happens too little, too late.

At the end of every year, every self-respecting TV network or magazine will review the most salient news and game changing events of the year. Invariably, it contains political, economic and social events *none of us had seen coming*. Election results surprises, unexpected M&A deals, regrettable deaths of celebrities or loved ones, freak accidents, etc. The few people that had adequately publicly predicted one of them correctly are put on a pedestal, and for some time solicited for their wise views of what's next. They are heralded as the new Nostradamus. Until also they fail, and are cut back in the media to the level of all of us, normal men and women.

Bloomberg, the financial data and news company, is bolder. It applies the new art of so-called superforecasting: making bold predictions yet accepting to fail dramatically[11]. It dares to publish its *Pessimists Guide* for the year to come, imagining a number of scenarios and events in the world that go against consensus expectations, yet would have a game changing impact. If you cannot get enough of superforecasting, enroll in the Good Judgment Project started in 2011. It is designed to leverage the wisdom of the crowds to forecast key world events[12].

They (models) are funny, aren't they?

Daniel Kahneman (and Vernon Smith) were awarded the 2002 Nobel Memorial Prize in Economic Sciences for their work on the psychology of judgment and decision making. Never since the inaugural year of the prize, in 1968, had the Sveriges Riksbank (Sweden's Central Bank) recognized this more psychology-driven part of finance and economics. Kahneman's empirical findings, published in accessible form in *Thinking Fast and Slow* (2011), challenged the assumption of human rationality prevailing in modern economic theory. It unveiled how our biases and heuristics underpin decision making and human error[13]. Until this award, the school of behavioral economics, and its subset behavioral finance, had been regarded with a sense of suspicion by the more quant-oriented colleagues.

Only fifteen years later, in 2017, a *second* member of the behavioral economics school got the same Nobel award: Richard Thaler, professor at the Chicago Booth School of Business. With no less than *eight* other Nobel Prize winners, Chicago is best known as *the* bastion of quantitative thinking and belief in the power of (financial) models. Just think of Merton Miller, co-author of the Modigliani-Miller theorem in finance suggesting the irrelevance of debt-equity structures, awarded in 1990 along with Harry Markowitz (modern portfolio theory) and William Sharpe (who was at the basis of the financial CAPM model). Thaler being the *ninth* award winner from this particular school can in itself almost be considered a black swan.

Thaler is so far the closest a more marketing-driven thinker was honored for his pioneering works understanding the engineering of human choice. Building on some of Kahneman's insights around the reflective and automatic systems of decision making, Thaler's book *Nudge: Improving Decisions about Health, Wealth and Happiness* (2008), cowritten with Harvard Law School professor Cass Sunstein, is a must read for anybody interested in learning how to actively influence consumer or societal behavior and perception.

Thaler & Co proved that people are predictably irrational in ways that defy the 100% rational *homo economicus* that still dominates economic theory. A nudge is a very clever push to convince you to slightly change your behavior. As a smart contribution to a better planet, and to their bottom line, most hotels will now ask you to only drop your towel to the floor if you really want it to be changed. In water-challenged areas, hotel showers will remind you to take the *5' shower challenge*[14]. Studies have shown the average person showers for 8' and consumes up to 20 gallons of water. By adding a simple tiny hourglass in the shower, hotel guests are playfully invited to shower faster than 5', thus saving at least 60% versus average. It makes you feel good, and everybody wins. Governments have used similar systems to collect more taxes, or to influence politics[15]. Marketers use nudges since ever to sell more (*buy more and save...*).

Why simple models work:
A Nobel Prize winner's viewpoint

1. The power of the rule of thumb
95% of people use mental shortcuts to make instinctive decisions. Simplicity matters. Depending on the task at hand, the prefrontal cortex only has time and place for so much.

2. The power of anchoring and framing
The best storytellers know how to leverage the use of stereotypes, anecdotes, analogies and references for maximum impact. They are emotional filters people used to process new events and concepts. The best value propositions in marketing reflect that same insight. Marketing bestseller author Seth Godin dedicated a book to it: *All Marketers tell stories* (2005). Well worth reading. And check the original title.

3. The power of asymmetries in markets in decision making
Whether that is in basic information leading to (mis)pricing, or other market inefficiencies. Supply and demand curves are seldom in an optimal equilibrium.

When asked how he will spend his \$1.1 million Nobel prize money award, Thaler, true to form, dryly responded he will *try to spend it as irrationally as possible*. Interviewed in Belgium later along with his fellow thinker, the Belgian professor Werner De Bondt, he again suggested to take any economic model with a big grain of salt: *They (models) are funny, aren't they?*[216]

Models will remain powerful in business decision making. Many company boards and leadership teams will keep *swotting* away, *run Five Forces* and deploy all sorts of modeling to help it chart a course for the future, or to help alleviate their tolerance of risk. But even the most sophisticated models today cannot guarantee for results. Not even the quant wizards working at hedge funds. Black swans and the irrational human being cannot be quantified yet.

The good news: even in galactic times, there is art, science and discipline (and some luck) in achieving extraordinary returns and so called *marketing miracle\$*. A good model will help increase your chances. The marketing model you will discover in Stage 3 aims to do exactly that: it will apply lessons from behavioral economics and finance, within its natural limits. Flying higher remains risky.

Breathing dreams like air.

F. Scott Fitzgerald

Chapter 9
From Marketing Dreams to Miracle$

Business marketers set dreams for their brands. Dreams move the company forward, and may one day lead to miracle$. Since the beginning of time, miracles sit at the crossroads of the epic battle between good and evil, between light and darkness, and between art and science. Why do we crave them? Why can nobody live without them, especially not business people?

The word *miracle* stems from the Latin word *miraculum*: a wonder, a marvel. Yes, Marvel Comics are all about superheroes performing miracles. The wonder years of one's youth are also full of miracles. According to Merriam-Webster, a miracle is any of the following three things:

1. An extraordinary event manifesting divine intervention in human affairs, like the healing miracles described in the Gospels.

2. An extremely outstanding or unusual event, thing, or accomplishment. A bridge could be a miracle of engineering.

3. Christian Science: a divinely natural phenomenon experienced humanly as the fulfillment of spiritual law.

Miracles can be *grand*.

Life itself is often called a miracle. Every time a child is born. Every time a patient beats debilitating disease. Every time a family survives the worst calamity. And you can scale miracles *even bigger*: when a nation performs an economic comeback. When arms remain quiet for a day in war zones. When humankind lands on the Moon, or discovers new life like ours.

Miracles can be *small*.

You did pass that exam despite fearing the worst after taking it. You crossed the finish line of a marathon despite suffering in the last miles. Your team had a last-minute win, despite being behind the entire game. And you can scale miracles *even smaller*: a baby's first words, making it back home in time for dinner, the butterflies from first love.

Miracles *happen everywhere.*

They happen both in our private lives and in every sort of professional life. For entrepreneurs, for example, it would be raising your first funds, surviving through Series A (less than 8/10 make that[1]), or finishing big (a successful exit, only less than 1% of startups ever get there). For researchers and scientists, it would be that first discovery moment, followed by ever more successful experiments proving the hypothesis, and ultimately a *law* or *lemma* named after you, if not the Nobel Prize.

You get the idea. Magic seems to happen everywhere, every day, since the beginning of time. Snake oil and wonder drugs have been sold for centuries for a reason. We need to experience wonder in our daily lives to feel good and to keep going, to give a reason to be alive. We generously *amplify* these good moments where we can, through storytelling in all forms. Not only in the traditional houses of religion, but via all platforms.

The visual and written arts are full of *based on a true story* narratives that make us awe and wonder, and as a result crave them even more. Music is another platform to celebrate and amplify miracles. Social media is our own personal platform. It is full of happy people experiencing and sharing seemingly endless magical moments, just like family Kodak and Polaroid pics used to sell the dream before. And all these forms interact to make any miracle so big we cannot *not* believe in them in the end. See more examples in the separate box.

Science and religion are closely intertwined in this definition. In the history of science, Archimedes created the famous *Eureka, Eureka* moment while pondering a question from his King related to a golden crown dilemma. *Eureka* is Greek for *I have found it*. Legend has it he exclaimed this word twice while stepping into a bath muddling over the King's quandary. Noticing the water level rose, he suddenly understood that the volume of water displaced had to be equal to the volume of his submerged body, which led to the Archimedes principle on buoyancy.

Many people claim they get their best ideas while taking a shower or a bath, or while being *in the zone* during sports. Neuroscientists have proven in the meantime that when the brain is induced to be in relative rest mode, i.e., when the prefrontal cortex is less active, neurons are flashing in all directions, and new synaptic connections are made. New ideas are born. Mini-miracles.

In normal life, eureka moments are also better known as *the aha moment*, that point in time, event or experience when one has a sudden insight or realization. It originates from the expression *aha*, signaling sudden awareness or comprehension.

Miracles in movies

Since 1936, in the black and white movies, miracles are at the center of many movie stories. *The Man Who Could Work Miracles* is a dark comedy where the superior gods bestow limited

Prometheus-like miracle powers on an inferior earthling, in this case a simple guy in Britain. Through the ever more cynical narrative and epic drama that ensues, including the end of the world as we know it, the director wants to prove mankind's inability to change the world order as is, even if we could. His moral point: any man given the power to do real miracles would in the end actually misuse that power only for himself, not for the benefit of society at large.

So much for giving any mortal the equivalent of Harry Potter's magic wand. But that has not stopped anybody from exploiting the miracle theme, in all languages, in every culture, and usually in a positive way. Robert Redford directed *The Milagro Beanfield War* in 1988. *Milagro* means miracle in Spanish. In 2004, *Miracle* depicted the true story of Herb Brooks, the man that coached the 1980 US Olympic Ice Hockey team to eternal glory over the seemingly unbeatable Russians. In 2016, a faith-based movie came out with this title: *Miracles from Heaven: A Little Girl, Her Journey to Heaven, and Her Amazing Story of Healing*, about the apparent miracle curing of a young Texan girl's crippling illness, after she reportedly visited heaven.

In 2010, acclaimed surgeon Atul Gawande published *The Checklist Manifesto*, an homage to the miracle of simple checklists to make complex tasks doable. The checklist concept had actually been an invention by the US Air Force, to fly even the most sophisticated aircraft safely. But when you watch the movie *Sully* (2016), you see a miracle of human intuition overruling this textbook. After the bird hits the engine, the pilot hero somehow safely lands his plane against all odds on the Hudson river in NYC, ensuring everybody lived to tell the tale. Another miracle.

Miracles in music

There is the miracle of listening to great music. And making great music yourself. And there is the celebration of miracles in music, to great commercial success. Hot Chocolate was a British soul band formed in 1968. Who has not danced to *I believe in miracles, where you from, you sexy thing*? Note this song was released in 1975 as a the actual *B-side* of a single. Miraculously, it was remixed and the rest is history. It became their best known song.

On their 1982 hit album *New Gold Dream*, the Scottish band Simple Minds *promised you a miracle, belief is a beauty thing*. It was the band's first chart hit in the UK, pushing them onto the TV show *Top of the Pops*. It catapulted them to a commercial success period of 21 hit songs in the UK and around the world.

Carlos Santana released his *Supernatural* album in 1999. It sold over 30 million and was awarded platinum 15 times. It ultimately became one of the best selling albums in the world, and continues to sell in the digital music age.

You get the drift. Throughout history, music is one of the most natural ways for people to express the sense of wonder that miracles inspire[2].

Miracles in books

There are many possible angles to entertain readers with a miracle. There are biographies and hagiographies, literally describing and celebrating miraculous achievement. There are books about magic tales of love and romance. There are thrillers in which the world is saved again and again from bad guys. And there are business books ranging from deeply researched models for success, to less serious *miracle recipes to get rich quick*.

Books and movies very often inspire each other, sometimes many years later. The above mentioned Simple Minds song inspired the eponymous title of a 2015 book written by Andy Beckett on early Eighties Britain's comeback from what he labeled the *failed Seventies*. The Eighties were a period full of miracles indeed. In 1981, for example, Prince Charles married Lady Diana. At that time, *the* miracle wedding of the century, and the subject of many TV movies afterwards (1982, 1992, 2011). The British monarchy is a gift that keeps on giving to the world: the miraculous long reign of Queen Elizabeth (watch *The Crown* on Netflix), the miracle weddings and family lives of William and Kate, of Harry and Meghan, etc.

Miracles in science and in religion

Miracles are an intricate, must-have part of every religion. In *The Book of Miracles: The Meaning of the Miracle Stories in Christianity, Judaism, Buddhism, Hinduism and Islam* (2000), religion journalist Kenneth L. Woodward says studying miracle stories is *a way of discovering how each religion discloses the meaning and the power of the transcendent within the world of time and space.*

Moses performs them for Judaism (parting the seas…). Allah's proximity to muslims itself is considered a miracle. Prophets like Mohammed can perform a *mujizah* via his divine inspiration. In Hinduism, with its millions of gods and goddesses, stories galore, and human mystics provide spiritual liberation and inspiration and levitation. In Buddhism, it is less about deities performing miracles, but all the more about the spiritual progress of the

From Marketing Dreams to Miracle$

individual, training their mind to make mind and body do unusual and extraordinary *miracle-like* things.

For Christianity, it starts with how God created man and Earth, how Jesus was born, and how Jesus performed around 30 miracles (like healing the sick, turning water into wine, walking on water, multiplying bread and fish…). The scriptures are full of miracles. In fact, Woodward describes how Thomas Jefferson once tried to eliminate all miraculous events from the New Testament just to get to the essence of the book. He apparently nearly cut half of the text. One cannot dissociate the miraculous from the broader belief structure. According to a 2011 Pew Research Center survey, more than 90% of evangelical christians still believe miracles take place.

Miracles in and around Space

Exploration is a field of dreams. A jump in the unknown, full of risks, full of ups and downs. Space exploration has been mesmerizing and awe-inspiring for generations. As rational as they were, astronauts always brought their lucky charms with them to support another mission miracle: specially designed patches on their uniforms. Every rocket Elon Musk sends in space has a four-leaf clover hidden somewhere inside. Rocket scientists are possibly the most superstitious people you will find.

Also on the ground miracles keep happening. Just ask the good people of Titusville, a little town next to Cape Canaveral in Florida, the holy ground of space. From a sleepy little place it started to brand itself in Barnum style as *The Miracle City* when the Kennedy Space Center and its legendary Launch Pad 39A came to full fruition[3]. The town hyped its *Miracle City Mall* where *miraculous profits await you*. The hyperbole magic went to dust when Apollo and Shuttle programs stopped 2 decades ago. But then, suddenly, there was Elon Musk and the private space explorers. Eager to carry on the flame from where it all begun, they completely revitalized the grounds as of 2014. Miracles keep happening in Titusville…

Last but not least…
Miracle$ on Wall Street

Achieving sainthood has become definitely much tougher than obtaining diamond status on airlines or *black card* level from your credit card provider, though some people may beg to differ. Achieving miracles on Wall Street is maybe the toughest of all. The world of finance expects miracles about every quarter.

87

Whenever CEOs don't deliver it in a smooth and predictable way, they suffer the wrath of analysts, whipped up by a business press out for blood. Going into 2018, Apple remains one of the most valuable companies on the planet, with a valuation expected to break the US$ 1 Tn barrier soon. To jog your memory though, here is a comment from an analyst grumbling about Apple's innovation pipeline after the Q1 2013 results release: *Tim Cook in particular and Apple in general have never given the impression of being a company that puts a lot of effort into smoothing out the quarters. I don't think they are going to manage the product cycle in order to deliver a nice flow of financials to Wall Street…there is a real and tangible risk this is as good as it gets.*

Tim Cook was under immense pressure and criticism at that time on quarterly earnings[4]. Many were doubting he was the right man to take over from the iconic Steve Jobs. Five years later, one assumes analysts and shareholder would recommend him for a sainthood. Maybe it is a miracle he is still there 5 years later despite the inhuman pressure on a modern-day CEO. But I would rather attribute Apple's results to a unique combination of deep values and personal competencies of the CEO and his top team, combined with sticking to and constantly nurturing their own distinctive *Apple Way of delighting consumers*. The root of miracle$ in business can usually be found in the excellence systems underpinning it (See Fundamental nr 8 in Part 3)

I wish to work miracles

Around 1482, Ludovico Sforza, regent of Milan, became Leonardo Da Vinci's patron. He supported his visionary works for nearly 16 years. Leonardo's cover letter to secure the position started with the ambitious words: *I wish to work miracles*[5]. He then went on to list the many new conceptual ways he could help the city be victorious in war.

Da Vinci's renaissance brought light after the darkness of the middle ages. Darkness is often associated with evil. *Darkness cannot drive out darkness. Only light can do that. Hate cannot drive out hate. Only love can do that.* One of the many famous quotes by Martin Luther King so many centuries later. Or picture the menacing scene in the Star Wars series: *The Last Jedi* (2017), when Supreme Leader Snoke announces *Darkness rises, and Light to meet it.*

Religion and science will continue to have their epic clashes. In Dan Brown's bestseller *Origin* (2017), the action-packed journey of his star Robert Landon starts when his friend and former student, the brash futurist Edmond Kirsch, challenges the fundaments of all world religions, and pays the ultimate price for it. But commenting further on similar earlier fights with the church and conventional wisdom by Galileo, Bruno and Copernicus, the author contends the fight is worth fighting, and will continue: *Science is banging on the door of religion again*. But each time it does, it comes at a cost.

Despite Greek philosopher and mathematician Pythagoras proving the contrary since 500 BC, there are still believers that the earth is flat. I am not referring to Thomas Friedman's provocative book on *Globalization in the 21ˢᵗ century* (2005). No, there are still *real flat-earth believers*. They believe NASA is being controlled by *round-Earth freemasons*. An eccentric character called *Mad Mike Hughes* is still serious about building his own rocket in California to prove them wrong, and recently survived his self-launch to 1875 feet[6].

The Devil's Advocate

In the church of Christ, performing miracles became one of *the* critical components of the act of canonization, i.e. the process behind declaring somebody a saint, which means de facto including a person in the so-called *canon*, or official list of recognized saints. When you reach this revered exclusive status, your name is added to the global liturgy, your tomb or altar may be revered and prayed to in a church, a day may be named after you, etc.

Sainthood status is not easy to get, and it was made much tougher over the centuries. Since 1983, a select number of specially trained clerics surrounding the pope in the Vatican will painstakingly assess if you are worth the honor. There are three evidence-based steps before sainthood: 1) *Servant of God*, 2) *Venerable*, 3) *Blessed*. Only when a martyr has passed these three, and then the fourth condition is also fulfilled, can the pope declare somebody officially a *Saint*. For that fourth condition, proof needs to be found of up to two miracles been performed during the person's life. And this evidence will be sternly debated between the Promotor of the Faith, and the Devil's Advocate.

In 1587, a little after Da Vinci's death in 1519, Pope Sixtus V installed the office of the Advocatus Diaboli, the now famous *Devil's Advocate*. His role was to prepare a case against the canonization of a person proposed by another top cleric, the Promotor Fideis, the *Promotor of the Faith*. The latter would ensure proper compliance with the intricate requirements prior to elevation to sainthood. The Devil's Advocate, almost to this day, has to argue why the person was/is flawed. The Pope would listen and then decide in the end if the person was worthy or not. Applying this renaissance spirit, I will argue as the Devil's Advocate in this book against my own model proposals, so you don't have to. But you are, of course, welcome to join that conversation.

Last, as the Devil's Advocate, it is also worthwhile to review the *opposite* of miracles. There are many stories or songs or movies about dystopias. They paint a dark nightmarish world we cannot escape from. A world with limited hope. Think about The Zombies, a 1958 successful English rock band, who had many a hit song over their lifetime. They also had a song called *I Don't Believe in Miracles* (1972). Never even close to a hit. Kid Ink may be a great LA rapper, but *No Miracles* (2014) was never his greatest hit.

With a few exceptions, like scary movies or Orwell's *1984*, true dystopia seldom outsells true utopia. Dark and somber movies that don't end well are seldom box office successes. Most successful dystopias have a very clear silver lining. Buried in the characters or narrative, they inevitably conclude in redemption, where light beats darkness in the end. The ultimate archetype based story being told (Think *Star Wars* or *The Hunger Games*).

The only place where negative sells more than positive seems to be in the business of news. *No news like bad news.* The premise behind the James Bond movie *Tomorrow Never Dies*. People have a morbid sense for scaring themselves. Probably to savor the next miracle even more, even if that is just the political leadership telling them that *everything will be OK*.

To be fair, darkness can have its miraculous sides too. Especially the darkness of space should be cherished and embraced, not feared. Beautiful and intensely deep darkness, like pure water, is becoming a scarce good with increasing value. Since 1988, the International Dark Sky Association made it its mission to protect the night skies for present and future generations. As a side effect of industrialization, excessive use of artificial light increasingly prevents stargazing, wondering and dreaming of miracles in the Universe[7].

With 80% of the world estimated to live under *skyglow* now, *light pollution* affects wildlife, our health (sleep, biorhythm…), energy consumption, heritage and safety. In central Idaho, the association was able to designate its first international Dark Sky Reserve in December 2017. One of the few places in the world you will be able experience the Milky Way in all its glory, as long as we protect it.

People *crave* Miracles

Bruce Springsteen best summarized the bottom line on miracles: *Countin' on a Miracle* (2002). People crave them. They will vote for the leader offering it. They deploy weird rituals and lucky charms to help enable it. They pray for it, and sometimes pay for it. They want every end to be a happy end. That is why CEOs and great marketers want to create miracle$.

You are about to graduate from base camp. A small miracle in and by itself. Ready for safe flight. Time to lift off. Please get ready to collect your business marketing wings on the next page.

Congrats, you got your business marketing wings!

A big congratulations for making it here. It is almost time to lift off.

For those who just skipped to this page. I am afraid you will not find the answers to the earlier 10 questions here. You cannot successfully build brands with shortcuts. You can not shortcut your way to investing in the best brands. You certainly cannot shortcut your way to flying rockets safely through the galaxy. Please go back to Chapter 4. Safety first.

Experiental Learning

A final note as you move on to stage 3. This book reflects the pedagogy insights from David Kolb, an American educational theorist and the father of *Experiential Learning* (1984)[1]. To anchor real learning, the *Kolb theory* suggests students need to go though a cognitive processing wheel that is composed of four different ways to learn: Feel, Observe, Think and Do.

Kolb Theory of Experiental Learning

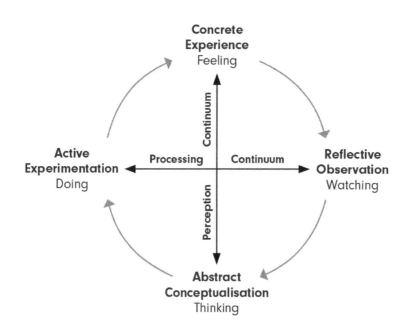

The *thinking* part, typically achieved by reading a book, is only about 25% of the learning. Starting to *play* with the ideas truly helps to internalize new concepts. Discussing it, or arguing over it, makes more neurons flash even more, and anchors more of the learning. Depending on how you learn most effectively as an individual, you enter the continuum where it fits your personality best. Kolb would argue that the learning will stick longest and most effectively when you have taken new ideas, like the two new models you will discover later in this book, through all four phases of learning, regardless of where you started.

So please feel free to digest this book in the way you feel makes most sense for you. As Aldous Huxley said in *Brave New World* (1932):

> **Experience is not what happens to you,**
> **but what you do with what happens to you.**

Congrats, you got your business marketing wings!

Personal Notes

LIFT-OFF: MARKETING IN A GALACTIC AGE

Get the
fundamentals
down, and
the level of
everything
you do will
rise.

Michael Jordan

Chapter 10
A new galactic marketing model

Discover the new Marketing Capability Rocket (MC-Rocket©), and Burggraeve's 8 fundamentals it is built on. A new marketing capability (MC) model for Space 2.0, increasing the probability to achieve marketing miracle$. A model built on Kotler and other leading thinkers, upgraded, amplified and inspired by rocket science.

End of 2012, as my corporate marketing career wound down after 23 years, the Wharton School of Business initiated the Wharton Future of Advertising Program (WFOA), under the leadership of prof. Yoram -Jerry- Wind and executive director Catherine Hays. WFOA resulted later in a book called *Beyond Advertising: Creating Value Through All Customer Touchpoints (2016)*. It had been cocreated with insights and ideas by 200+ thought leaders, innovators and visionaries from a breadth of disciplines and from all over the world. Each contributor was invited to briefly answer two simple questions:

- What could/should *advertising* look like in 2020 *(so eight years from 2012)*?

- What should *advertisers* do now for that future?

When Catherine invited me to join that discussion, I sensed that too many contributors again equated *marketing* to *advertising in a narrow sense*. So in my contribution, I argued from the start that advertising is only a part of marketing itself, and therefore we should rephrase the 2 questions above accordingly.

- What could/should *marketing* look like in 2020?

- What should *marketers* do now for that future?

Below is a paraphrased summary of the Wharton WFOA article I wrote end 2012. It details what I considered would never change in marketing, and what possibly would. The thoughts below became the theoretical basis for this book and the underlying models it will propose.

Why: The essence will not change. Learning to better market *in societal context*, and *purpose-driven*, will be the key new skills.

Peter Drucker famously remarked: the objective of marketing is to make selling unnecessary. It is about creating people's willingness to pay, ideally paying more for more over time while the business grows too. Yet *context* matters more than ever. As marketers, we need to consider the ever evolving societal context in which we operate. Consumers, stakeholders and shareholders are all empowered more than ever with influence (social media, governance, regulation). They all expect more in return for trusting us with their attention, affection and cash. The key question for marketers becomes: how do we connect and interact better with all stakeholders, guided by our purpose?

What: The essence will not change. Marketers need to move the needle on hard *outcomes* (brand health), not on easier to control *inputs* (like creative material) or *outputs* (likes, clicks, GRPs…).

Marketing essentially remains about finding the insights that drive brand health, as measured by *behavior* and *attitude* changes. Attitude is about how much you know and love me. Behavior is about how much you actually consume or use me. Marketing is all about strengthening or changing existing behavior and attitudes. Or, in the case of new category building, it is about the creation of new habits and perceptions. *Inputs* (like creative material), are typically easier to measure than outputs, which are influenced by many factors. *Outputs* (GRPs, likes, clicks…) can also be easily measured. It is therefore only human for most to succumb to creating a dashboard on inputs and outputs. While it is good to have that visibility and tracking ability, this should never replace the most essential dashboard of all: the one that regularly measures *outcomes* in terms of behavior or attitude. Measure how hearts and minds are changing, and how that impacts willingness to pay.

Who: The essence will not change. A better balanced profile is required. And marketers will need to become (Wall) street smarter.

If marketing is indeed about art, science *and* discipline, then great marketers are a mix of Mad Men, Math Men and Method (Wo)Men. With continued advances in technology and biology, science is entering the world of marketing faster than ever. Big data, neuro-marketing, and other science-based disciplines will shift the mix of Mad/Math/Method from an average of 80/10/10 in the middle and late 20th century, to something more like 20/40/40 today. As ambiguity increases to new levels, resourcefulness and good financial foundations will be critical new skills for the marketers of tomorrow. And vice versa, CFOs and CEOs need to understand marketing.

How: The essence will not change. Many tools in the toolbox need to scientifically upgrade with the times as we strive for excellence.

Most marketing processes are typically covering three time horizons, and they each have specific tools designed for them.

- **Long-term thinking:** handles brand aspects that should change less often, and includes tools segmentation, positioning, portfolio decisions, etc.

- **Short-term calendar thinking:** handles a more operational view of the detailed connection and activation plans, typically on a rolling X months/year basis. This is where most marketing budget is invested.

- **Continuous Renovation and Innovation:** A process to develop future sales and handle idea pipeline management.

It is in the subsegments of these latter three areas that most revolution and change is happening, and will continue to happen. This is where most ink will flow, where hype might ensue on the latest tech gimmick, and where new seminars will be created: experiential marketing, social media platforms, community management, influencer marketing, big and small data science, e-CRM and m-commerce, neuromarketing, lean thinking, GDPR, etc. There is an incessant stream of new tools and techniques and regulations marketers need to become familiar with and experiment with to stay current, and to stay ahead of their consumers. This is the area that risks to overwhelm marketers, and suck up all their time. This is the Silicon snake oil area to watch out for.

In summary, I concluded marketing's fundamentals remain largely unchanged. However, to be a galactic *business marketer* in 2020 and beyond, we need to evolve again our skills and competencies in each element of the Why, What, Who and How of Marketing. So what could be the blueprint and clear jargon for such a galactic marketing capability model? A model, like SWOT and Five Forces, simple enough so *both* marketers and investors would remember it, understand it and apply it with ease. Built on the basics of behavioral economics.

For the Cartesian left brain – inclined among you, here is the simplest possible matrix version to refocus marketers back on the fundamentals:

Burggraeve's 8 Fundamentals

Why	**What**
1. Pricing Power	3. Brand Health
2. Purpose	4. Value Proposition

Who	**How**
5. Business Marketers	6. Power Toolbox
	7. Insights
	8. Excellence Models

■ Evolve carefully   ☐ Evolve regularly

Some of the marketing fundamentals would be subject to much more change, as the context changes. Based on my experience, I would venture that the degree of change is (and should be) substantially higher for the *who/how* parts than for the *why/what* parts. Of course I am not 100% absolute in that delineation. Everything in life is at one point subject to change. At the very end of this book I will even argue why indeed marketing as we know it may truly be redefined by Artificial Intelligence (AI). If I were to arrange the 8 fundamentals through the lens of change, here is what we would get:

Evolve very carefully

- Fundamental 1 (Why) - Pricing Power

- Fundamental 2 (Why) - Purpose

- Fundamental 3 (What) - Brand Health

- Fundamental 4 (What) - Value Proposition

Evolve regularly to stay in tune

- Fundamental 5 (Who) - Business Marketers

- Fundamental 6 (How) - The Power Toolbox

- Fundamental 7 (How) - Insights

- Fundamental 8 (How) - Excellence

The number-one focus of anybody interested in building a sustainable business model, the focus of *any* first discussion between a new CMO and the CXOs, is on the two *why* parts. This is where the magic of sustainable top line growth happens. This is also *the* area analysts should focus on first when they look at a company's relative strength in marketing, as a proxy for future top line growth. If an investor starts talking with the CMO about the *how* parts like social media campaigns, or worse, about percentages of Net Sales invested in marketing (an analysts' eternal favorite to judge marketing excellence), you are both lost from the start.

Lift-Off

I trust everybody can remember the above simple 8 fundamentals matrix. Now, I *am* a consumer scientist with a passion for space. There had to be a way to also translate the above matrix in an equally memorable metaphor that fits the galactic canvas we are painting on, appealing to those right brain people among you. No worries, throughout this stage 3, and in stage 4 of this book, we will merge both left- and right-brain views.

It is my pleasure to introduce you to the **MC-Rocket**©, short for the first iteration of a Marketing Capability Rocket for the new Galactic Age:

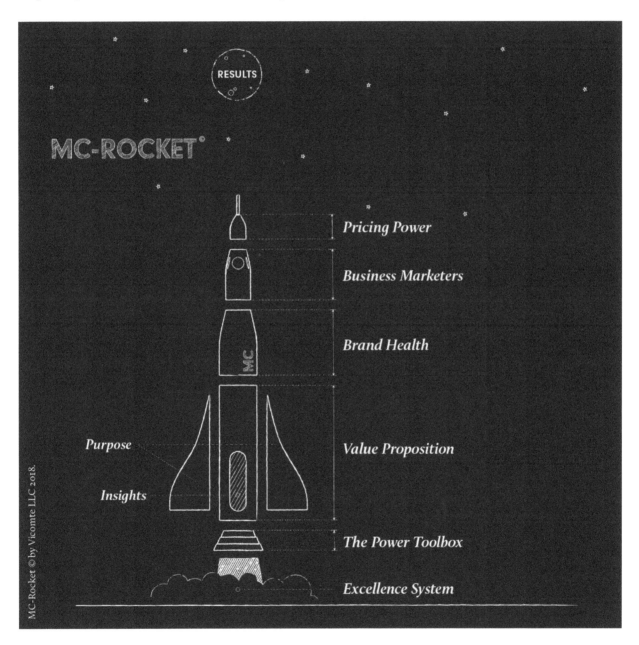

Many people read Antoine de Saint-Exupery's *Little Prince* (1943) in their youth, one of the most translated books in the world[1]. It is a poetic tale, in which the stars take on different meanings for explorers (*a guiding light*), for businessmen (*a number to count and own*), for kings (*subjects to rule*), and for the pilot in the story (*the presence of the little prince on another planet*). In the words of the little prince before his final departure: *All men have stars, but they are not the same things for different people.*

In this visualization of the marketing model, **the stars are a clear proxy for the tangible business growth results we strive for:** revenue, EBITDA, volume and value share, mindshare, share of wallet, ARPU (Average Revenue Per User), etc. The MC-Rocket is designed to help you reach the stars. Your stars. The **MC-Rocket©** is a simple metaphor that has already helped finance-driven marketers and investors interested in brand-driven companies to better understand and apply the proven 8 fundamentals of marketing.

Over the next eight chapters, I will decompose these eight rocket components in a conceptual order, and recompose it as we progress. It will feel like the legendary Airfix model planes or LEGO spaceports many of you may have built in your youth, before you let them fly in your mind to infinity and beyond. Starting with the *Why*, I will systematically show how these fundamentals interact, and how their sum—or better, their multiplication—results in a powerful exponential whole with massive forward thrust as the rocket climbs higher. At the end of each rocket component I will ask three self-reflection questions relevant for the CEO/CMO/CFO, and maybe for the board. In each chapter, questions I will try to answer are:

- Do we have tools that define and/or measure this Fundamental?

- Is that tool *wired* with other relevant fundamentals? Which metrics connect this with other fundamentals?

- Is this tool or model a proven one? Do we have demonstrable evidence that it works?

- Can the entire organization rally behind this fundamental?

- Is this tool the right one for our organization at this stage?

Belgians in Space

Tintin is a globally famous comic character created by Belgian cartoonist Hergé. Tintin's *Destination Moon* (*Objectif Lune*) was published in 1953, but serialized earlier in the Tintin magazine in 1950. The story was told in two albums, the second being *Explorers on the Moon (On a marche sur la lune)*. The iconic Tintin red and white checkered rocket adorns kids rooms around the world ever since its introduction (including mine).

I could be the *third human* of my original home country Belgium to be in space, standing on the shoulders of two men I consider *real* astronauts and rocket scientists.

- The first was viscount **Dirk Frimout**. As astronaut number 268 in the world, he *went up* with the NASA Space Shuttle STS-45 for 8 days and 22 hours (1992). In September 2018 I had the chance to meet him in New York, at the occasion of the Belcham Lifetime Achievement Award ceremony. He passionately spoke about why and how we should now aim for Mars.

- The second was **Frank de Winne**, who went up twice (in 2002 and 2008-9). His first time lasted around 10 days. On his second round, he became the first astronaut from the European Space Agency (ESA) to command a space mission which lasted six months in the ISS.

In true renaissance spirit, if I play the role of the Promotor of the Faith (see Chapter 9), then you, as the critical reader, should play Devil's Advocate. This is an open invitation to cocreate. Based on earlier teaching experience in TRIUM, and at other schools and at companies, people easily grasp the rocket metaphor. But as you read on, take notes, don't hesitate to send me constructive opinions about how to fine-tune the proposed *fundamental eight* components, about their relative importance, or about their interconnectivity. You may have other or better case studies to illustrate them. You may believe I overlooked another core concept that belongs among the fundamentals. Happy to talk about that too. Let's build the best possible rocket out there together over time.

The design of the MC-Rocket as it looks today is copyrighted by Vicomte LLC. However, all the key visuals and more info are downloadable for free from

vicomte.com/galactic

There is no catch. As per the Kolb theory of learning I discussed before, use the blueprints, play with them, redesign them, argue over them with your colleagues as you check your organization versus this model. Design your own rocket if you have to.

Let's now explore Burggraeve's 8 fundamentals, starting with the first two *why* ones. The purpose of most rocket science is to launch rockets. The purpose of the galactic marketing company is to create *sustainable* pricing power.

Marketing is not rocket science

Why the idea to bring rocket science into this book? By now you know I love anything to do with planes, flying, space, and the universe[1]. Space is not just cool. It is about the future of humankind. If there is one industry that has benefited society as a whole in more ways than people imagined, it is the business of space. Air and space transport can and will continue to transform and lift societies as a whole.

Consumer scientists can learn a lot from rocket scientists[2]. A number of authors would even claim marketing is rocket science[3]. Others claim it isn't[4] at all. Nobody[5] claims marketing can guarantee miracles, let alone miracle$ with a $ sign at the end. I am actually in the camp of those who believe creating renaissance brands in a galactic age is *not* rocket science, and we *can* increase the chance to create marketing miracle$. That does not mean it will be easy though. It will require serious art, science and discipline.

Building true marketing capability is *much* more than just being great at advertising, managing digital media smartly, or being a great trade marketer. Having great sales skills are not an automatic qualifier to be a great marketer. Like many professions, marketing is a profession. Mastery is the result of experience on many levels, across many brands and categories, across many geographies and contexts. It involves having lived through success and failure. It is a *metier*, as the French would say. It is not just a two-year stint on your resume to look good. I agree 100% with the idea that everybody *should* be a little bit of a marketer in a brand-driven company. I agree 100% that marketing is too important to be left to the marketers alone. However, I disagree 200% with the notion that everybody *can* be a top marketer. Not everybody is made to be a great CEO or CFO either.

Below are two brief personal stories linked to aviation and space that have colored some of the insights and thinking of this book. My real focus is to help create as many marketing miracle$ as possible here on planet Earth, in the orbit where a consumer scientist can make a difference to the world of marketing and finance. Marketing is *not* rocket science. But letting yourself be inspired by rocket science can definitely increase the probability of creating miracle$.

Seabird Airlines:
Turkey's first-ever seaplane company

This is the rollercoaster thriller story of how some friends and I tried to create and scale a Canadian Twin Otter – based seaplane company in Turkey. It was called Seabird Airlines, the brainchild of a dynamic young Turk called Kursad Arusan. Back in 2010, Kursad's dream for Seabird was to become the first and only company in the world to get Turkish government permission to land on the Bosphorus with a seaplane, right in the very heart of Istanbul. From there, the idea was to reapply business models he had observed in places like New York, Miami, Vancouver and the Maldives. Seabird Airlines would pioneer a never-seen-before water-based point-to-point airline model. Seabird's *purpose* was to unlock and democratize the economic potential hereto unserved or underserved destinations through new forms of air connection.

I lived and worked in Turkey for The Coca-Cola Company in the mid-Nineties and early 2000s. The Seabird idea grew on me, despite it being clearly very, very risky. I knew already how hard the restaurant world could be. With Cem Pasinli and Asli Durukan, two of my most entrepreneurial former Coke Turkey team members, I had the honor and pleasure to cocreate a boutique restaurant business group in Istanbul over the last 15+ years, called Soul Group[6]. Battle-hardened in the ups and downs of restaurants, I decided to join Kursad in his seaplane dream. No guts, no glory and no regrets whatever the outcome. Without people taking risk, society does not progress.

The mid-2012 inaugural Seabird flight was simply magical. It had actually been a small miracle, two gut-wrenching financing and regulatory nightmare years in the making. We had persevered against all odds. Turkey knows nothing about water planes, so we had to teach all stakeholders about them, from government to consumers. You don't just buy an AOC (Airline Operating Certificate) in the store It had taken enormous grit, blood, sweat and tears, and a massive dose of rocket science, with many thick manuals to prove it. When we saw the Bosphorus and Istanbul's majestic towers and mosques disappear in the sunset, we knew it had been absolutely worth living and fighting for.

Seabird started to perform what would become thousands of safe flights to other coastal areas from that magical spot over the next three years. Like Uber, we created new behavior, disrupting old ways of travel. Once travelers heard about us (*awareness*) and overcame their fear for a completely new type of plane most had never flown on in their lives (*trial*), people loved the new *more for more value proposition*. We delivered on our intent to become an affordable luxury people actually *wanted*. They saved easily up to six hours of travel time for a little more money. Super convenient, fun and safe, for only a little more. We built the confidence to invest to bring in a second plane, and then a third one. Our analysis showed the country could easily justify 50, possibly up to 100 planes to fly in Turkey and its neighbors —warranting even local manufacturing and maintenance. The plans for that were advancing between the Civil Aviation Authority, and both Turkish foreign partners.

Then, mid-2015, our world changed in six months. Looking back, it was probably the biggest Icarus moment of my professional life.

Explosive geopolitics in the middle east made any expansion financing dry up in no time. Government and finance postponed all plans, putting themselves in *wait & see* mode. Such behavior is a killer for a scale-up in full expansion. The old airline joke became reality again (to a degree). With a heavy heart, we were still able to safely send the leased planes back to Canada, and to put Seabird more or less decently on ice end of 2015. For all the people who worked so hard to get there, it was one of the saddest moments of our lives. Kursad is running his own small new venture now, but he could restart the Seabird dream anytime the government wants him to. The business case is still there. We are sure these birds will fly again. As they say: *nothing as powerful as an idea whose time has come*. Had we been too early?

Virgin Galactic:
Defying the sun even more

In 2011, while helping to create Seabird, I had also decided to bet on an even more risky startup in the world of flight. I booked a ticket for suborbital spaceflight from Richard Branson's (then) embryonic Virgin Galactic.

I look forward to one day experiencing a thrilling rocket motor ride, weightlessness in zero gravity and the incredible views of our precious planet against the black sky of space. Maybe we even make it to the Karman line where deep space begins, 55 miles or 100 km above the Earth. But the Virgin Galactic dream, its *purpose*, was/is not about servicing the eccentric needs of a few space tourists. At scale, the intent is for prices to lower fast, and to help usher in a new chapter of fast and democratized global travel and space travel for all—the next frontier. That is the dream I was happy to become part of. Being part of the Virgin Galactic Future Astronauts group has been humbling, all while literally and emotionally pushing me out of my comfort zone. I already got physical training for body and mind:

- learning how to breathe through the very serious G forces in the NASTAR centrifuges

- experiencing the thrill and skill of Mars and Moon gravity, as well as total weightlessness on Zero G flights;

- sitting through serious presentations by real rocket scientists and colorful space nuts

This future suborbital flight has made me reconsider life on Earth. The variety of preparatory experiences to date brought back the wonder years. As an example, mid-summer 2017, about 150 aspiring Virgin Galactic Future Astronauts from all walks of life were blessed to see the *total* solar eclipse in the open camping fields of Idaho, US, with the Grand Teton mountain range as a mighty backdrop. Stargazing at night under a pure dark sky, seeing Saturn and its rings through powerful telescopes. It sparked many a conversation on the plausibility of other intelligent life out there.

I am looking forward to my Virgin Galactic (VG) suborbital flight in the coming years. As far as I know, I might be the first CMO in space. What I really hope though is that, thanks to all these new projects, we make exponential progress to democratize space over the next decades. Everybody should benefit from the promise of the Universe.

DNA of Flight
© 2018 Virgin Galactic

I think I'll try, defying gravity and you won't pull me down.

Wicked

Chapter 11

Fundamental 1 (why) – Pricing Power

Marketing is not a popularity contest. Marketing is finance, a core competency at the heart of brand-based business models. Galactic marketers will focus on delivering the true purpose of marketing: making selling unnecessary in the new space age. Their absolute number-one focus will remain to create pricing power.

Sergio Zyman was The Coca-Cola Company CMO when I joined from P&G in June 1995. A larger than life personality, he was idiosyncratic, brash and colorful. In business, ferocious, unapologetic and intense. One of those leaders you could love and hate in the span of a minute. Not surprisingly he was nicknamed the *Aya-cola*. But he definitely knew his marketing stuff. Before there was the Coke Way of Marketing (called DNA) end of the 1990s, there was definitely an unwritten *Sergio's Way* in the 1980s and early 1990s.

Sergio held deep beliefs, but equally promoted the agility of the scientist to course-correct when results dictated one should. He was the best marketer I had met in my life by then, and still among the best I have seen to date. His genuine passion for the art and science of marketing has deeply impacted how I *ate, slept and drank* marketing since meeting him. Any aspiring business marketer interested in truly understanding the fundamentals of marketing is well advised to read his seminal book *The End of Marketing as We Know It* (1999), written after he stepped back from his second tour of duty with Coke. Written *before* the digital revolution, but because of that all the more focused on this core idea:

*The sole purpose of marketing is
to get more people to buy more of your product,
more often, for more money.*

Before anybody jumps out of his or her chair, and claims 1) more is not always better, 2) that we should not push over-consumption on society, or 3) that being purposeful is most important, let me add the following. The commercial priority of creating pricing power is not incompatible with being purposeful. *Purpose*, as we will immediately see in the next chapter, is a very necessary, and morally required *necessary* condition to be successful. But purpose is not the *sufficient* condition to be successful as a brand-based business. Being purpose-driven is what will ensure marketers create *sustainable* pricing power. A very critical extra word. We will dedicate a full extra chapter to it, and also tie both ideas together after.

Marketing is *not* about advertising or complex research definitions and media jargon. It is *not* about winning awards, nor about Superbowl popularity or Facebook likes. They all may help, but they are small parts of the mechanics and tactics. Marketing in itself is a means to an end, not an end in itself. It is about business, about creating pricing power. Period.

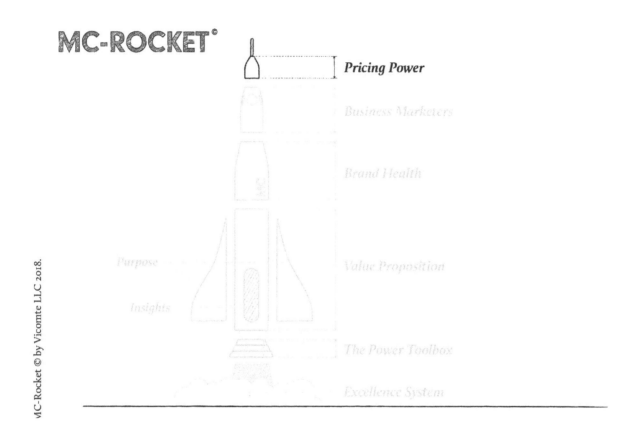

Back to pricing power as the critical base test. Just ask P&G, J&J, Kimberley-Clark, and a number of other big CPG firms[1]. Their classic top-line growth model is under pressure, and cost cutting is not going to save them. End of 2017 P&G had to discount many of its top brands for the first time since 2011 to reset their value proposition and potentially to gain back share[2]. The pressure is on in its core US market: fundamental shifts in its traditional family target composition, declining birth-rates, new private label competition from discounters (Aldi, Lidl…), deep-discount e-commerce and m-commerce route-to-markets (Amazon…), new disruptive brand models (Dollar Shave and Harry's versus Gillette), etc.

During the end of Jan 2017 quarterly results conference calls between P&G and analysts, lots of the discussion centered around the declining pricing power of the top brands, and what to do about it. If top brands raise prices too much without having the brand health strength underpinning it, they open the door for alternatives below it. There is only one way out of this: do the hard marketing work of rebuilding brand health based on re-architected value propositions, all while you also reinvent new business models, or buy them. The Danish startup Organic Basics is out there inventing more environment-friendly *Silvertech* underwear that, so they claim, does not need washing for six weeks[3]. That is a straight attack on a profitable detergents category. Non consumption has always been one of the most dangerous forms of disruption[4].

Willingness to Pay

I am happy to argue with anybody that Sergio's seemingly hyper-capitalistic definition of marketing's number-one fundamental remains valid. It still largely stands, even as, like the CPG companies above, The Coca-Cola Company itself may not be its best student anymore. By and large, this number-one fundamental has proven itself time and again for the brands I had the privilege to serve. It still guides all my consultancy, investments, teaching and speaking today.

Marketing is finance is business. Any branded business model should aim to optimize the value captured by the firm. The company should try to create value both on the supply and the demand side. On the demand side, the company should optimize its pricing in such a way that the value captured by the consumer/customer is approximating zero, the point at which they pay exactly what they are willing to pay. The wider the gap between willingness to pay and actual price paid, the more the company is leaving money on the table.

Marketing is Finance:
Help Optimize Value for the Business

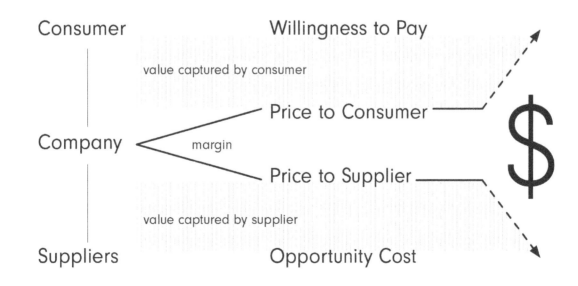

Let's look at two examples of pricing many of us are familiar with: Amazon Prime and Netflix. Both have a way to carefully nudge consumers along to accept higher prices. These two excellent mini cases demonstrate how much psychology there is at play in consumer behavior and a company's pricing decisions. In both cases, the companies leverage their brand equity to get us to accept an increase without impacting their brand health.

Amazon Prime

The price of the monthly Prime membership increased from US$ 10.99 to US$ 12.99 on January 19, 2018[5]. That is an incredible +18% increase. Amazon's rationale to justify this increase: 1) the number of items eligible for free two-day shipping increased in recent years from 20 million to more than 100 million items, 2) Prime Free Same-Day and Prime Free One-Day delivery was expanded to more than 8,000 cities, 3) More Prime Originals, included with Prime Video, and more Prime Music, Prime Reading and exclusive products. Oh and by the way, the annual package remains US$ 99 should you want to switch (it was last raised from US$ 79 in 2014).

Amazon hopes you will not run away, and likely you will not. First, Americans love free shipping. Amazon has built up a lot of equity with Prime. There is willingness to pay here. Yet an estimated 19% (by CIRP, Consumer Intelligence Research Partners) are still paying monthly. It incentivizes you to shift from monthly to yearly subscription, and then will raise that yearly each year. By making the monthly cumulative annual total, consumers have a real reason to move (I did). If anyway you plan to use Amazon in the next 12 months, you save about US$ 57.

With this clever move, Amazon achieves a double objective: 1) it acquires working capital upfront, but more importantly 2) it creates priceless loyalty and builds a lifelong habit. It builds a sustainable *sticky* business model. CIRP estimates Amazon has already crossed 90 million Prime members end 2017. Critically, Prime members spend on average US$ 1300 on average per year, versus US$ 700 for non-Prime customers.

And guess what happened just five months later: early May 2018 I was kindly informed that the annual Amazon Prime would increase from US$ 99 to US$ 119 as of mid-May 2018. But in my case it would only increase as of the January 2019 renewal, as I just had changed a few months earlier to the current annual package. These guys are good. But I will be watching.

Netflix

End of 2017 Netflix raised its prices for the first time in two years, increasing the cost of its most popular plan by $1 to $10.99 monthly[6]. Netflix last raised prices in October 2015, when the two-stream plan increased from $7.99 to $9.99. Its justification: the increased cost to bring you more and unique content, and better overall user experience. Netflix also seems to have brand equity strength to capitalize on. The company stock price hit all-time highs again, valued early 2017 at US\$ 110 Bn[7]. It keeps adding subscribers, hitting above 120 million worldwide since end 2017. Curiously, it burned US\$ 6 Bn cash and is not profitable.

Like Amazon, the objective is to lock you in first, make Netflix a habit, and then slowly start raising prices. In class, I have been asking students for five years how many people are Netflix users. First nobody, now about half of the global student class. Many had not even noticed the last price increase though. Then we started a discussion on elasticity: would you pay US\$ 20 / month, \$30, \$40? What are alternatives (from free to all other streaming video models)? What price level would Netflix need to be profitable? And what Value Proposition would convince users to stick with Netflix. Will they compete with the cost of a fun night out at the movies? Conclusion of the class: as much as Netflix has equity, it may not yet be at the same level of Amazon Prime. Students perceived there was much more risk in the Netflix model.

Let's see over the next few years who is right. Mid-2018, Netflix was still winning. Investors seem to support the current low price strategy to maximize users first, and worry about profitability later. By mid-2018, that believers story still held, and even accelerated. Netflix valuation soared above \$US 170 Bn, even though any projections for being cash positive are not expected before 2022[8].

How high is up?

Successful price increases are not as easy to make happen as many management teams think. According to *Simon Kucher*, a pricing specialist consultancy, only 32% of price increases stick. They typically see 7 key challenges with price increases, with each having a potential solution:

1. *Overambitious targets:* be realistic with how strong your brand equity is

2. *Across the board increase:* versus a segmented and SKU-based approach

3. *Poor communication:* set clear guidelines and escalation rules

4. *Limited sales preparation:* prepare all customer-facing functions

5. *Lack of reaction planning:* simulate *what if* scenarios in advance

6. *Lack of monitoring:* versus close tracking and setting incentives

7. *Giving in too early:* versus holding firm and believing in brand strength

How high can you set your price? In economic terms, this means you are testing the inelasticity of the demand curve. Any company should always test how high is up before they lose volume or share or have other unintended consequences. Absent of doing that, they leave top-line revenue on the table. Every 1% matters, as most extra pricing flows through 100% to the bottom line. The introduction of the Apple X was a great example here, testing a previously unimaginable US$ 1000 price barrier for a smartphone. It was the springboard for Apple to become the first-ever company valued at US$ 1 Trillion[9]. The Apple X is a so-called *Veblen* good, named after the Norwegian economist who invented *the theory of conspicuous consumption* (1899)[10]. Expect Apple to test as soon as it can products of US$ 2,000 – 10,000. Why not?

The stronger the Brand, the lower the Price Elasticity

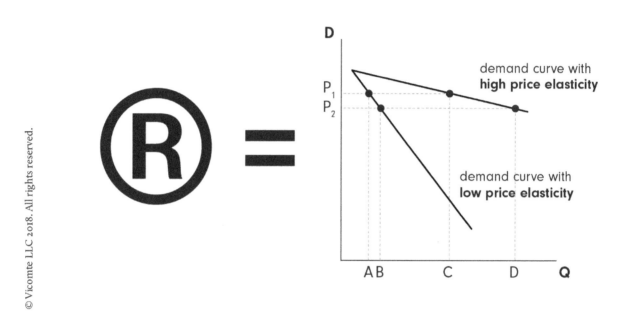

Most luxury brands apply this theory: higher prices create the perception of higher quality, status, taste and wealth, and in turn spurs demand among a clear segment of people interested only in *The (perceived) Best*. The stronger the brand, the lower its price elasticity. The longer the waiting line and FOMO effect *(Fear Of Missing Out)*, the more inelastic your brand becomes, the higher the consumer's willingness to pay. To maximize value for the firm, the best marketers will then continuously test how high they can go before consumers turn elastic again.

Dreaming of breaking thru magical price barriers is a favorite sport for many. One million, 1 billion, 1 trillion, 1 quadrillion, etc. These are the financial miracles we referred to earlier. We crave them. To a degree they inspire, while at the same time chasing such numbers can open new questions about the morality and purpose behind it all (see next chapter).

The Scarcity Race to US$ 1 Bn

Brand strength can be developed in many ways over time. But one proven way is to increase the *perceived* scarcity of your offering. If and when combined with a deliberate strategy *and* with an ability to unlock the true willingness to pay among the broadest possible group of interested market actors, the sky is the limit. Narrow supply for a huge demand. Here are seven examples across different categories of pricing gravity being defied beyond human imagination:

Art

The auction of Leonardo da Vinci's painting *Salvador Mundi*, ultimately selling for US$ 400 million plus a whopping US$ 50.3 million in auction house fees[11]. After an unprecedented 19-minute bidding war at Christies on November 14, 2017, Da Vinci's brand is proving to be the strongest of any artist ever. Over half a millennium after his death, the creator of other masterpieces like *The Mona Lisa* and *The Last Supper* stuns the world again. The painting can now be admired in the new Louvre in Abu Dhabi.

No museum or art curator in the world had seen this one coming, with some calling it *obscene*. Curators, in a self-serving move, already warned other owners of old masters not to think they will get the same for similar works. But they are not the buyers. What we saw was elasticity and scarcity at work. There are more ultra high net worth individuals on the planet than ever, yet there was only one Leonardo da Vinci. And, this was (so far) his last painting *ever* for sale. Its status value was galactic. Christies *captured lightning in a bottle*. By creating a unique Value Proposition, it created a marketing miracle. With the above new price anchor, imagine what the Mona Lisa could be worth, *if* it was ever put up for sale?

Sports

The purchase by the oil-rich Qatar-backed Paris Saint Germain soccer team of Brazilian striker *Neymar* from Barcelona for an unprecedented US$ 220 million, setting a new high watermark for top talent in the soccer world[12]. We will see many more expensive trades as a result, and the valuation of the top soccer teams keeps rising too as a result[13]. Because no broker worth his keep can now accept a deal below US$ 100 million for any great star, now can they? In July 2018, Uniqlo signed a US$ 300 million over 10 years deal with Roger Federer, supplanting his 24-year Nike relationship. It shows the perceived eternal commercial value of *legend* status[14].

Cars

Bentley already had its SUV Bentayga for US$ 200K+. The Lamborghini Urtus SUV sets you back US$ 230K+. We can top that in style, Rolls Royce must have thought, when it finally launched its minimum US$ 325K new SUV RR Cullinan in May 2018. Why on Earth anybody would pay so much for a vehicle to bring you from a to b is the wrong question. It is a fantasy on wheels for a niche public that values the status the vehicle communicates.

The only big car brandname left now without an SUV is… Ferrari. I am speculating here, but they owe it to their image to launch a galactic US$ 1 Bn vehicle. Probably a fast flying car of some sort?

Fashion

The US$ 1 Bn valuation of teenage lifestyle brand *Supreme* (since 1994), versus previous teen idol brand Abercrombie (A&F, since 1892), as a result of a 50% stake sale to private equity group Carlyle[15]. Supreme only has 11 stores, with undisclosed revenue, versus A&F generating US$ 3.3 Bn with 900 stores, and being valued below US$ 0.9 Bn.

What explains the difference? Just surf to social media and see how much teens and young adults are willing to pay for (perceived) unique and limited-edition Supreme gear. Check its pop-up store in London in partnership with Louis Vuitton. Come and talk to people who stand in line around the block every day at its Lafayette store in NYC. Its pricing power is mind-boggling for the type of goods it sells. It is pure Veblen in action, for as long as its cult following lasts. As A&F found out, (young) consumers are fickle beasts. The second you become too abundant you lose your cool, and it is game over. Check again on Supreme in five or 10 years.

Real Estate

No place like New York to test how high can be up. Mid-2018, the penthouse at the historical Crown building was in contract at $180M, making it the most expensive apartment ever sold in NY at US$ 14,000 sq ft[16]. This price nearly doubled the previous *it cannot ever get higher than this record price* ever paid for an apartment in NYC: the One57 penthouse sold in 2014 for US$ 100.5 million to tech billionaire Michael Dell.

The buyer for the Crown penthouse is rumored to be a European investor who owns multiple homes around the world. Again, with these new high watermarks, US$ 10 million for a small apartment means nothing all of a sudden. I am sure there are architects dreaming of creating the first galactic US$ 1 Bn penthouse in Manhattan.

Movies

Unlike the examples above, movies is a category where we are not talking astronomical access numbers out of reach for the average person. Many people can afford an occasional movie. But there is scarcity at work nonetheless. Disney's early 2018 *Avengers: Infinity War* movie broke all movie opening weekends with over US$ 630 million[17]. The previous record was held by Universal's *The Fate of the Furious* at US$ 541 million.

Here is the interesting part: the average pre-sale ticket price in the US on Atom Tickets hit a record US$ 15.45, an amazing +72% versus the average movie ticket of US$ 8.97 end 2017 (itself an all-time high, according to the National Association of Theatre Owners). As you can see, every extra cent matters here. Strong advance ticket sales are a good proxy for potential interest and success. The secret ingredient of why people were willing to pay *a little more for much more*: it is not every day you can enjoy a never-seen-before 20+ Marvel superheroes for the price of one. Or actually, for *almost* the price of two movies, but people don't calculate that way. This is classic behavioral finance at work.

In the not too distant future we surely will see the first truly galactic *opening weekend* passing the US$ 1 Bn high watermark. A combination of a great idea appealing to lots of people, and probably testing in one swift upward move about US$ 25 for *a unique experience*. The keen observer will correctly say it may be difficult to find an even catchier movie title than one that already used *infinity* in the title. What could beat that? Nothing better than creating fear to never see them again. How about *The End of the Avengers: Galactic Armaggeddon*?

Wine Estates

Chateau Petrus was already among the world's most expensive and storied wine estates. In Pomerol and Bordeaux, people woke up in a different galactic world when they found out the US-Colombian Santo Domingo billionaire family bought 20% of the estate for an estimated US$ 200 million, valuing the estate at US$ 1B, a level never seen in the wine world[18]. It creates a new watermark on the price/hectare for any vineyard.

Of course not all brands can play the scarcity theory to the above extremes. These examples just serve as a clear reminder that brand managers should strive to make their offerings perceived as unique as possible. And consumers will always surprise on how priceless things can be perceived.

The more you are interchangeable, the more you are a commodity, the higher the price elasticity, and the lower willingness to pay.

How low can you go?

So let's argue the opposite case as well. Are there goods and services that are becoming more elastic, with more downward risk on price? There are many categories facing downward pressure, even in branded goods. Just picture frozen foods like pizza. How many choices do you have? But a great supplier choice is not enough to guarantee low prices.

Consider for example the suggested downward pressure on education cost. An American four-year undergraduate study at a top school costs you as much as a house in many cities. Student education debt is ballooning above commercial debt. Larry Zicklin, a clinical professor at NYU Stern argued in 2017 that the era of paying more than US$ 200K for a business school MBA education is over. He wants faculty to spend more time on teaching, and avoid students pay for *scholarship and research that nobody reads anyway*[19]. He claims that future generations of students will not be willing to pay anymore for that non-added value, which today is baked in the overall cost of tuition. He hopes MOOCs (massive open online courses) and other tech solutions will help create the change and put on the pressure.

Part of me hopes Larry is right, though it will come too late for my family (I already paid). But barring some form of smart regulatory intervention or real societal uprising, I am not sure consumers will prove him right, even if there is lots of talk about it not being right, nor equitable. Still many students and parents accept the ecosystem with all its inefficiencies of today, and so far everybody pays, grudgingly. The power of the brand dream presented by the best universities is proving too compelling.

Even if there are many choices, the perceived right education has a powerful effect on future income, as suggested by award-winning Harvard economist Ray Chetty's research (2011): *if a student in primary school is lucky enough to be taught just even one year by an excellent teacher, it will push that student's later income by 2%*[20]. So think about the cumulative effect of a full top-class education. The power of *making it* thanks to that superb education. And the American Dream is a Universal Dream, with massive waiting lines of non-Americans willing to pay to get a western education.

I cannot see the natural levers to change elasticity on education soon. Education is not pizza, even if there are technically many suppliers one can chose from.

Galactic Pricing Theories

Chetty's most cited work is actually related to pricing policies for small shops[21]. One of his widely cited findings: if they advertise prices including VAT, they lose customers. Customers want to see the net price and decide based on that, even though they know there are taxes on top of that lower price. We will discuss the importance of behavioral finance and marketing even more in the chapter on Value Proposition.

Pricing is a rich and contentious field we can easily talk about for many more chapters by itself. In 1968, Elizabeth Marting already edited the book *Creative Pricing*, a collection of papers by 19 scholars and pricing practitioners on creative pricing approaches. There are a number of books available since that time, combining marketing and finance, and on pricing in particular. They will cover classic subjects like *cost-based pricing versus price-based costing* (key in space contracts, as we will see later), and pros and cons of *monopoly and oligopoly pricing* (just think tolls on highways, utility yearly price increases, etc.).

But with the digital revolution and the rise of behavioral economics, there has been a transformation in terms of how we understand pricing and pricing power over the last 15 years. Virtually no book or curriculum really reflects the latest thinking in terms of pricing philosophy, argues David Moran from Eversight in Palo Alto, California. David is a former McKinsey consultant and former AB InBev colleague specialized in the dark art of *revenue growth management*. His job was to help us translate increasing brand equity of our beer brands into sticky pricing in the markets around the world. In a modern world with plenty of new business models and experimentation opportunities, experts like David make you discover pricing strategies in a galactic world. Here is just a brief list of examples:

- SAAS (Software as a Service) business models have their own pricing power dynamics, and many businesses start to copy such *as a Service* models, asking target customers to pay a little each month or year for a particular offering instead of one big lump sum.

- The B2B technology, marketplace and e-commerce terminology of *CAC* (Consumer Acquisition Cost), *LTV* (Lifetime Value) and *ARPU* (Average Revenue per User) is expanding fast.

- Evolved or new disruptive pricing models emerge: new *subscription* models, new *bundles*, *freemium and upgrade* models (video games), *externality-based* models (you are the data, service free or almost free, like 23andme or Catalina), *auction* models (Google, Facebook), *rank-and-file* models (Salesforce), *layer cake* models (combinations of skimming, maximizing and penetration pricing like practiced by Tesla, Porsche), etc.

- New pricing testing models are now possible, like *dynamic pricing, price transparency and showrooming effects, A/B price experimentation* and *price personalization*.

Other big things that no book covers at this stage in David's view, and critically important in more classic CPG/Retail pricing in the new Space Age:

- Competitive conduct planning/game theory/hoteling theory

- How to measure price elasticity across different categories and products, frontline and promoted

- An evaluation of the pros/cons of various research techniques (discrete choice experiments vs. econometric regression vs. a/b testing, etc.

- The interplay between brand, pack, channel, region… all those basic tools like brand ladders, pack price curves, catchment analysis, etc.

- Longitudinal impacts of promotions on brand health and promotional effectiveness decay

- Trade terms and B2B deal structures/performance drivers

- Price change sell in stories/price communications

- Margin pool analytics, including corporate affairs and tax strategies

- Tools and software landscape.

There is much more to unearth in terms of pricing (power) research from the Journal of Marketing and scholars.com, all the way to consultancies like Periscope by McKinsey Solutions[22]. But the base point of this chapter was to demonstrate the prime objective of the business marketer, as fundamental number one: creating pricing power.

Now, let's turn to that second fundamental *why* in the MC-Rocket model. The purpose *yin* to the pricing power *yang* (or the reverse, if you prefer). Galactic marketers should not just be focused on creating pricing power, but on creating *sustainable* pricing power.

Three pricing reflections for the CEO/CFO/CMO:
1. Do we see evidence of net pricing power on our key brands?
2. How do we actually make and cascade price increase/decrease decisions in our company? How much are they leveraging brand equity?
3. How high is up for our key brands? How do we create scarcity?

Personal Notes

People don't
buy what
you do.
They buy why
you do it.

Simon Sinek

Chapter 12

Fundamental 2 (why) – Purpose

Can business be a force for good? Can you be driven *and* be financially successful? How to define purpose versus these other jargon words: Vision, Mission, CSR, Sustainability? Discover why purpose is a galactic marketer's True North: a necessary, but not sufficient condition for *sustainable* brand building. How can a Brand create sustainable pricing power?

Red Bull may give you wings, but *purpose* is what will keep your MC-Rocket on course to your destination. *Purpose* is a big jargon word in marketing, and one that is often mixed up with vision and mission. I will tackle that first. Later I will show the difference with CSR and sustainability. Sometimes people confuse purpose as well with Value Proposition, which I will discuss in depth in Chapter 14.

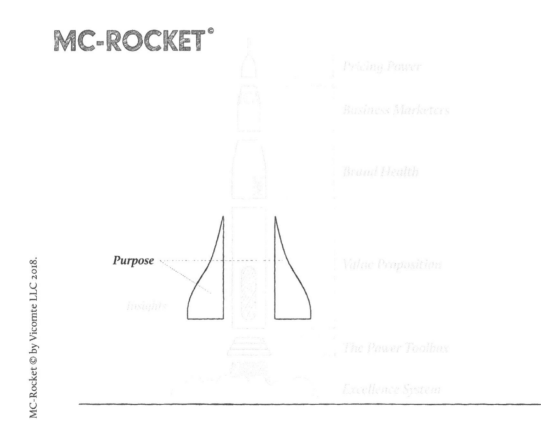

A vision is like a picture of the future you want to get into people's minds, as a rallying cry to help them understand your strategic choices for the period to come. Vision is time bound. Your company vision may be to be X by date Y. For example: *a computer in every home in 10 years*. Mission is about *how* you would get there. Purpose goes deeper. It is about the brand's positive impact on the world. The answer to an existential set of questions. It is a brand's *True North*. The gyro control of the rocket. Its Polaris. Its guide in the darkest of times.

Here is how I propose a brand or company to think about the word purpose. Five different ways to help you come to the purpose answer:

- What business are we in?

- Why do we exist in the lives of the people we serve?

- What added value does our brand offer to the societies we operate in?

- If we would *not* exist, what would people *really* miss?

- What were the deepest motivations of the founders of the company?

IKEA's purpose

After founder Ingvar Kamprad (1926 – 2018) created IKEA, he increasingly developed a *vision* to have a store in every major growing metropolis of the world in X years. Since 1943, they make that happen with evangelical zeal, opening the first store in Sweden in 1958. It grew to be a US$ 37.3 Bn company end 2016, operating 370 stores in 47 countries. It received 783 million physical store visits and 2.1 billion virtual ones during that year.

But why does IKEA exist? Answer: to offer everybody a sense of pride and confidence, a sense of freedom, a feeling you can stand on your own feet as you define your own life. IKEA's enduring *purpose* was always centered on creating a confident middle class by democratizing design.

Despite some darker stories in the past of Ingvar Kamprad, most cities will welcome IKEA to open stores as a vector of wealth creation. It is seen as an endorsement for their city or area to be part of an upwardly mobile trajectory overall. Local governments seldom refuse IKEA a license to open a store. It will be interesting to track how it may evolve and reinvent itself following the death of its founder[1].

Purpose sits at the heart of a company or a brand's social license to operate, which is the necessary, but not sufficient question to be successful. Brands and companies never operate in a vacuum. They need societal endorsement, even official permission in many cases, to be in business. Your purpose helps you get and keep that license. Then you can build on that to make your brand as great as possible, thru effective and efficient marketing. Purpose alone will not keep a CEO in his or her seat though. It is Purpose as a basis for Profit. It is all about results, ideally *sustainable* results.

Social license to operate

During my CMO period with AB InBev, early 2008, I joined the Executive Committee of the World Federation of Advertisers (wfanet.org), the preeminent global marketing industry advocacy group. I became an active EC member, and had the honor to be elected a few years later to serve as its President (2010 – 2013). The WFA, led since many years by its charismatic Managing Director Stephan Loerke, significantly colored my perception of what great marketers should and should not do in how it interacts with society at large. It is the marketing world's leading advocate for responsible self-regulation. My thinking on the role of purpose is inspired by the many great discussions I was able to have with senior marketers, and with leading regulators and stakeholder representatives. Purpose is a key condition for self-regulation. Marketing Capability can only work taking *societal context* into account.

Founded in Europe back in 1953, but in the meantime truly global and well over 65 years young, WFA is the only global association to truly represent the interests of Marketing companies between them, and with the key global and local regulators and stakeholders. It gave me phenomenal insight in the two key conditions to become a world-class marketer:

- **The necessary condition: How to keep earning our social license to operate?** Hence, to maximally earn our society-endorsed freedom to connect and engage with the people our Brands serve; since the last few decades, every brand and category needs to understand this first.

- **The sufficient condition: How to continue to be most effective and efficient in our technical marketing field?** This is how the WFA started originally. It was a technical expertise group, sharing best practices. Making marketers smarter and more confident in their core profession.

Purpose works

Purpose is not just an expensive feel-good buzzword. Cynics may keep arguing that *purpose is overrated*. However, it is proven to drive business, and CEOs on both the company and investor side focus their organizations on it. Michael Porter started the academic discussion back in 2006 on how companies could connect their success with social progress, launching the idea of *creating shared value*[2]. Back in summer 2014, that same HBR published *The Ultimate Marketing Machine*, the result of the biggest ever Marketing 2020 study among a sample of the estimated 2.1 million marketers around the world[3]. The M2020 objective was to separate the strategies and structures of superior marketing organizations from the rest. The study was lead by EffectiveBrands (now Kantar Consulting), in partnership with the Association of National Advertisers (ANA), the World Federation of Advertisers (WFA), Spencer Stuart, Forbes, MetrixLab and Adobe.

Here are the M2020 results related to purpose. The companies with superior results also scored statistically better on the purpose related questions.

M2020 results related to purpose

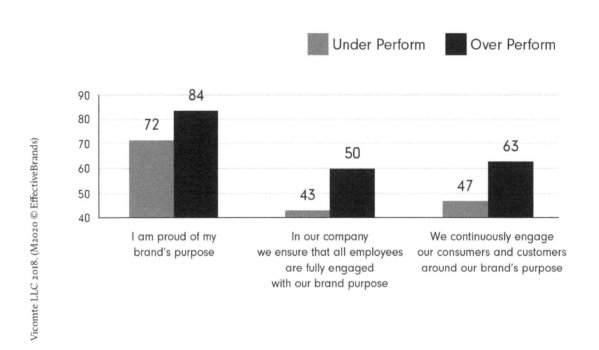

The original M2020 work evolved further into Insights 2020, and in 2017/18 there was a specific Purpose 2020 follow up[4]. That latest study has the merit to clearly articulate one definition for purpose, explains the difference versus other concepts, gives many examples, offers a playbook on how to implement and roll-out, and further details the business case behind purpose: not drives (millennial) consumers demand (+84%), investors require it (see further: Blackrock), and employees love it (it helps retain people 3x more). End September 2018, during a CMO round table on this study in NYC, Bob Liodice, President and CEO of the influential ANA and co-sponsor of the work, emphasized the business case in this introduction: *Purpose is also about profit and growth. It is about your money.*

Diego Scotti, CMO of **Verizon**, and Meredith Verdone, CMO of **Bank of America**, shared inspiring examples of how their respective teams drove their companies to embrace a purpose-driven business agenda over the last four years. They explained what started it, the pitfalls and successes, and the change management needs to support it. Mind you, as with everything, neither were overnight successes. It took nearly four years to define and truly anchor purpose. Both CMOs have been in their role all that time, supported by their CEOs, so they could anchor a key building block for the long term. As I mentioned before, CMOs that are only 1 – 2 years in role can seldom create a truly lasting impact. Just like this book tries to decode the 8 overall Fundamentals, Kantar Consulting has been decoding how to become purpose-led. Companies will likely go thru the following four phases.

1. **Articulation:** purpose as an isolated tactic

2. **Infusion:** purpose as a societal brand promise (here is where CSR and sustainability start becoming mission-critical)

3. **Amplification:** purpose as an aligned company-wide strategy

4. **(For Few Companies):** purpose as a business-led **movement**

The Verizon and BofA cases showed real life is never as linear or as neatly as depicted above, but picture in your mind a general trend line with a number of milestones in each of the four boxes, as you progress. At the request of members, the ANA is setting up a Center of Excellence related to Purpose. It will be a great source as well for the 82% of its members-practitioners that claimed they need help in this area.

The study and brand cases corroborated earlier evidence collected before by former P&G CMO Jim Stengel in his first book *Grow* (2011). In partnership with global market research company Millward Brown, Jim looked for the stock market performance over the first decade of the 21st century between public companies with a clearly articulated purpose (which he dubbed the *Stengel 50*), versus the rest of the market S&P 500). His conclusion: purpose drives performance and company value[5].

The Stengel 50 vs. S&P 500

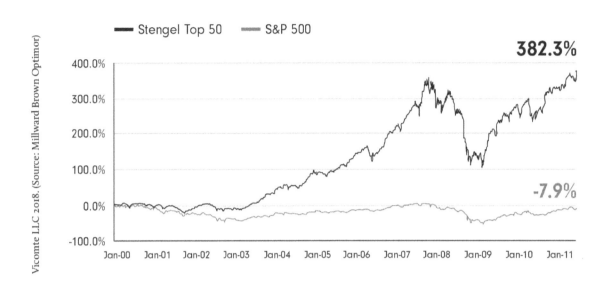

There is more and more consumer evidence that purpose is one of the fundamentals of anybody's MC-Rocket[6]. Here are a number of statistics from various global and US-based consumer surveys[7]:

- 75% of global consumers expect brands to contribute to our well-being and quality of life (Havas, Meaningful Brands 2017)

- 75% of global consumer agrees companies can increase profits while improving economic and social conditions in their community (Edelman, Trust Barometer 2017)

- 84% of US consumers believe businesses have a responsibility to spur social change (Cone Communications, CSR Study 2017)

- 70% of US consumers think corporations should stand up for what they believe in politically (Global Strategy Group, 2016)

Would all this doing good translate in good business? Here are some more stats from Global Strategy Group (2016) and from Nielsen's The Sustainability Imperative (2015)

- 89% are likely to switch to brands they associate with causes

- 80% would support issues by buying from socially conscious online retailers

- 76% would refuse to buy from a company that supports issue contrary to their beliefs

- 66% of consumers would pay more for products from more socially responsible companies

The last claim is the key one for brand marketers. **In surveys, consumers always tend to say they would pay more, but would they really?** It is one thing to confess to supporting a Better World on paper. In my own testing and in-market experience, I saw many times that when push comes to shove at purchase, consumer's willingness to pay extra was suddenly much less evident, or limited to a few percentage points. Niche groups would, and can afford to, put their money where their mouth is. Among broader masses, price elasticity was inevitably always much higher.

Is purpose only applicable to the higher-end part of the brand pyramids? Not necessarily, but we should not approach it with a niche-only mentality. Brands need to find a way to address the wishes to combine consumption with their sense of doing good for all layers of society. Consider Nike an example of a purpose-led mass brand. By taking a clear stand on the contentious NFL quarterback Kaepernick asking attention for racial issues, Nike made a choice. Its business responded positively (+30%), despite an early outcry from detractors[8]. Those who crack the purpose code will be the galactic winners of tomorrow.

CEOs (start to) get it

Successful business leaders are increasingly aware of the critical need to sharply define the purpose of their company. Let's continue to align on the jargon. We know jargon matters. *Purpose* should also not be confused with *sustainability* or with *corporate social responsibility (CSR)*. The 3 concepts are naturally interlinked. They all support the idea of building enduring (Galactic) Brands. In an attempt to keep things simple: purpose is the foundational existential idea that inspires strategic and tactical translation via sustainability and CSR plans on a more corporate or individual brand level. Allow me to illustrate, using examples from Unilever, AB InBev and l'Oreal.

Paul Polman, CEO of **Unilever,** is probably the most outspoken one among of the top CPGs on the above subject. He has inspired and remodeled a sleepy Unilever to reflect a proactive ethos called *Crafting Sustainable Brands for Life*. Polman makes sure this purpose transpires in all what Unilever does, even in M&A. An example is Unilever's acquisition of Kensington and Sons, a small NYC-based scale-up that makes *condiments with character*: premium ketchup, mayo and mustard, and now also ranch dressing[9].

Sir Kensington's clearly articulated its own purpose *to bring charm and integrity to ordinary and overlooked food*. It never makes compromises on the finest ingredients. When it develops new products, it specifically looks to address overlooked sustainability issues (e.g., food waste). In one of its breakthrough innovations, it turned what was previously seen as just a waste product—aqua faba (chickpea water)—into an emulsion for a new pioneering product called Fabanaise, a great-tasting vegan mayo. Consistently living this purpose over years was one of the main attractions for Unilever to acquire this brand in April 2017. Mark Ramadan and Scott Norton, its co-founders, are now purpose-change agents inside Unilever.

Another example is **AB InBev**. Here is Carlos Brito, CEO since 2004 of the world's largest brewer, during the 2017 Fortune Global Forum in the southern Chinese city of Guangzhou, at the occasion of opening the largest brewery in China: *People look for more than products, they look for experiences*, he says. *So it's very important to provide consumers with entertainment where beer, beverages and food are at the center of it.* AB InBev pairs brands with globally popular entertainment, e.g. major sporting events like the FIFA World Cup and Wimbledon, or the mega Belgium dance music festival Tomorrowland which attracted 70 million Chinese to its 2017 online broadcast.

Brito makes sure we know there is much more at play. He understood early on that creating great *experiences* are the sufficient condition for a marketing-driven company, but he stresses there is a necessary condition of great marketing first: *Today, consumers want you to have products with innovation and added value, but they also want to know what you stand for. Talented Chinese people want to join a company where they see a purpose.*

Not only in China of course, but everywhere great talent wants to see evidence of a company being purpose-driven. When I was at AB InBev I was proud of our Dream (purpose), especially after we evolved in 2009 from the too financially and internally focused *Best beer company in the world* to a more externally balanced *Best beer company in a better world*. Today that Dream is simplified even further to squarely focus on external stakeholders: *To bring people together in a better world.* A good evolution (see also further in Chapter 19). Through brands and experiences that bring people together, the company aims to drive growth and provide better living for more people in more places. Through its scale, resources and energy, it strives to have a positive impact on the communities in which it lives and works. Its Better World platform focuses on three *Worlds* for which concrete targets and plans are being defined: a *Growing World*, a *Cleaner World* and a *Healthier World*[10]. AB InBev should not be shy communicating more about it.

At the January 2018 Word Economic Forum in Davos, AB InBev announced its overall 2025 sustainability plans. Sustainability is supporting ABI's purpose. It is mission-critical. *Sustainability is not necessarily something we have to do that will have a cost that doesn't help the business. Sustainability is our business. If there's no water, there's no beer; it's that simple*, said Brito. *Our consumers and our people also want to know where we stand on those issues.* Within its evolved Dream, the company set out for the *second* time a long range series of sustainability goals by 2025. The new objectives build on targets published the first time in 2009 (when we launched the Better World idea). However this time, the KPIs will extend to external partners, including entrepreneurs whose ideas AB InBev hopes to tap through ZX Ventures, its disruption arm. It includes plans to see all of its beer sold in returnable or recycled packaging and all of its electricity coming from renewable sources by 2025 (versus 17% in 2017). You can find the seal on specific Budweiser bottles since Spring 2018[11].

CSR Examples at AB InBev

- During his speech in China Brito further expanded on various CSR partnerships that underpin AB InBev's overall sustainability goals:

- **Stella Artois**' latest selling line is *Be Legacy*. As a global beer brand consuming water, it is not a surprise it meaningfully connects for years with water.org to help empower families with access to safe water and sanitation through affordable financing. For every purchase of limited-edition Stella Artois chalice, water.org can help secure five years of clean water for a person.

- Other global brands do their bit, consistent with their brand positioning. **Corona**'s fights to conserve beaches and oceans. **Budweiser** continues to make efforts toward responsible consumption and deep commitment to the community. That commitment was even at the center of its Superbowl 2018 commercial, sharing how the brand can always be relied upon to unconditionally help people in areas struck by disaster with water relief (stopping to brew beer).

It is easy to be cynical about CSR or sustainability, or *all that purpose-driven fluff*. Critics will claim it is *just another marketing trick*. Actually, like pricing, this is one of the hardest parts of the MC-Rocket to get right, and to keep consistent over time. Most brands at their core genuinely want to strive for a Better World. From personal experience I can assure you these new targets will be taken as serious as anything else, if not even more serious. All these big companies are run by parents of children too. They become a natural component of many people's individual incentives. They will be monitored again by neutral third parties. Reducing carbon emissions for example will be audited by the Science Based Targets initiative, a partnership including the UN Global Compact and World Wildlife Fund.

Here is another example of how sustainability starts to be built in business performance. At leading cosmetics firm **L'Oreal**, brand managers used to be focused on cosmetic and economic performance only—finding the right balance between beauty and price. Under the leadership of its CEO Jean-Paul Agon, as a rule, they now also have to focus on sustainability performance as part of brand renovation or innovation. As a clear nudge, 10% of their bonus is linked to it. They are incentivized to really focus on the planetary impact of their brand decisions, all while making sustainability sexy[12]. Healthy competition from purpose-driven cosmetics scale-ups will keep them on their toes. Global brand owners need to stay ahead of consumers' demands for big businesses to make a positive contribution to society, especially in a time of unprecedented transparency where bigger brands are often under pressure from smaller rivals branding themselves as more responsible alternatives. Frederic d'Alsace, associate professor marketing at HEC Paris, provocatively defined it as follows: *if marketing is the daughter of globalization, then marketing will be the mother of sustainability*[13].

Investors (start to) get it

Wall Street is watching too. Whilst shareholder value creation remains its top focus, the biggest investors in the world start to understand that doing good is good business. And then there was the famous letter of Larry Fink, CEO of BlackRock, the world's largest institutional investor investing US$ 6 Tn, in his unprecedented yearly letter to CEOs at the occasion of BlackRock's 30th anniversary[14]. Here are a few client excerpts:

> ### Title: A Sense of Purpose
>
> *...As a fiduciary, BlackRock engages with companies to drive the sustainable, long-term growth that our clients need to meet their goals...*
>
> *...Society increasingly is turning to the private sector and asking that companies respond to broader societal challenges. Indeed, the public expectations of your company have never been greater. Society is demanding that companies, both public and private, serve a social purpose. To prosper over time, every company must not only deliver financial performance, but also show how it makes a positive contribution to society.*
>
> *...Without a sense of purpose, no company, either public or private, can achieve its full potential. It will ultimately lose the license to operate from key stakeholders...*
>
> *...a company's (diverse board + executive management – my addition) ability to manage environmental, social and governance matters demonstrates the leadership and good governance that is so essential to sustainable growth, which is why we are increasingly integrating these issues into our investment process...*[15]

The message cannot be clearer than this. Purpose is now a concept ignored by companies at their own peril versus potential investors. The cost of not having one is likely to be high. In *WEconomy* (2018), co-author Holly Branson (yes, daughter of), sees purpose as *miracle grow for business*. It is the role of company leadership, amplified a lot by the senior leadership, to infuse a sense of purpose throughput any organization. Then it is up to each employee to carry their part of the burden of greatness—for the collective to succeed.

Under pressure from their own investors, various sovereign wealth funds make purpose-driven thinking a must-have criterion for investment. They increasingly value the role of ethical impact investing or ESG criteria: **Environment, Society and decent Corporate Governance**. Note, that does not mean investors expect less return. The for-profit world is not just about charity. It still expects that doing good should be good business too, if not *even better* business. In this sense it is interesting to explore the ascent of the new *global impact* funds, and of the certified B corporation format.

- At US$ 2 Bn, *the Rise Fund* is the world's largest impact fund of its kind—aimed to combine financial performance with specific social and environmental benefits[16]. It includes celebs like Bono, but is managed by professionals from TPG. The fund makes sure it is not seen as feel-good investing. This is about doing even better. Other similar funds include the likes of Bain Capital Double Impact Fund.

- In essence *a B Corp is to business what Fair Trade certification is to coffee or USDA Organic certification is to milk*[17]. For example, **Patagonia** became the first California B Corp back in January 2012, joining over 500 certified B Corporations in 60 different industries. B Corps are for-profit companies that obtain certification by the global nonprofit B Lab to voluntarily meet the highest and most rigorous standards of social and environmental performance, accountability and transparency. **Sir Kensington's,** the Unilever subsidiary I mentioned before, obtained B Corp status in September 2018.

When *Big* becomes *Bad*

Not just the traditional so called *sin* categories are under pressure. *Every* category needs to *combine sin with soul* (see detail after this chapter). If your category starts to be called *Big* in the press, it means social dark clouds are coming. Untouchable and societal darlings for many years, *Big Tech* has recently come under serious societal scrutiny for hubris, for controlling our lives in ways we do not want anymore, as NYU Stern professor Scott Galloway recounts in *The Four* (2017). The Big tech leaders Apple, Amazon, Facebook and Google. Mobile phones risk to be cut out of schools (in France) as they start to be seen as hampering learning instead of enhancing it. Parents don't know anymore how to handle their kids' (and their own) real addiction to Facebook and their iPhones. Society's answer to unregulated consumption is often nonconsumption.

Mark Zuckerberg is facing pressure on both sides of the Atlantic. In Europe, Facebook is trying to placate stakeholders for its unfettered invasion in our lives, but that will not stop assertive privacy protection regulators in various countries and at EU level to start aiming straight at the heart of its business model: collecting personal data that help Facebook sell advertising. Facebook, like Google, or any TV network, is not your friend. It is an ad-based for-profit near-monopoly, in which your data is captured for free (potentially abusing dominant market positions), and leveraged for profit in return for the service they give you. In the US, Facebook is challenged by a group called *Time Well Spent*, whose stated purpose is to reverse the digital attention crisis and to realign technology with humanity's best interests[18]. Interestingly, one can suddenly observe a lot of spin articles appear in the mainstream press touting the creativity-enhancing potential of screen time, arguing kids should spend even more, to less, time.

Facebook is not alone against the ropes of enhanced societal scrutiny. Amazon is increasingly at odds with the good citizens of Seattle, who decry *Amazonians* for having taken over their bohemian town and rendered it soulless, without giving back. While Apple surges to a trillion dollar stock market valuation following the Trump tax plans, some of its activist investors see the writing on the wall, and are taking up social causes. Jana Partners and CalSTRS, the huge California State Teachers Retirement System that manages the pensions of the state's public schoolteachers, both Apple investors, sent Apple a letter demanding that it focus more on the detrimental effects its products may have on children[19]. In other words: it asks to become again more purposeful. As a basis for *sustainable* pricing power (and stock market value).

No category can take anything for granted. As I saw during my time at the WFA: pharma, banking, insurance, cosmetics, telecom, agriculture, mining, food & beverage …each category has its own set of regulatory versus self-regulation challenges. In each category, companies need to always *sit at the table* with regulators and stakeholders, or, as the saying goes, *become part of the menu*. Sometimes the stakes of the debates become truly existential, when a usually small but vocal part of the population wishes your company to simply disappear. As an example: following successful moves on tobacco in Australia, alcohol and soft-drink activists are now demanding plain packaging in these categories too. This may cost the industry nearly US$ 400 Bn in sales as it would make the most recognizable global brands unrecognizable[20].

Purpose starts Personal

There is a growing literature around purpose, detailing inspiring brand examples. I can recommend books (or TED talks) like Simon Sinek's *Start with Why* (2009), or *Conscious Capitalism: liberating heroic business* (2013) by WholeFoods co-founder John Mackey (and others), or the much deeper existential ones like Viktor Frankl's *Man's Search for Meaning* (1946). Many top agencies have their own methodologies to help you find your purpose, as they need it to translate in creativity.

While a category and a brand need purpose, and even a country needs purpose, in the end, each one of us needs to find his or her own personal purpose in life. The Japanese call it *Ikigai*[21]. Why do you wake up in the morning? What keeps you busy while giving your life personal meaning? The concept was distilled from research around why some people live happy and healthy to 100+, like the people living in places like Okinawa and other blue zones of the world. If you have not done it already, consider writing down the answer for yourself applying the simple schematic below:

Ikigai: Personal Purpose

Ikigai, personal purpose. It is the existential fuel that keep us going. It is our personal North Star. It is what defines us. We define the wings of our own personal brand MC-Rocket. I never forgot this fantastic passage by Founding Father Alexander Hamilton challenging his nemesis, in one of the opening songs of the namesake hit musical on Broadway (*Aaron Burr, sir*):

Burr, the revolution's imminent, what do you stall for?
If you stand for nothing Burr, what'll you fall for?

Three purpose reflections for the CEO/CFO/CMO:

1. Do we have a clearly articulated purpose for the company brand, and for each one of our key brands?
2. How do we actively cascade these internally and externally? How much time and energy do we really invest to generate inside-out passion around our purpose?
3. How are we ensuring our purpose remains relevant for each upcoming generation? Who carries that torch?

Personal Notes

Balancing Sin & Soul

For many stakeholders, profit is seen as sin, and purpose is soul. Acclaimed writers like Yuval Noah Harari warn: _It is dangerous to trust our future only to market forces, because these forces do what's good for the market rather than what's good for humankind or for the world_[1].

Can we combine Sin & Soul? The answer is yes. Not only is it possible, but it is also a _must do_ for marketing in a galactic world. Purpose is the base for recurring profit. Both need each other. It is critical to always find and keep a balance between capitalism and consciousness, between the invisible and the visible hand.

Sin & Soul:
Balance Responsibility with Commercial Viability

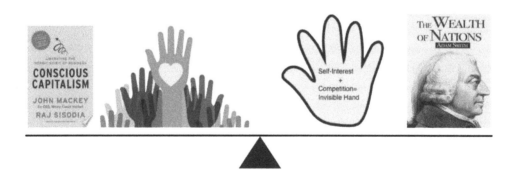

Based on my corporate career and WFA presidency insights, I have become a big proponent of _self-regulation_ as the first option for industry to tangibly demonstrate its responsibility towards societies. I equally respect the principle of _checks and balances_. To ensure pressure, I agree with Margarete Vestager, the European Union Commissioner for competition, that we need to maintain the principle of _Trust, but Verify_. The possibility for corrective regulation is a must-have societal tool to avoid what she calls _the jungle_[2].

I worked in categories where this balance was increasingly like walking on a tightrope. From household products to soft drinks to beer. I had many discussions over the years with stakeholders (consumers, employees, regulators…) on the tension between profit and purpose, especially on alcohol. Beer is like religion. It has many faiths, and it is a favorite subject of heated debate. Beer is a 9000-year-old category, and yet has brought more enemies and friends together than any other product. As a consumer goods marketer, there are only a few categories that are so intense, so controversial, so risky, and yet so emotionally rewarding to work for as alcohol. Until I discovered even bigger societal emotions behind a fast-growing *historical comeback* category: cannabis.

It forced me to review again all what I hold true in the Sin & Soul debate. Most of the medical and enjoyment products we know and use in our lives are already there since a long time (except smartphones, only about two decades young). Coffee, chocolate, sugar, soft drinks, alcohol, cars, tobacco, gambling, gaming and so many more are usually 100% legal and overall reasonably well- regulated. Activists for or against spill a lot of ink each year to move regulation on these categories a bit more to the left or to the right. But by and large we seldom ask how the huge commercial markets they represent today emerged over decades or centuries, and how they ultimately found balance between profit and ethics.

Cannabis offers a historical chance to (re)shape a new category from scratch, with all the societal tension that comes with it. Following nearly 100 years of curious prohibition in many countries, cannabis is going through a remarkable renaissance around the world. The cannabis-related hemp plant was discovered at least by 27,000 years BC. It is medicinal, but, like alcohol, it can also be about social bonding. It is among the fastest growing categories on the planet today, among *all* categories. There is a long way to go with plenty of surprises for sure. All stakeholders are moving faster than many imagine, pulled by society at large (consumers and business). By 2025 the US market is estimated to be worth US$ 75Bn. The global market potential figures keep being revised upward above US$ 250 Bn[3].

CANNABIS IN THE US

The story of why cannabis even became a so called *schedule 1 drug* in the first place is intricately documented, amongst others, by the British writer and journalist Johann Hari in *Chasing the Scream: the first and last days of the war on drugs* (2016). The author weaves storytelling and facts together in a dark and gripping picture of the key personalities behind it all. We come to look deeply into the soul of Harry J. Anslinger for example, the man who lead the massive police force that was suddenly out of work after alcohol Prohibition was finally over.

In 1933, Congress repealed the 1920 18th Amendment by passing and ratifying the 21st Amendment to the Constitution, ending national Prohibition. In 1930, Anslinger had already maneuvered smartly to become the first United States commissioner of the US Treasury Department's Federal Bureau of Narcotics (FBN), a role he would hold for 32 years. Hari describes vividly how Anslinger needed something new to fight against, to justify his own power, as well as to keep his massive police force at work. He recounts step by step how Anslinger cleverly manipulated (fake) science data and public opinion to get his way. He became one of the pivotal players in the prohibition and the criminalization of drugs, including the prohibition of cannabis.

Alcohol Prohibition was essentially over after 13 years, closing an unsuccessful social experiment that had essentially benefited the Al Capones of the world more than society at large. Yet Cannabis Prohibition started soon after. One failed social experiment replaced with another even more disastrous one, leaving a trace of racial injustice and many non-violent incarcerations for possession. The second one has lasted already nearly 90 years. But it is not unlikely that also this one will end in the coming years, with significant impact in both the cannabis medical and recreational space, as well as in the wider Consumer Packaged Goods space at large.

Pew research shows how an ever larger majority of the American public are firmly for, or not against, relaxing cannabis laws[4]. The same research shows that even among 8,000 police officers, always more conservative in such maters, a net 68% are supportive. Mark Zuckerberg found out on his 2017 tour of America that opioids and hard drugs like Fentanyl were an exponentially bigger issue to worry about[5]. Facebook was full of opioid ads, which he vowed to remedy. Michael Pollan, the very influential provocateur in the food industry when he wrote the *Omnivore Dilemma* (2006), recently went even further in *How to Change Your Mind*: *What the New Science of Psychedelics Teaches Us About Consciousness, Dying, Addiction, Depression and Transcendence* (2018). Expect that in a few years we may be discussing rescheduling of LSD and other substances in more mainstream circles.

Canada descheduled and legalized cannabis October 17. 2018[6]. When the US will follow remains unknown, but the stars are aligning. From a regional cottage underworld stoner industry, living in the dark, marijuana is fast transforming into a professionally run and mainstream FMCG brand-driven category, properly taxed and regulated, living in the light. Society will finally learn a lot more about the pros and cons of what these plants can do *for* us, and *to* us. As always, we will need to learn to consume in moderation. We will learn about how to best (self-)regulate to the benefit of consumers and society at large, around the world.

Products like cannabis are often seen in a fearful way for potentially being addictive, despite the fact that the neutral and critical WHO (World Health Organization) declared it not be a gateway drug based on serious global research[7]. But what about smartphones? Or what about watching TV/video, for decades one of the key causes for an overweight and sedentary lifestyle, unlike the popular perception of eating too much sugar. What is *Big TV* (classic and online) doing to help eliminate obesity in the world? I am not saying sugar does not play a role, but is society holding producers and owners of smartphones and TVs responsible enough for their contribution to this sedentary behavior?

What about *Big Coffee*, which keeps the work day going for many, but which is becoming fast one of the biggest pollutants of our oceans with the omnipresent throwaway coffee cup and plastic straws. The category may be called upon (and taxed) to help address this serious environmental challenge[8]. Why would society allow any company to reap benefits unchallenged without them taking responsibility for the cost of the externalities they cause? Companies cannot expect society will endlessly allow them to privatize the benefits and socialize the losses. You cannot sin without saving your soul.

Constellation Brands, the second largest brewer in the US invested US$ 191 million for a 9.9% minority stake in the Canadian medical marijuana company Canopy Growth[9]. They took an option of purchasing additional stakes in the future, and not even nine months later surprised everybody by investing an additional US$ 4 Bn[10.] The company's objective was to leverage Canopy's deep legal, regulatory and product expertise to cocreate cannabis-infused beverages for sale around the world, as a fourth line of business besides beer, wine and spirits. A very bold bet on the future, based on early consumer trends. A new chapter in how consumers will socially bond seems to be in the brewing kettles too.

Constellation's moves were/are considered by many a very risky move for its reputation. In the US, cannabis is still a schedule 1 drug, part of the Controlled Substances Act, and therefore federally illegal. Trump's White House and his Attorney General Jeff Sessions' Department of Justice is not necessarily seen as marijuana-friendly. However, the market reacted overall very positively. It applauded the foresight of Constellation management to look beyond corners and buy themselves a seat at the possible tables of the future. It is the type of move a bolder number 2 should do to close the gap with number 1. It is a historic move by a major player that pushes a big societal debate to a national level.

On the other side, the fast-growing global cannabis industry, while fascinating, is in need of a sense of purpose to ensure society will grant a permanent social license to operate. The National Cannabis Industry Association (NCIA) and other advocacy groups in the US (the Marijuana Policy Project and the Drug Policy Alliance) have made incredible strides on a state-by-state basis. There remains serious work to do before the category earns a Congress majority that will truly set it free.

In the meantime, massive new money is flowing into cannabis, betting it will become a profitable growth category. Everybody is coming in. In search of positive alpha, even the most conservative family-oriented companies are dipping their toes in CBD, like my beloved Coca-Cola Company[11]. They should have done it earlier, as consumers wanted it for a long time. Because people want the choice of how they live without the state telling them how they can. That may include all forms of reasonable stimulants and relaxants (and even a debate on hard drugs), all forms of technology, etc. But now investors are potentially giving permission. The risk is diminishing, but so are returns. Coke will not enjoy the same returns as early pure play companies like Tilray, though there we may see signs of markets entering irrational exuberance[12].

Cannabis got on my radar the first time as part of a research company Five Forces analysis exercise on the beer industry. It was only a blip on the radar then. At that time, so-called *craft* beer and other non/low-alcohol opportunities bubbled up as much closer challenges and opportunities to deal with for the company. I kept track of the category dynamics, intrigued by its possible role as a complement or substitute, or both, to beer's promise as a social lubricant. As futurist Amy Webb articulates well in *The Signals Are Talking* (2016), the future does not arrive in a nice package wrapped in a bowtie. *It emerges step by step. It first appears in seemingly random points around the fringe of society, never in the mainstream.*

I have never smoked cannabis in my life. I don't smoke cigarettes. I do enjoy an occasional cigar in summer, outside, with friends, at the pool, with a drink. As a believer in experiential learning, I decided the best way to learn was to get skin in the game. Since Q1 2016, well before the Trump election on November 7, 2016, I made two bets in this category. With the clear intent to help shape it where I could, as a marketer, and as a father. In a Bloomberg interview that went viral and global in a heartbeat, I shared the idea that *Green is the new Craft*[13]. All of a sudden, a new chapter of Sin & Soul had opened...

Responsible Scale-Ups

My first investment back in March 2016 was to cofound a consumer product portfolio company called *Toast Holdings*[14]. Our intent is to create a series of affordable luxury brands, inspired by the likes of Moet Hennessy[15].

Toast's origin was all about the fundamental reinvention of the good old *joint*, replacing it with a proposition of a carefully dosed pre-rolled 100% tobacco- and pesticide-free high-quality pure cannabis cigarette (*a Slice™*), in a stunning vintage packaging. Nespresso meets cannabis. Toast balances CBD and THC in such a way that every Slice offers the buzz equivalent of a drink: Toast Classic is akin to drinking a simple cocktail, Toast Gold is like a glass of champagne, and Toast Reserve is similar to enjoying a smooth bourbon. Toast Emerald will only have CBD, no THC. So only a mild body relaxation effect.

Toast is all about responsible consumption. The brand slogan says it all: *be social, be mindful*. Our prime goal was to ensure consumers were again in control of their enjoyment experience. By offering dosed experiences, the company successfully challenged the prevailing potency paradigm of the stoner world. It offers an increasing range of smokables designed for carefully curated segments of newcomers to cannabis, as well as for people already enjoying the product. Toast's purpose is clearly to be a positive and responsible agent of change in the wild world of cannabis. It will expand its promise in many more relevant form factors beyond a smokable version (like oils and beauty).

My second investment came in Summer 2017 in *greenRush*, nicknamed the Amazon of cannabis[16]. GreenRush is the largest and fastest-growing cannabis marketplace in the US. This is a bet on technology that connects consumers, brands and dispensaries in the most convenient and modern way possible. It is built on the thesis that, like in other categories, consumers seek convenience, and the demand side of the category will increasingly rely on mobile ordering and delivery solutions.

Punit Seth is the CEO of Toast. My cofounders are David Moritz and Eddie Miller. Four muske-teers. Paul Warshaw is the CEO of greenRush. All cofounders and their teams, and all sharehold-ers we invited to join in the (ad)venture, are deep believers of responsible marketing principles. I frankly hesitated in the beginning to be too exposed and visible with my opinions on this conten-tious category. Then I also figured out that by leveraging my previous experience and reputation, I actually can and will help shape the debate more than if I just stood by. No guts, no glory. I prefer to sit at the table, and to create the menu.

Indeed, I quickly found out that as the former CMO of AB InBev, stakeholders were actually eager to learn more about why we did what we did in the new cannabis world, and how we did it. On behalf of the two scale-ups, I have become a more visible ambassador in the media and on stages globally, spreading the gospel on how we create vanguard cannabis brands intent on doing the right thing. In the process we have met a lot of great new people with incredible new insight. It is a very healthy, and often very humbling, process. Our own biases and assumptions are constantly being challenged. But that is exactly what makes us progress further as new Brands.

In a galactic world where many more new categories will emerge, these Sin & Soul discussions will multiply (think cryptocurrencies, AI…). Each time, the focus will be about patiently building sustainable pricing power, about balancing Sin & Soul. The two core *why* components of the MC-Rocket.

Personal Notes

Price is what you pay. Value is what you get.

Warren Buffet

Chapter 13

Fundamental 3 (what) –
Brand Health

What gets measured gets done. But we naturally measure what is easiest to measure and to achieve. That is why most marketers measure only inputs and outputs. Not the hard outcomes (brand health): the real changes over time in behavior and attitude towards our brands. Yet exactly that is what you should do, as brand health today is top-line tomorrow. And it impacts (galactic) valuations more than you ever knew.

When an investor would ask what the senior marketers in a prospective company are incentivized for, they will often hear things like creating advertising, or running social media campaigns. If that is what a company says, think twice about investing. They may not have grasped the idea of Brand Health yet, defining marketing too narrow. We need to make a clear distinction between marketing *inputs, outputs* and *outcomes*. Incentives and targets should be linked to *outcomes*, not to *inputs* or to *outputs*. Outcomes is another word for Brand Health.

We need to keep building and measuring both components of Brand Health. How we measure will likely get more sophisticated and more convenient as technology evolves, as we get into the hereto hidden parts of the brain that make the purchase decisions, and as cost of measurement declines. Whatever investment we do in the marketing mix, in the *how*, it somehow needs to be tied back to the *outcome* of the decision(s).

Marketers need to remain first and foremost outcome-centric, and link that to the why of sustainable pricing power. Marketing is primarily about business, not (just) about entertainment. Hollywood is about entertainment, as a business. Here is how *outcomes* is different from *inputs* and *outputs*:

- **Inputs:** any and all forms of conceptual thinking and creative material to help Brands connect with consumers. This ranges from long-range planning and thinking around a brand's segmentation approach, its positioning statement, brand book, all the way to creating *all the important stuff* to bring the brand alive to the people it wants to engage with: TV ads, websites, social media accounts, printed.

- **Outputs:** any measurable impact of the connection between brands and the people or stakeholders it targets, often referred to as *touchpoint* measures. This includes measures like reach and frequency, TV GRPs, likes, clicks, purchase funnel metrics, conversion rates… But importantly, it is not because people saw and liked your Super Bowl TV ad that you won the battle in their mind. Equally, a lot of likes on social media does not mean you have a strong brand. It just meant people thought that cute kitten picture was indeed cute. It meant you engaged them, but what you don't know is whether you built relevant brand equity in their brain and heart.

- **Outcomes (Brand Health):** measures your relative brand strength inside the head of the people you are trying to sell to. It is the cumulative effect of any and all marketing (and nonmarketing) actions you undertook, and the ones of all your direct and indirect competitors/suppliers/distributors, in a given overall societal context, after some time. This is the real acid test for any sticky branded business model.

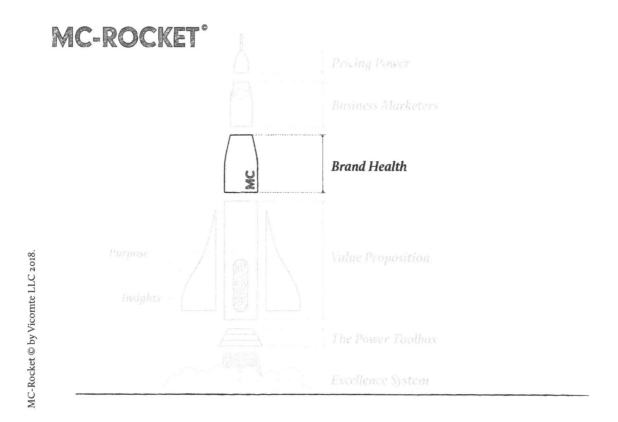

How can you measure such outcomes? There are plenty of market research techniques to unearth what goes on in theming the consumer, translating it in numbers or emotions. This is where leading brands systematically prioritize smart investment in quantitative tracking systems, to find out what is truly happening in the head of the consumers, as opposed to what they claim, or what you can just observe from sales or from outputs. These outcomes can be observed in two pyramid forms:

- <u>**Perception (Attitude – how much do you really love me?):**</u> Measures as a first step the number of people who have at least heard about your brand (aided or unaided *awareness*). Subsequently it checks deeper how much they really would proactively chose you out of a competitive set if they could (*consideration, favorite brand*), all the way to finding out how many would strongly *advocate* only for you (true *brand ambassadors*). Brand advocates can become your strongest future salesforce if managed well as a group, a theory beautifully explained in Joe Jaffe's book *Flip the Funnel* (2010).

- <u>**Behavior (Experience – how much do you really use me?):**</u> measures the number of people who have really tried/consumed/experienced your brand at least once in their life, and subsequently it measures repeat. *Repeat* is the lifeblood of a brand, as this means it is used in whatever frequency makes sense for your category, all the way to (multiple) daily usage (if that makes sense). Enduring brands are only built on repeat behavior, all while expanding their footprint (see also Byron Sharpe, in Part 2). As CFOs know, you cannot take attitude to the bank. Except if you can license the brand, e.g., market Coca-Cola T-shirts. If you can charge a royalty for the brand name, that could be a nice extra revenue stream. But it will never replace the real business income from the sale of the brand itself (the drink Coca-Cola).

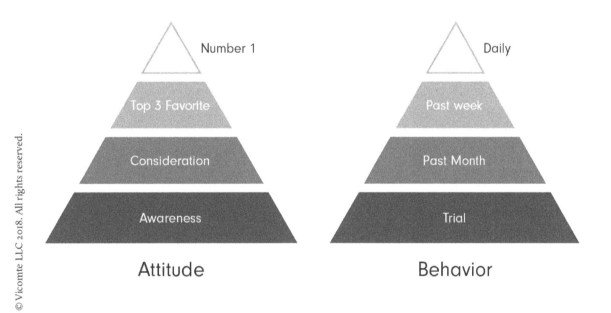

As a quick and easy example anybody can do: build the brand strength of a global brand like Coca-Cola among a group of colleagues in a room. Likely you will hit 100% awareness and a very high, near 100% trial, so two of the broadest pyramid bases possible. So far so good for regular Coke. But then proceed to check behavior. Ask who drank a regular Coke in the last month, then in the last week, and today since the morning. Quickly you will see a fast shrinking percentage—and maybe only 5% of the near 100% trialists will prove to be a daily drinker.

And similarly, for attitude, you can ask who would consider Coke during the next break in the office as a refreshment alternative, then if it would be one of the top three favorites you would chose from (imagine a fridge with options) and finally, who would go out of the office to go buy a Coke in the shop next door in case there would not be Coke in the fridge. A true Coke ambassador would do that. Again you will see that from 100% awareness, you would shrink possibly to a single digit number on the top of the pyramid.

Imagine now this exercise to be done scientifically on a statistically relevant sample in every country every month or quarter, and you get a quantitative reading of what consumers around the world truly think and feel about Coke. You have now visualized brand health. Of course there always is some bias and some noise in the data, but it is about detecting relative strength, and relative progress. It allows Coke brand management and the leadership to compare across markets and learn from best practice from one another. And to decide by country or area if growth in brand equity (and willingness to pay) can be translated in higher prices at equal or higher volumes.

Brand Health shapes narratives

Every brand needs regular re-invention to stay healthy over a long life. Pundits, especially financial analysts, love to say that brands have lifecycles. They need to do their job as a sell or buy side analyst —which means add a sense of drama in their report narrative, to create volatility in the market. Analysts are about spotting or generating buying and selling moments and so-called *inflection points*. On a personal level, each one wants to assert his or her place in the hallways of masters of the universe that can move markets, putting fear in any investor relations team.

Analysts do their job as best they can. Many do it in an incredibly professional way, despite the lack of data or insights of a company or industry insider. Back in 2004, during the TRIUM Global EMBA classes on corporate finance from Prof. Aswath Damodaran at NYU Stern, he made me write a full analyst report on PepsiCo, because I was marketing director in Germany at that time. He challenged me to spin my own story: where did I think PepsiCo stock would go over the next 9 – 18 months, and why? It was one of the best ever exercises of my MBA.

I took it seriously, and spent real time on the report. It was a great chance to get under the skin of the target company, and to combine narrative with numbers to tell a compelling story. To my own surprise, maybe sheer luck, I got remarkably close to what happened in reality in the stock market in the months after. I also used brand health data in the analysis. I should have followed my own advice and actually buy the stock. Eat my own dog food. I did not, out of loyalty and moral support for the company I was working at (Coke). It taught me again how clinical investing and effective brand management are two different skills. Yet the experience really opened my eyes to always take clinical external observation as a great source of input for more positive change inside.

Which Young Company to invest in?

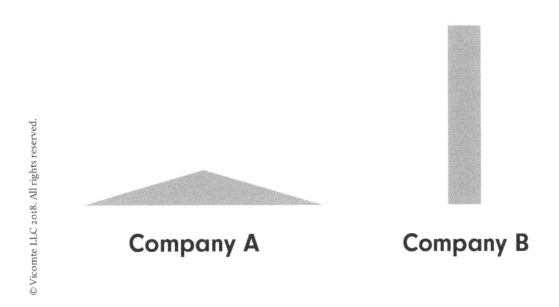

Company A   **Company B**

Here is how brand health pyramids can help you save money or make more money. Picture just the *behavioral* pyramid of the above two young companies. Two scale-ups with different brand health profiles. Company A has a broad base, but a very low top. Company B has a very small base, but a very rectangular and high top part. How would you think about valuation? Which company would you invest in? Who is the better marketer?

It usually creates interesting debates in class. The better marketer is likely to be Company B. It has created a sticky model. It is able to convert trial all the way up to 100% repeat business. As an investor, any proceeds of your investment will likely go to expanding the base, with the knowledge that quickly your small rectangle will become a large square shape. This is the shape of a very strong brand. On the other hand, Company A seems to have built a very large trial base, bigger than Company B. But for reasons to be found out, trial did not translate in an equally successful repeat.

This should alarm any investor. It is an indication that the marketing efforts so far were able to convince a broad group to at least try, in itself not bad, but you would want to better understand why these trialists are not coming back. If you by a company like that, not knowing why, you may have to completely reinvent the brand later on, a very costly venture and a nasty surprise. Investors can avoid *buyer's remorse*, the pain of a wrong purchase, by being more diligent on checking brand health. The above example was just on behavior. Check attitude too.

Which Mature Company to invest in?

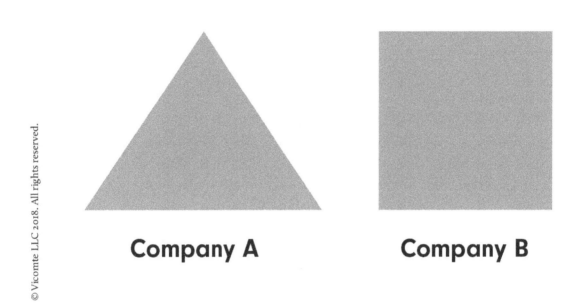

Company A　　　**Company B**

Now picture just the behavioral pyramid of the above two more mature companies. Two established businesses with different brand health profiles. Company A has a broad base, and a very decently developed high top. Company B has a very large base, *and* a very developed top part. Now a different question: How would you think about valuation? Which company would you still invest in and why?

Again, many interesting debates in class. The better marketer has likely been Company B. It has created a very sticky model. It was able to convert trial among a large base all the way up to a 100% repeat business. But as an investor, you are likely going to have to pay a lot for such a strong brand, assuming the owners will let it go in the first place (depends on how much cash it throws off each year). The key here is to find out its further up-pricing and expansion potential. Any proceeds of your investment may likely go to expanding the base, maybe leverage this brand in other categories or adjacencies, etc. Or you may bring synergies to lower the cost and increase the brand profitability even further. Due diligence should focus on checking if nobody can undermine or disrupt the stickiness of the brand business model, on the current and future Brand P&L, and other areas that can preserve and grow what seems to be a goldmine brand.

Company A is not necessarily bad either. It is a more classic brand case. Well run so far, but with upside to move from a pyramid to a square shape. Understand what drove its success today, and where the current brand ownership sees the opportunities and challenges to broaden the top. Sharpening the value proposition (see also next chapter), or better segmentation, may be the first things to look at here.

Brand Health shapes Valuations

Oscar Wilde taught us *beauty is in the eye of the beholder.* In business, that translates as *Value is what a damn fool will pay for it.* If analysts succeed in imposing their narrative over yours, that is *your* problem as a company. You are the brand owner, and you can use *your* brand health data to design the right narrative. You should create the right perception in the market among stakeholders, however hard that is. If you chose not to engage, you will be positioned anyway. *If you are not at the table, you will become part of the menu.* If you as a company get lazy, or intimidated, or short-term-oriented submitting to quarterly thinking, the brand's future will be a self-fulfilling prophesy. Brand health is a long-term concept, and it is a reflection of the mindset of its owners.

Behavior is what builds profitable brands. Every marketer should read *The Power of Habit* (2012) by Charles Duhigg. For the more tech-oriented habit-forming, there is *Hooked* (2013) from Nir Eyal. There is a watchout here as well. Tech companies have come under increased scrutiny for using *behavioral cocaine* to tie people to screens[1]. The social media platforms get accused of deliberately engineering the experience in such a way it *hooks* people in spending a lot more time than they should. It is the job of marketers to find ways to build habit and preference, to *nudge* people along in Thaler speak. But there is a fine line between a habit, a routine and *addiction*. Nicotine is addictive, and builds a proven unhealthy habit. As per the mantra of being purposeful, behavior building should be done in a morally correct and sustainable way.

As we saw in Part 1 already, brands *don't* have lifecycles *if* we allow them to stay young and topical. Brand managers tend to have shorter lifecycles than great brands. CXOs certainly have lifecycles. So eat or be eaten. Be the dog, not the tail. Build and measure brand health as much as makes sense for the rhythm of your business. Connect long-term incentives to it. Brand health *does* translate in pricing and in valuation—and both seller and buyer should be on top of this data to support their case.

Brand health today is top-line tomorrow. It creates the core set of facts to keep the entire company on the right course. And if done properly, it drives (galactic) valuations more than you could ever imagine.

Net Promoter Score: a proxy for Brand Health?

Every time you have flown **Delta Airlines**, you are asked to rate your experience related to overall flight experience, seat comfort, cabin service, food and beverage, entertainment and Wi-Fi. Given the millions of clients and thousands of daily flights, Delta can monitor customer satisfaction on a daily basis. A great and practical base to start to measure brand health, albeit not a complete one: you measure perception and future intent. You don't measure actual behavior, nor any specific brand equity drivers. Nevertheless, **Net Promoter Score (NPS)** is a very useful and relatively easy to implement base tracking tool to start gauging the loyalty of a consumer's relationship with a brand.

NPS: Net Promoter Score

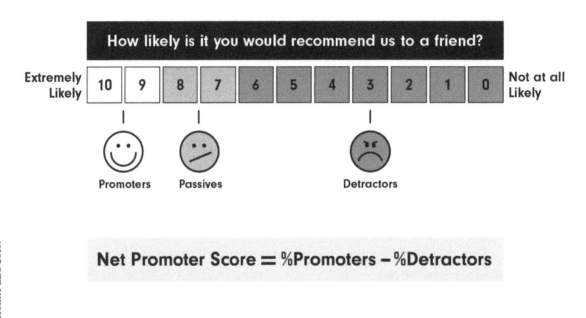

Vicomte LLC 2018.

The metric was introduced by Fred Reichheld from Bain & Company in a 2003 HBR article called "One Number You Need to Grow." NPS is calculated based on responses to a single question: *How likely is it that you would recommend our company/product/service to a friend or colleague?* Scoring is usually on a 0 to 10 scale. *Promoters*, who answered 9 or 10, are considered likely to buy more in the future, to remain a customer for longer, and, importantly, to become *brand ambassadors* making positive referrals to other potential customers. *Detractors*, who answered 0-6, are expected to do the opposite. You obtain the final NPS by subtracting the percentage of detractors from the percentage of promoters.

Passives (7 - 8) matter as well: they count towards the total number of respondents, thus potentially decreasing the percentage towards zero. A brand that only evokes passives is possibly very weak. It means it evokes limited to zero emotions. More akin to a commodity nobody truly cares about. Ullie Hoenes, the longtime president of German top soccer club Bayern Munich, once told me how he always stayed cool over the millions of people that loved *and* hated the *Rekordmeister*. Hoenes: *a real brand can never feel like a smooth sphere. It always needs to preserve some sharp edges (Ecken und Kanten – in German) to evoke emotions.* Adding with his egregious smile: *as long as you evoke more positive than negative emotions!*

NPS claims to be correlated with revenue growth and has been widely adopted. It can range from –100 (every respondent is a detractor), to +100 (everybody is a promoter). A positive NPS (above zero) is already good, and an NPS >50 suggests an excellent relationship. As an example, despite all its delivery and other PR issues, Tesla's public NPS on indexnps.com seems to be a stunning 96, highest among many automotive brands. This compares to 84 for Porsche and 73 for Lexus.

Three brand health reflections for the CEO/CFO/CMO:
1. How do we track evidence of brand health on our key brands?
2. How do we leverage brand health data in pricing decisions?
3. How do we leverage brand health data in valuation decisions (buying and selling of brands)?

Personal Notes

What we fear doing most is usually what we most need to do.

Ralph Waldo Emerson

Chapter 14

Fundamental 4 (what) – Value Proposition

The most challenging part of any business plan or brand promise is to define a sharp value proposition. How can you find the right balance between *perceived value* versus *perceived cost*, as compared to a meaningful *reference*. Critically, how do you avoid your biases as you define a value prop relevant to your consumers stakeholders, not just to you?

The heart of a TRIUM global EMBA is a 12-month Capstone Project, where self-organized teams of students mostly start a new company of their choosing. They use the Business Model Canvas (see Part 2) as one of the very practical constructs to help organize their entrepreneurial thinking. As a Capstone Director, and as an entrepreneur myself, I have gone through many sessions using this model. My observation is that the core Value Proposition area remains the most puzzling one for aspiring entrepreneurs, and one where a better mastery of the marketing fundamentals can be of immense value. Because if you don't get the Value Proposition right from the start, the risk is high that your entire business model will be flawed from the outset. And either you will need to *pivot* later, or the business will go nowhere.

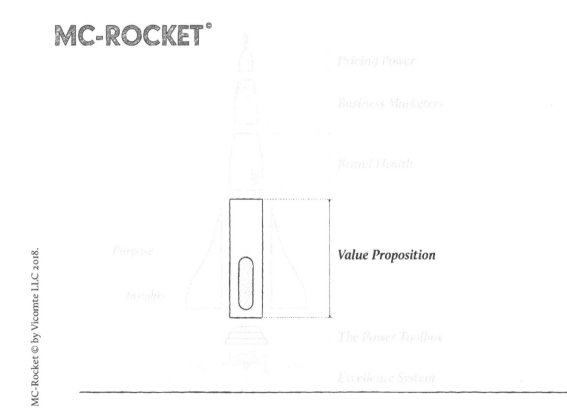

Value Proposition

In marketing jargon, what is a Value Proposition really? In its simplest form, it is a statement that describes the relative (perceived) benefit(s) of your new or current brand proposition, balanced versus its (perceived) relative cost. To help articulate what that a truly **winning** value proposition statement looks like, we need to play with the words *More, Less* and *Same.* I learned a lot in this area from Sergio Zyman during my time with Coca-Cola.

The crux of writing great Value Propositions: determining the right, unbiased *Reference.* This can be a *real, existing or obvious* comparison. Equally, it can be a reference that is to be *invented, imagined or imposed.* The human brain always looks for an *anchor* to frame something new. If you don't give it to people, they will make one up. And you better give them a relevant one, based on *their* world view, not on *your* biases. This is also where the world of insights start playing a role (see next chapter). Here are the most important value proposition permutations:

Winning Value Propositions

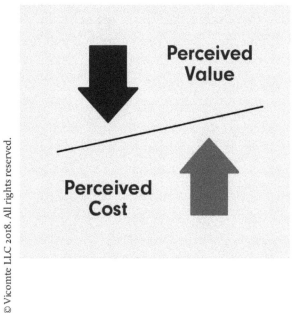

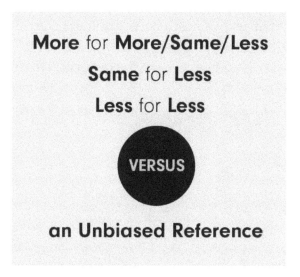

- **More for More,** is what most branded models strive for. The second *more* stands for an above average price versus the key competitor, or versus the category or segment in which you compete. Creating pricing power is all about creating More for More. Super premium luxury brands will strive to convince you to pay *Much More for Much More.* But the words don't guarantee a successful *profitable* business model. Everything depends on the cost structure of that super luxury model. The Value Propositions we work on in this chapter all deal with the top line part of the P&L.

- **More for Same,** is what many branded models compete on, especially in a crowded brand category with leaders and followers. Just look at the number of brands in any category to determine who is the category leader, and who are the category followers. The critical question here is then: *Same* versus who? *More* on what features and benefits? The reference question is critical here. The follower will usually position himself versus the leader.

- **More for Less,** seems to be the Holy Grail of Value Propositions. As a consumer, you get to have the proverbial cake and eat it too. All the benefits at the lowest cost. Any company that achieves that Nirvana is likely poised to control big market shares and ditto profits. But again the tricky/critical question is the cost side: Less versus who?

- **Same for Less,** is the typical private label model, but there are very successful brands built on this model too (see IKEA below). It aims to convince consumers that the cheaper retail brand offers the same benefits, but *without paying for the advertising* of the real thing. Off patent generic pharmaceuticals, retail brands... The good part of private-label models is they ensure there are checks and balances on the siren song of monopolistic pricing behavior by the strongest brands. If a strong brand increases its prices too much, it may create room for others below. Consumers benefit from company greed.

IKEA

What product and services does this brand sell? What can you actually pay for as a consumer? There are essentially four big revenue streams:

- Core: flat pack furniture (and tons of ancillary products)

- Assembly services at home (to avoid that one missing screw)

- Food & Beverage services (Swedish meatballs, anyone?)

- TaskRabbit services (acquired in 2017)

What is IKEA's *Value Proposition?* On its core product, IKEA offers you the same great-looking design furniture to create a great home, at prices well below those of top designers. Its Value Proposition can be defined as:

Same for Less
(versus the reference of design furniture)

Same for Less also often makes a lot of sense for the retailers, as private label profitability can help slim retail margins. However, it is seldom a sustainable long range play for the *suppliers* to these private labels. Private label brands piggyback on cost-intense category or brand development, on innovation invested in carefully by real brands. Private label is de facto subsidized by the innovation sweat of the real brands. So real brands don't help themselves by falling for the lure of extra short-term sales, often pushed by overcapacity or retail customer pressure. Once consumers find out, they de facto kill the original real brand. Why pay more if you know for a fact the products are (nearly) identical from the same supplier? In my own career, and in my consultancy, I always try to steer clear of mixing a private label with a true brand strategy. As a real brand lover, I hate the practice of outlet malls.

- **Less for Less,** is what most discount or value brand models shoot for. Cheaper airlines and retail automatically come to mind. Don't be misled by the name though. Less for Less are often the most profitable business models. There is a lot of money to made from frugal offerings, and many people who can technically afford more will self-select such offerings depending on the occasion. A business person usually loves to fly business when they can (and when the company pays). When he or she needs to fly privately, or take that full family holiday, and pay out of their own pocket, everybody flies Ryanair (the excuse: *not to spoil the kids at a too young age*).

The key combination absent from the above list is obviously **Same for Same.** That is the quintessential definition of a **commodity**, and commodities only compete on lowest cost. There is no real Value Proposition for a commodity, as there are by definition no (perceived) real benefits to leverage. Commodities are 100% interchangeable. You do *not* want your brand to be perceived as, or to become, a commodity.

Equally, as the smart observer will have understood already, **Less for Same** or **Less for More** are not recommendable positions to be in either. **Unless Less can be reframed as More.** The absence of a negative can be a fantastic positive. Think about the many products claiming *no fat, no cholesterol, no gluten, no artificial ingredients, no tobacco, no GMOs, etc,*

When Less can be More

Over the last decade most coffee bars had to start offering a costly extra benefit to its consumers: *free Wifi*. This was *More for Same*. Some coffee bars in San Francisco consciously have *no WiFi*.

The absence of this traditional consumer wanted/required free extra benefit is turned into a new and relevant benefit for a subsegment of coffee drinkers. What these coffee bars are saying to their patrons is: we value your true real person-to-person conversations, just like in the old renaissance philosopher salons. In our coffee bar, your experience will be purely human.

So No Wifi can be a perceived benefit, turning Less into More, smartly saving the extra cost and boosting the bottom line.

Eliminate Bias

The key in the above framework is to find the right *reference* to position yourself against. To do that, you need to dive into the mind of your prospective B2C consumer or B2B customer, and see the world through their eyes. The reason is we are all subject to bias. Our brain is cumulatively prewired to see the world in our particular way. Examples of biases and heuristics in human cognition are many. Here is an example list I once saw at a wonderful presentation during my Executive Program week at Singularity University back in early 2014:

- Confirming evidence bias: failure to challenge assumptions

- Saliency bias: focus on dramatic events versus seeing the whole picture

- Sunk cost bias: protecting earlier bad choices (as opposed to letting go)

- Overconfidence bias: failure to challenge assumptions

- Framing bias: posting the wrong question

- Status Quo bias: failure to consider alternatives to what is

- Base rate bias: neglecting relevant baseline information

- Linear rate bias: assuming linear versus exponential change

Our World View

If you want a fun exercise on bias, just compare the three world maps depicted on this site

http://infographics.economist.com/2014/ProjectionsSwiper/Projections.html?n=&w=595

Same world, different maps in our brain. You will see how different cartographers designed the map of the world. The first one was designed in 1569 by Gerardus Mercator, the Belgian geographer. The Mercator projection is a cylindrical map projection that distorts the true size of many land masses away from the Equator. In reality, Africa was always much bigger than enlightened Europeans (wanted to) believe in those years. In their mind, Europe was anyway the center of the world. Only much later did world maps start to show the true relative size of all continents.

The other map shows the Americas in the middle of the map. This is the map all North and South Americans grew up with in school. And the other map is the Australian perspective of the world. For Europeans and Americans, it seems they turn the world upside down.

Same world. Different perspective.

Shifting references

The reference in terms of benefits and cost can be inside your own category, or outside. As an example, during the early days of **Coke's conquest of Central Europe and Russia** in the mid-Nineties, the obvious first reference would have been Pepsi. The cola category was a low per capita one to begin with, but Pepsi had been the communist cola of choice since the mid-Seventies. Pepsi concentrate had been bartered with Stolichnaya vodka for years. After the Berlin Wall fell, Coca-Cola entered in the mid-Nineties with *Freedom Coke*. We achieved market leadership in virtually the entire area after a few years of hard work.

But then, Coke had to change its reference again. In the minds of our consumers, the relatively expensive Coke they loved to get was now coming at a serious opportunity cost: paying for a mobile phone (during those years). The average consumer only had so much money in their wallet. Our battleground was shifting from competing *versus soft drinks*, which you could see as a *share of stomach* fight, to competing for *share of wallet* versus (perceived) higher order needs of the average consumer. Our competition became the much deeper need and desire for (mobile) connection. We learned we could not beat that need, but we could join it. So we started to change our value proposition. We shifted our advertising and promotion tactics. For example: we started to use co-promotions with newly emerging mobile phone companies, offering free minutes as you bought Coke, and free tickets for the bus. We remained more for more, but worth it.

In a recent example in **Japan, Coke** now offers a new *Laxative Edition* more for more value proposition since end 2017[1]. Yes, you read that right. *Zero-calorie Coca-Cola Plus* retails for US$ 1.50 for 470 ml, and features a governmental coveted gold label approved special ingredient that helps the bodies of aging Japanese absorb less fat from food. This is new *Foshu* (Food for Specified Health Use) that competes with pharma references and helps lower cholesterol and prevent osteoporosis. Remember Coca-Cola started in a pharmacy in Atlanta in 1886. It knows a thing or two about pharma references. The category is growing fast—already US$ 6 Bn in sales. Pepsi now has Pepsi

Special, and Kirin offers Mets Cola. Soon the value propositions will have to be shifted again to keep driving brand health and to create pricing power.

Competing with *Free*

Everything is about finding the right reference. Arguably the toughest reference to compete with is... *free*. End 2017, I attended a CEO summit in Brussels organized by the Belgian family fund Verlinvest (where I am an operating advisor). During one of the many inspiring panels, prolific investor and entrepreneur Shakil Khan recounted how he became the first investor in Europe's unicorn pride **Spotify**, the music streaming company created by Daniel Ek in 2008.

When asked why Spotify is so good at what it does, Shakil was very clear: from the start Ek decided to primarily compete with piracy, with *free* music. That has always been Spotify's reference, to keep it honest and sharp. Of course Spotify has had to compete with many other music streaming models over the years (Napster, MySpace, 999, iTunes, Tidal...), and the competition remains fierce. Apple Music is coming back with a vengeance, narrowing the gap quarter by quarter[2]. And Amazon Music and Google Music are not gone either. On top, they have their respective voice assistants to add as a secret weapon to *their* value proposition.

Shak believes Spotify is a pure play focused only on music experiences, and will ultimately win the race. Under Ek's leadership, he claims, 3500+ people wake up every morning obsessed to create the best music experience possible, as opposed to employees at Apple's iTunes, where management focus is the iPhone and iTunes needs to additionally compete for attention with watches, tablets, laptops, TVs, headphones and self-driving cars, and whatever else Apple will focus on soon.

Spotify is a classic *More for More*, one that made it ultimately worth more by itself than the entire US music industry[3]. With over 140 million active users around the world, its valuation a few months post its direct listing rose to around US$ 30 Bn (end May 2018). Certain investors (self-servingly) already predicted valuation to grow to US$ 50 Bn within 2 – 3 years, assuming the team could maintain/accelerate current momentum[4]. It would be a rare European tech unicorn miracle indeed.

Now, with the *why* and *what* understood, *who* will fly your new MC-Rocket?

Three value proposition reflections for the CEO/CFO/CMO:
1. What is/are the Value Proposition(s) for our company brand and for our key brands?
2. How do we communicate these internally and externally?
3. How do we keep them relevant for new generations and segments?

Personal Notes

Life is too short to hang out with people who aren't resourceful.

Jeff Bezos

Chapter 15

Fundamental 5 (who) – Business Marketers

In any company that claims to be brand/consumer-driven, the CEO and CFO need to be true business marketers. Investors should expect they understand marketing's fundamentals. But the focus of this chapter is to clarify the role of the CMO. The old mindset: the CMO is the advertising Superman or Wonder Woman. The galactic mindset: you need somebody at the helm of business marketing teams with a set of future-centric competencies, based on a 20/40/40 balance between art, science and discipline. And with a good dose of MacGyver *ZBB* agility.

Companies have extraordinary expectations from their SuperCMO. Unfortunately, rarely is your CMO superman or superwoman. So who are the best marketing astronauts to navigate your new MC-Rocket? What kind of team would they lead? Who are the new rocket scientists behind the expected marketing miracles?

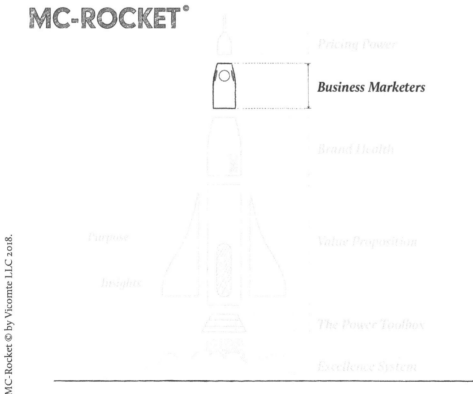

Headhunters keep propagating the archetypical image of a superhero that came in and made it all happen. The *Unicorn CMO*. Spencer Stuart's latest research called for *The Disruptor CMO*[1]. There is no doubt that individual talent can make a difference. One genius soccer player can turn a game, but they only win the full championships over time as a team. One may argue that in individual sports like tennis, it is only Roger Federer or Rafael Nadal who can influence the outcome. Even in their case, it takes a village. They have coaches and support staff. One gifted player does not win trophies each year for the team.

The lonely hero is an archetype of the past. Equally, the CMO is not Superman or Superwoman, but the leader of a team that needs to combine multiple personas to lead a brand in a galactic age. Well balanced, diverse and complementary teams are proven to win the marketing challenge over even the best of individual talent. Even in Marvel Comics and others, you will have the lonely superhero conics, but the bestselling ones are about superhero teams who win the war against the bad guys: The Avengers, The Fantastic Four, The A-Team, The Dirty Dozen, The Expendables, The Three Musketeers, Teenage Mutant Ninja Turtles, etc. Even James Bond cannot win without the wisdom of M, the smarts of Q, and the quick wit of Moneypenny.

If they should make any appearance, top marketers should go defend and sell their record especially at investor meetings, not only in advertising creativity festivals. In that sense, some of the introspection and pullback of worshipping in Cannes at the altar of marketing creativity is a good thing. I will come back to it later: real creativity does drive results. However, too many marketers were seeking glory and eternal fame in the eyes of the global agency ecosystem. Indeed, one should steer clear of investing too much in companies where the wunderkind hero cult is rampant. As seductive as it may be, nobody builds a sustainable company alone. It is far smarter to invest in an innovative and entrepreneurial team with the ability and agility to adapt and adjust to fast-changing landscapes.

Galactic CMO

Choosing who will be on the bridge of your MC-Rocket will remain one of the most important discussions a CEO will make, whatever name you give the leader (CMO, Head of Marketing…). Who will lead, what competencies does he or she needs to have to serve the business for the next phase of its development, and what kind of team will work with that CMO.

Enough articles have been written on the ever changing role of the CMO of the future, each one more provocative then the other, and each one arguing the CMO name should be changed to some other variant. I started to list all the old and new things that were expected from the CMO, and quickly filled over two full pages of competencies and skills. I won't bore you with the two pages, but here is a flavor of what I mean. When judging the CMO's team character traits, one could be inspired by how Luke Johnson, a regular FT columnist, described how he as an investor would look at a prospective entrepreneur:

- Self-discipline

- Honesty

- Numeracy

- Confidence

- Industriousness

- Enthusiasm

- Optimism

- Decisiveness

- Commitment

- Ambition

- Domain knowledge

- Frugality

- Understanding of risk

- Hands-on approach to operations

- Sense of urgency

- Belief in kaizen, or continuous improvement

The above laundry list is illustrative for the many *ideal candidate requirements* one encounters on elaborate job descriptions for CMOs. Johnson admitted as well that making a call on the above list was very hard to make for anybody, especially with limited time and not experiencing the person firsthand in action. Let's try this shorter list of how one could select the CMO of tomorrow: an all-around athlete with six competency areas:

- Thought Leader

- Growth Hacker

- Strategist

- Brand Marketer

• Culture Builder

• Product Marketer

If you step back from the above, we still risk getting back to Superhero territory quickly. Let's make our definition even shorter to get to the essence of what we want from galactic CMOs, inspired by how future leaders competencies are framed in Singularity University's Exponential Leadership terms:

• Innovator

• Technologist

• Humanitarian

• Futurist

Elon Musk Deconstructed

Elon Musk is an increasingly controversial figure. His summer 2018 tweet antics around the Tesla share price and the subsequent interviews on not sleeping enough caused many to take a second look at somebody who was previously given demigod status by the media[2].

However, Musk is worth studying deeper. Here is how Peter Diamandis would identify the three secrets behind Elon Musk's entrepreneurial success (February 18). He knows Musk since nearly two decades, and still calls him *arguably the greatest entrepreneur of our age*. Fans of Jeff Bezos and others may disagree, if only on absolute wealth results to date. I would also recommend to study the fascinating bios of Bezos, Branson and others. But Peter's blog was so good, I decided to summarize it here below. It is a must-read for future galactic CMOs. Yes, Musk is human after all, but he remains a very inspiring profile to learn from. Also for CEOs looking for a great CMO (and to reflect on themselves).

1. Deep-Rooted Passion

I didn't go into the rocket, car or solar business thinking 'This is a great opportunity.'
I just thought, in order to make a difference, something needed to be done.
I wanted to create something substantially better than what came before.
— Elon Musk

Musk only tackles those problems where he has deep-rooted passion and conviction. After selling PayPal, with $165M in his pocket, Musk set out to pursue three Moonshots, and subsequently built three multibillion-dollar companies: SolarCity, Tesla and SpaceX. This passion allowed him to push forward through extraordinarily difficult times and take big risks.

You might think it was always easy for Musk, but back in 2008 he was at a lowest low: SpaceX had just experienced its third consecutive failure of the Falcon-1 launch vehicle, Tesla was out of money, SolarCity was not getting financed, and Musk was going through a divorce. Musk borrowed money for basic living. Traumatic times. Despite the 2008 economic crisis at the time, he bet every penny he had, and eventually everything turned around. Ultimately, it was his passion, refusal to give up, and grit/drive that allowed him to ultimately succeed and begin to impact the world at a significant scale.

2. A Crystal Clear Massively Transformative Purpose (MTP)

Fundamentally the future is vastly more exciting and interesting
if we're a spacefaring civilization and a multiplanet species, than if we're not.
– Elon Musk

Part of Musk's ability to motivate his team to do great things is his crystal-clear MTPs, which drive each of his companies and organizations. Most remarkable breakthroughs in science and technology are backed by a powerful MTP. Musk's MTP for Tesla and SolarCity is to accelerate the world's transition to sustainable energy. To this end, every product Tesla brings to market is focused on this vision and backed by a master plan Musk wrote over 10 years ago.

Elon's MTP for SpaceX is to backup the biosphere by making humanity a multiplanet species. He has been preaching this since the founding of SpaceX back in 2002 even when he was experiencing numerous rocket failures. These MTPs are like a north star for Elon and his employees. They keep all efforts focused and aligned, which helps his organizations grow cohesively even in times of chaos.

3. First Principles Thinking

It is important to reason from first principles rather than by analogy.
The normal way we conduct our lives is we reason by analogy.
– Elon Musk

First principles thinking is a mode of inquiry inspired by physics, designed to relentlessly pursue the foundations of any given problem from fundamental truths.

For example: Elon has deployed this thinking strategy to give himself an unfair advantage when developing new batteries, a key component for both Tesla and SolarCity. Most people believe battery packs are really expensive at US$ 600 per kilowatt hour, and that's just the way they will always be. If so, this means it's not going to be much better than that in the future.

With first principles, you challenge and check the material constituents of the batteries and their stock market value. Batteries contain cobalt, nickel, aluminum, carbon, some polymers for separation and a sealed can. Break that down on a material basis and check what they would cost on the London Metal Exchange today. It's more like $80 per kilowatt hour.

So clearly you just need to be resourceful, and think of more clever ways to take those materials and combine them into the shape of a battery cell much cheaper than anyone realizes. First principle thinking works so well because it gives us a proven strategy for editing out complexity, while also allowing entrepreneurs to sidestep the tide of popular opinion.

Inspired by all the above, and going back to the two key *whys* of the MC-Rocket, allow me to propose the simplest job definition possible for the person you select to lead your brand portfolio into the new Space Age:

The (galactic) CMO inspires all internal and external stakeholders,
to deliver *sustainable pricing power* across the brand portfolio over time

The CMO is Captain Kirk or Picard, or Han Solo, or whoever is your commander role model on the bridge of your MC-Rocket in your preferred space movie. Like these leaders, they would be nothing without a kick-ass team. On a macro level, what key competencies should one seek in a winning galactic marketing team?

Business Marketing Teams

In Chapter 10 we already referenced the evolved 20/40/40 marketing competency split between art (Mad), science (Math) and discipline (Method). The split between these three has dramatically evolved over the last decades as a result of the digital revolution. Based on 30 years of observation, I would venture: from roughly 80/10/10 to 20/40/40.

We may have a big generation gap to close here. Many people in charge of marketing and businesses today were raised in the old paradigm. A balanced 3/3 is hard work to catch up with for the last of the Baby Boomers and Gen X leaders. As a young brand manager in the early Nineties, I was definitely raised in the first split. I *had* to evolve to the new split, or become obsolete. It requires real learning agility, and commitment to stick with the times and understand what is relevant for ever-new generations (Millenials, Z, Alpha…).

Art, Science & Discipline

From "80/10/10" to "20/40/40"

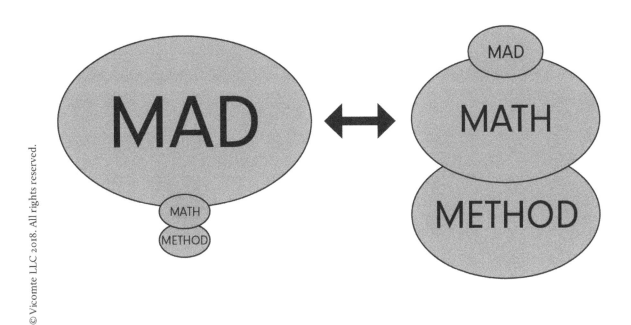

Marketing *science* has evolved dramatically. We will discuss the new power toolbox in the next chapter. But it is the *discipline* part that now matters more than ever. The *method* component should be the true focus of the CMO and CEO. What matters is get the routines and the everyday culture right, to turn Marketing Art & Science into progress towards the creation of sustainable pricing power. The 99% perspiration part people dread, versus the 1% inspiration everybody loves. *Grit* is the major differentiating factor to drive teams to high performance over years. How do we teach our kids grit, so they are prepared for this in their working life? For inspiration on the subject of grit, watch Angela Lee Duckworth in her famous TedX talk[3].

Grit: Learn from *As Can* Training

Another idea to prepare our children for the future: just like any new university graduate should have at least basic coding experience, inspire your business curriculum with lessons from astronaut candidate training *(AsCans)*.

To train talent with future-proof competencies, there is a phenomenal lifelong learning opportunity for pioneering universities. If they were to move too slow, the broader training, development and recruitment ecosystem can monetize this. AsCan training rigorously covers the following technical, psychological, health and safety areas over a minimum of two years before a mission, during basic and advanced training camps[4]:

- Launch and landing (space motion sickness, orthostatic intolerance, cardiovascular events)

- Internal on-orbit systems (from spacecraft propulsion on the body, thermal control, life-support systems)

- External on-orbit systems (mechanics, science experiment handling, earth observation, geology, astronomy…)

- The team is drilled in hazardous event simulation due to the extreme circumstances inside and outside a vehicle (e.g., pressure issues, fire, radiation, isolation, confinement…)

Find a *basic astronaut* way of the above to test students outside the classroom comfort zone. To teach *grit*, and on how to look up. To challenge all their paradigms on Earth. Experiential learning will generate new galactic mindsets. New mindsets will lead to ideas and worlds hereto uncovered. Which MBA or corporate university program will be the first to strike a partnership with NASA (US), ESA (Europe), JAXA (Japan), CNSA (China), ISRO (India) or Roscosmos (Russia)?

To lead brands and marketing teams in the new Space Age, there is more than one successful method to inspire your teams every day. Here are two possible extremes on the continuum of possibilities: Elon Musk versus Jeff Bezos.

- Elon Musk is all about swagger. His SpaceX company mantra is: ***Head Down. Plow Thru the Line***. Musk fires up his troops every day to set seemingly impossible targets, and then solve for them. Same for Tesla. Such a motto can backfire as we have seen, but it is how these companies have chosen to live. It *is* their idiosyncratic culture, and it *has* created incredible and awe-inspiring achievements for humankind. Decades ago, Leo Burnett, the famous founder of his namesake advertising agency, used to say: *if you reach for the stars, you may not quite get one, but you will not come down with mud either.*

- On the other end of the spectrum is Jeff Bezos. The Latin slogan behind how he prefers to do things at Amazon, and especially at Blue Origin is: ***Gradatim Ferociter (step by step,*** *ferociously)*[5]. Bezos is a fan of the Navy Seal approach, as it fits his tortoise approach: *slow is smooth and smooth is fast*[6].

Pick whatever method that suits your company culture best. But pick one and work it consistently. Your teams need to know *how things are done around here*. In the new post digital galactic world, hitting the old Art part is not enough anymore. Even 2/3 is not enough. A well balanced 3/3 team is the future.

MacGyver: Mr. ZBB

When it comes to team competencies, there is one extra competency the whole marketing team needs to demonstrate, to anchor the idea that marketing truly *is* finance truly *is* business. The fourth dimension is a financial dimension. For the team to become truly galactic business marketers, it needs to adopt as a group the frugality spirit and the resourcefulness of legendary 1985 TV action star MacGyver[7].

The series was relaunched in 2016, yet without the smash hit success of the original. Still, MacGyver remains the old TV embodiment of what one can do with a simple Swiss army knife and duct tape. He symbolizes agility. While at AB InBev, my Brazilian colleagues would refer to a ginga[8] attitude. In dancing *capoeira*, it means moving the hips freely and loosely, with swagger. In business, it means being flexible and street smart.

Competencies
of Galactic Marketing Teams

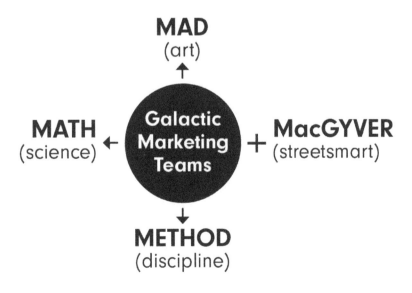

That is why we add MacGyver's low-cost problem solving skills to the competency model—as a fourth dimension to Art/Science/Discipline. In business, this competency is best reflected in the classic budgeting concept of *ZBB*, which stands for *Zero Based Budgeting*, a concept invented in 1970 by a Texas Instruments accounting manager[9]. AB InBev swears by it, and turned it into a true way of life. More and more companies follow ABI's lead, but seldom with the same intensity and rigor. Living ZBB as it is meant to be can feel very hard for many people. Few employees love a constant pressure on the money they are entrusted. But when done right, it actually does free up lots of inefficient or wasted resources the company leadership can chose to reinvest elsewhere in the business, or to give back to shareholders. For a galactic business marketer, ZBB simply makes sense.

ZBB is very often wrongly confused with plain cost-cutting. Cutting travel and saving paper clips. Rubbish. If you study its core principles, you will see ZBB means you are first to reason, like Elon Musk, from first principles. You don't propose a next-year budget based on this year plus some percentage, doing slightly more of the same but maybe slightly more efficiently. With a ZBB mindset, you defend the most economical way to achieve your marketing objectives—starting from zero *every year*. This includes making clear distinctions between so-called *working* versus *nonworking* money: between money that directly matters to the end consumer buying your brand (which you try get measured ROI on), versus money that serves intermediary cost (which you try to minimize). Your galactic team becomes a tight-knit group of street-smart marketers with an *owners* mentality, not a big budget spending machine happily investing *OPM, Other People's Money*.

Adopting ZBB does not mean at all the marketing budgets should all be zero everywhere. There are many legitimate reasons and business cases to invest hundreds, millions or even billions in marketing. Brands are built over time, patiently, step by step (again: think Jeff Bezos' mantra). What we are talking here is *mindset*. If you work for a big company, why (continue to) pay for million-dollar commercials if you can get the same or better effect these days with US$ 10K or less? I have learned the best way for a CMO to make true business marketing teams become more creative and efficient is to take away the comfort of big budgets as a principle. With a ZBB mindset, you will see who can strategize and improvise with less. *Starving artists create the best work.* Anybody can spend big budgets, but not necessarily can they spend it wisely. Matthew Bull, one of my former highly respected agency partners, has been on a crusade to reinvent the old agency service model. His **Solo Union** group of creatives works under the motto *Pay for the heads, not for the overheads*.

I always get asked: what is the ideal marketing budget? How much should I invest? Think about it. Visualize a P&L in your mind. Picture the line item that says *Marketing*. If you had your *own* business, how much would you *ideally* want to see on that line item…? I do co-own a series of restaurants in Istanbul and in New York since 2003. Everybody welcome. Restaurants owners and operators know the ideal marketing budget is… *zero*. You want to avoid investing in advertising to bring in patrons. It is all about location, experience and customer service. Investing in these drivers is smart business marketing. If you get this right, your regulars will become your brand ambassadors.

When you find ways to flip the old AIDA funnel we discussed before, turning current brand users into evangelists who work for you for (nearly) free, then you start thinking like MacGyver.

In space, as *The Martian* movie showed so well, astronauts have no choice but to be extremely resourceful. On Earth, the new privately run space contractors *had* to learn to be more frugal than the incumbent space contractors like Lockheed Martin and Boeing. In *the good old days*, these incumbents used to bill NASA on a *cost-plus system*. That meant there was *zero* incentive to be frugal, or to think differently for that matter. The incumbents became slow and fat. Launches happened, yet true progress stalled. Today, the new privately funded space challengers like SpaceX, Blue Origin and Virgin Galactic work for NASA on a *price-based costing* principle. To survive over time, that means these companies *had/have* to be scrappy and frugal by design, *without* compromising quality and safety. The Federal Aviation Commission and NASA will see to the latter. Ownership and frugality worked to break one of the industry's oldest paradigms: the *reusability* of rockets. By eliminating the most dramatic cost factor of launches in the past, launch costs are reduced by a factor of 10X, with more reductions to be expected as Moore's Law kicks in.

STEAM rules

As a CEO, you now know how to select the next galactic CMO and his/her team. Business marketers focused on creating sustainable pricing power, blending Elon Musk's focus on first principles with Jeff Bezos discipline. I would like to share one major watch-out for the CEO, CFO and CMO as they and their teams get to work. Protect creativity. Protect Art. Science is expected to progress more and more. We need to protect that 20% Art part as long as we can.

So far, humans continue to beat machines when the challenge is to go beyond boundaries. In the epilogue, I will share how that may change in future, and how all bets may be off then. For now, as long as galactic business marketing teams continue to consist of mostly humans, they need to not just have STEM capabilities, but STEAM capabilities[10]. The *A* is a critical factor behind the *imagination economy*. It stands for that unique human capability to blend liberal arts and humanities with science, tech, engineering and math. Intuitive and creative thinking will likely continue to create economic value by humans, while logical and rational thinking may get increasingly outsourced to robots. Maybe one day we end up with a dystopian 0/50/50 split. George Orwell's Big Brother vision would have won.

Let's see when a robot can out-agile MacGyver? Can we make them such they never will? In the meantime, as a CEO, CFO and CMO, encourage the business marketing teams to unleash their *Mad* DNA. We need to keep evangelizing and celebrating the need for *that special magic* that makes ordinary ideas and campaigns potentially extra-ordinary. Allow risk and experimentation. Its unpredictable powers remain key to create marketing miracle$.

Three business marketer reflections for the CEO/CFO/CMO (+ also for the Board):

1. What real understanding, competencies, skillset and track record do we have in our senior leadership (board + management) in terms of marketing and finance fundamentals?
2. How do we actually train our senior leadership in marketing and in finance fundamentals?
3. What marketing/finance skillset do we (board + management) require to promote senior talent to the company's top leadership levels, especially to the CEO level?

Personal Notes

Let Earth go

I very often get the question of how I *planned* to become the CMO of a company like AB InBev. My answer is always the same simple one: I never planned anything like that, nor could I have, even if I had wanted to.

When I was a young student in Leuven in 1982 – 86, the CMO title was not known yet. And AB InBev would not exist till 2004. Even its predecessor combinations did not exist yet (InBev, Interbrew…). In fact, during my student days, the local leading Belgian beer brands Stella Artois and Jupiler were the fiercest rivals. Today, (only) three decades later, Jupiler is by far the leading Belgian beer brand, and Stella Artois is one of the rare global beer jewels.

I did however embrace an *international* life from the start, and allowed that idea to underpin my personal journey. The wanderlust must have come with the mother milk. I was born in Africa, in the Democratic Republic of Congo. My father worked there as a science and math teacher in the early Sixties. I have always dreamed of far destinations. After a lot of InterRail travel through Europe in my student years, it all started to get serious in 1989 when I won a Prince Albert Fund (PAF) fellowship in Belgium[1]. It eventually landed me setting up the new office for a small Belgian consulting firm in Charlotte, North Carolina.

The US is where I discovered my passion for the field of marketing. A completely new world opened up, and I never looked back. The only thing I knew for sure was that any further career choice would involve building brands, ideally on a global scale. That became the north star in any further career decisions, a filter I kept even in my post corporate life.

Before you are CEO

In 2016, a fellow Belgian called Peter Vanham released a book called *Before I was CEO*. He also had studied economics at KULeuven, and I had been his official mentor during *his* Prince Albert Fund (PAF) fellowship in NYC. Over a joint passion for biking and beer we had become better acquainted. Peter was restless in those days, dealing with the key question many young talented people face in their early career phase:

What choices do I make, or should I make, to be successful?

In the end, I urged him to settle on answering that question himself. He went to ask a bunch of very inspiring and successful senior corporate leaders about the key choices they had made in their early days that, with hindsight, they believed had gotten them to the top in their field.

I don't consider myself a classic big company CEO. Peter interviewed me anyway, as CEO of my own consultancy, post a CMO career. I let you discover the overall lessons his book has to offer, except for one striking one. There was a clear common characteristic between virtually *all* the people he profiled in his book: *being open to the world*. They all built their their phenomenal careers by living and working internationally. They *all had learned to let go*, both physically and mentally.

I could never have done what I did, or what I do now, by staying in Belgium. Don't get me wrong: Belgium is a great (small) country. A wonderfully complex and sometimes surreal city-state. I am eternally grateful for the education it gave me, and I have been giving back to it wherever I could through my nonprofit work. However, I learned early on that only when you truly enlarge your horizons, new doors will open. You don't really know what lies behind each one. When you chose to find out, magic happens. It is truly like the inspiring Delta Airlines 2018 *Runways* campaign. It challenges the conventional wisdom that good things come to those who wait. Instead, Delta suggests the best (travel) experiences will happen *to those who go…*[2]

Your appetite for risk plays a critical role in all the choices you make. In your career, in your financial bets, in life in general. How much risk you are willing to take as an individual is entirely personal, and utterly depending on the context of the decision. More often than not, the knowledge we have holds us back more than we think. A friend at university once introduced me to the works of Elias Canetti, the 1981 Nobel Prize winner of Literature. I turned one of his provoking aphorisms into a poster that has traveled with me since. The quote loosely translates as:

> *What is important is not what we think about daily,*
> *but what we have NOT thought about daily.*
> — *Die Provinz des Menschen* (1973)

That is true for financial investments and career choices, but de facto for whatever major choice you make in life. You have to break eggs to make an omelet. You may take calculated risks, or just go with the flow and follow your gut. By doing so, you may find yourself sometimes backed in a corner, with nothing to lose, facing high risks and a sense of urgency. Henry Kissinger, a man of many high-stakes diplomatic situations, said it well: *the absence of alternatives clears the mind marvelously*. As a business marketer, and as an investor, if you want to truly create alpha, you have to take risks. Get out of the comfort zone. That is where the magic has a chance to happen.

History is a great reference point and context provider. Worth studying and learning from. But even more important for the galactic marketer is to learn to move away from all you know, without losing your soul. If I had three lessons from spending time thinking about these galactic futures, it would be these:

1. Carpe Diem

Enjoy today with as much intensity as you can. For people like me, the risk is tomorrow tends to always be even more exciting, especially as you can help shape it without legacy issues to deal with (yet). But today is pretty awesome too. If you never appreciate to live in the here and now, you will forever be unhappy chasing a better tomorrow. If you taste life today to the fullest, and keep a sense of wonder for what is coming, the surprise may taste twice as sweet. No regrets.

If Stephen Hawking is right on his climate change predictions, our planet has about only 600 years to go before it becomes a giant fireball[3]. That is only about the same time from Da Vinci's renaissance till now. Hawking's advice was to accelerate the deeper discovery and colonization of Alpha Centauri, the star system with possible earth-like living conditions closest to us (4.22 light-years away). Let's hope active climate change management will prove Hawking wrong. Nostradamus also missed a few prophecies some centuries ago.

2. Black swans keep life worth living

Not only is it pointless to try to control the world, but it might render it also boring as hell. Who wants to live in an Atlantis or Utopia where everybody is happy all the time? Not that I am a buddhist, but the Buddha already taught the world: how can one be happy if one doesn't know what sadness is? Each time humankind, or some of its delusional leaders, thought they found the secret to world dominance and mind control, something happened that forced a full rethink. James Bonds in Guy Fawkes masks rose to restore order. Action gets reaction. Thesis, antithesis, synthesis.

This book's core is about systems and models to help predict marketing capability better, and to make better investment bets. If I am honest, I also want marketing as a profession to keep a delicate sense of unpredictability and risk, as life should be. Marketing should still remain at least 20% unpredictable art (Mad), besides the more predictable 40% science (Math) and 40% discipline (Method). An occasional black swan will keep life interesting, and it will keep us all on our toes.

3. Let it go

My favorite Disney *Frozen* song. Let all biases go, and you may not only recognize faster what comes, but also understand it better, and possibly even enjoy it more. For the high achievers among you, Mark Manson has some controversial advice in *The Subtle Art of not Giving a F*ck (2017)*: the more you obsess to become excellent, the harder it will be. The more you accept your mediocre, *average* starting point, and the more you naturally work in manageable increments from there, the more extraordinary results may actually come.

So today I would slightly reframe my *go international* advice to whoever asks for it. Today, I would tell anybody wondering about what choices to make: *go live a galactic life…* even a *BFG one* if you have the chance for it. Before she joined Facebook, when a very smart and successful yet (self-declared) very risk-averse Sheryl Sandberg considered *not* moving to to Silicon Valley, Google's Eric Schmidt convinced her as follows:

**When you're offered a seat on a rocket ship
you don't ask, *what seat?*
You just get on.**

Personal Notes

Let Earth go

We become what we behold.
We shape our tools.
And then our tools shape us.

Marshall McLuhan

Chapter 16
Fundamental 6 (how) – The Power Toolbox

Welcome in the MC-Rocket engine room, where rocket propellant is converted in high-speed propulsive jet. Since the advent of digital, the toolbox for marketers has changed dramatically, even if some core tools remain unchanged, at least conceptually. Discover the basic toolbox for the galactic business marketer.

Car enthusiasts discussing *traction* will often use the analogy *where rubber meets the road*. In space, it is the opposite: it is all about *rubber leaving the road*. It is all about liftoff, about defying gravity before escaping velocity into orbit. Classic rocket engines are reaction engines, generating forward thrust in accordance with Newton's third law of motion (action equals reaction). As we lift off, better understanding and mastery of the galactic marketing toolbox secures the required net forward thrust of your MC-Rocket. A similar exercise could also be done for the finance toolbox, but I leave that to a CFO to share best practice. To manage your expectations: this chapter is the core subject of many brilliant marketing books. I will only discuss the high level that is relevant within the context of the MC-Rocket construct. For people wanting to discover more in depth, surf to vicomte.com/insights.

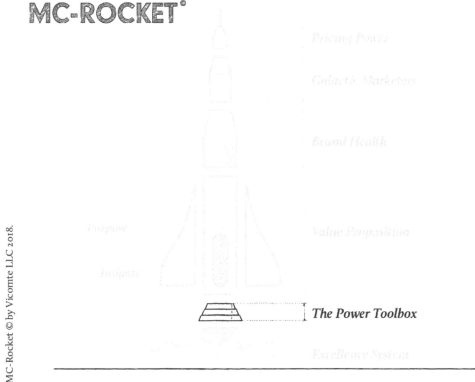

The Power Toolbox

The most critical gravity challenge for the modern marketer over the next decades remains *mastery of the new digital world*. According to 2017 survey by OC&C Strategy Consultants and Experian, leading a broad digital transformation remains by far the number-one issue keeping nearly 60% of the CMOs up at night[1]. That may be surprising to you, after nearly two decades of broad internet availability. However, consider how many pieces of content are sent each second or minute these days, and you start to understand why. Here is just a small snapshot (early 2018):

- 204+ million emails/minute

- 3.2+ billion Facebook likes per day

- 2+ billion digital image being uploaded every day

- 300+ hours of video uploaded every minute on YouTube

- Average attention span watching a video on social media: 2"

It only gets exponential from here[2]. The fully digital Gen Z natives are rolling in to replace Millenials, followed by an even savvier Generation Alpha[3]. One can only imagine how they will connect with each other. It is a paradox for marketers: never before were the connection tools so accessible and so democratized. The internet leveled a lot of ground between big-budget brands and no-/low-budget brands. Yet never before was there so little signal through the exponential noise level. How can one be heard, let alone be noticed at all against this noise level? Answer: by being clearer than ever on the fundamentals, before you engage with the latest tools. Do not let the tools confuse your focus on the fundamentals.

In terms of connecting with people, the challenge marketers need to focus on remains the concept of *Reach*. The issue for galactic marketers is to find ever-new ways to break through the clutter with consistent messages and engaging stories that anchor your value proposition in consumers' minds. The challenge is not to add to the noise with stuff, but to break through its brand relevant messaging that builds brand equity over time. And that is easier said than done.

Zegna's fourth generation Edoardo Zegna discussed why he was pushing for more radical change inside his family company: *Millennials and generations after them don't want brands to talk to them, they want brands to help them have a relationship with their friends*[4]. Edoardo faces the law of inertia among his colleagues, as all need to learn the complexity of connecting in the new media landscape. In another example, consider the exponential power of e/m-commerce to reach and sell to the newest generations around the world. On November 11, 2017, 180-year-old Henkel's brand Schwarzkopf became the number-one shampoo brand in China thanks to betting on this new channel, a bet that was different versus its classic rivals legacy distribution models. Still, overall, Henkel changes its ways slowly. Pascal Houdayer, former EVP Henkel Beauty Care, summarized the issue facing many established brands as follows: *The fear of pain is still bigger than the pleasure of gain*[5].

Digital Snake Oil

The galactic marketer power toolbox consists essentially of three big sets of tools we will discuss in detail below: long-term tools, short-term tools, and the ones you use continuously. Virtually all of them have been digitized over the last years. So there is no point anymore in making any distinction between analog and digital tools. For example: all video is *de facto* digital these days. But that does not mean all digital video is used optimally for smart connections with an ever more digitally savvy consumer.

Some tools, especially the so-called short-term tools, do keep changing at a breakneck speed, causing marketers to react like squirrels chasing the latest shiny object[6]. Think programmatic buying, big data, virtual reality, augmented reality, neuromarketing, and lately AI. It seemed at some point that if the CMO could not speak fluent Python or R, he or she was out of sync with reality. Big tech players like IBM, Oracle and Salesforce are small new markets and amplify the new tech hype[7]. They worship the CMO even more than the CIO now. They sell massive database and personalization capabilities. Every year, a new tech hype gets massive media and seminar attention, and gets added to the Gartner Hype Cycle[8]. Some eventually break through and will make it past the *Peak of Inflated Expectations* on the Hype Cycle—like data science and AI—but most don't.

Gartner Hype Cycle

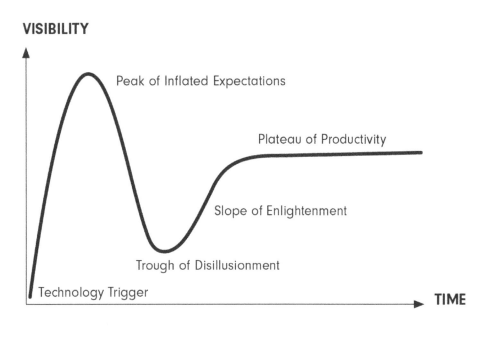

Great marketers need to separate the truly useful from the hype, and watch out for *digital snake oil*. Internet brought us many good things, but already in 1996 software engineer Clifford Stoll warned us to beware for technocratic *Silicon Snake Oil* [9]. We need to stay open-minded and agile, like MacGyver, and keep an attitude of experimentation and learning about the value of each new discovery as it comes. But we also need to refocus on the fundamentals each time the latest *new thing* hits the mass marketing shelves and the lecture circuit. Galactic marketers need to keep focused on building sustainable pricing power, brand health and value propositions. They need to ensure the new tech truly serves core KPIs that matter the most to brand owners:

• Customer recruitment: how to drive new clients to your brand?

• Customer retention: how can I best retain existing customers?

• Employee engagement: how can I use my assets to acquire and retain scarce talent?

Got *Seaters inside?*

Clever new tools solve classic marketing challenges better, faster, cheaper. Marketing is finance is business. Let me make a plug here for a brilliant secret marketing AI tech solution I invested in years ago, unique in the world. A tool every galactic brand should consider having in their modern toolbox. **Seaters** is a hidden gem, a Belgian-American company founded by Belgian Jean-Sebastien Gosuin back in 2012-2013.

Its client roster is growing: the biggest banks of Europe (like BNP Paribas), major telcos (KPN, Proximus, Telenet…), CPGs (AB InBev, Coca-Cola…), national lotteries, media companies and sports companies (like ASO Tour de France). BNP France deployed Seaters tech already twice on its biggest global asset platform, the Roland Garros tennis tournament in Paris. On a stage like that, nothing can go wrong. It has been driving client prestige and awareness for the bank for four decades. But now, thanks to Seaters, Roland Garros also tangibly converts that same asset investment directly in significant new account openings. Turning passion into business. Seaters helps drive clear asset ROI on your brand. Seaters is about you as a brand, not about Seaters. It is like *Intel Inside*. To test Seaters, mail its founder: js@seaters.com. A no-regrets move.

Seaters was a little ahead of its time. Like many breakthrough tech solutions, it took some time to position itself as a clear value add for brand-driven companies: how to sell it and price it in a way a brand can adopt easily as part of its modern toolbox. The classic startup/scale-up search for product-market fit. It would have been easy to give up, but with Bezos in mind we kept improving, step by step. We kept iterating, and Seaters finally hit its sweet spot in 2017. Its ever-growing and loyal client roster is the best proof. It is now super easy to test and adopt. Brands can prove its business case fast on the core KPIs mentioned above. The software efficiently upgrades pre-digital dinosaur processes, in a GDPR compatible way. Seaters will evolve and learn from other Belgian-American trailblazing scale ups in the sector, like **Showpad**. The brainchild of Louis Jonckheere and Pieter-Jan Bouten offers sales enablement software that reinvents how marketing is leveraged by sales forces in the field. It is already used by a 1000 companies around the globe, and they guys just got started.

Seaters was my first bet on marketing tech. I learned a lot from the experience. My second bet was **FlashStock** in 2014, a Canadian start-up created by serial entrepreneurs Grant Munro and Michael Scissons. I met them during their first venture in the early days of social media. AB InBev had been one of their first clients experimenting with it. After a few successful years, the venture ended with mixed results after investors forced a too rapid expansion. I decided to bet on the now even more experienced jockeys, and on what I thought was a big new problem they intended to address.

Flashstock's genius insight was to solve the brand marketer's fast-growing new problem to acquire brand relevant social media content at scale, with all digital rights covered (to avoid being sued), and at low cost. Again, it took a while before we figured out how to sell this new solution to brands. Defining the pricing architecture was a constant fight, until we eventually landed on a workable SAAS model brands felt really good with. After the first 18 months I could honestly not have predicted we would actually sell 18 months later to **ShutterStock** for a great price. But after weighing all pros and cons, we did. Welcome to the wonderful and unpredictable world of entrepreneurship.

Brands need to watch out for the increasingly fake side of social media[10]. Fake followers, fake clicks and fake reviews are rampant, despite calls for transparency and threats of shifting budgets back. The media supply chain is murkier and murkier. The World Federation of Advertisers has cautioned marketers worldwide since a while to take back control over the media eco-system, to protect brand equity long term[11]. As an example, *influencer marketing* can only work sustainably as long as these influencers are seen as real and authentic, not just as another purchased ad medium. Kylie Jenner may have 111 million followers, and receive more than US$ 1 million per post. But this is the same like paying for classic TV reach. Except for some die hard fans, few people believe her support for brand A or service B is authentic. It is just advertising. Old wine in new bags. Brands paying for reach, for eyeballs.

The galactic marketer toolbox

The medium is the message[12]. A famous aphorism by University of Toronto professor Marshall McLuhan, making him one of the most influential communications theorists of the 20th century.

His conviction was that media shapes the way we think, and that the printed book was fated to disappear. He was right on the first, not on the second. Marketers need to stay focused razor-sharp at all times on the fundamentals, and therefore on using and shaping *all three sets of tools* in the toolbox below, not just the toolset focused on the short term. You will not win in the new Galactic Age by thinking and acting short-term only. You need to keep redefining the tools to serve you, not the opposite.

1. Building the long term

You use these tools once or a few times per year, across your brand or portfolio to ensure a strategic underpinning of all your tactics. This is where senior leaders focus their time, and ensure in-depth discussion.

- Strategic insights, pre-search

- Segmentation, targeting, positioning

- Portfolio management

- Brand architecture

- Occasion-based marketing driving a broader user base

- (Corporate) strategic brand planning

- Visual brand identity design (VBI)

- ...

2. Building the short term

You use the short-term-oriented tools continuously during the year, across your brand or portfolio, to ensure a tactical translation underpinning of all your strategic thinking. This is the part of the toolbox where most digital hype activity takes place as well, and where marketers need to balance staying in tune with smart experimentation (and not early overcommitting) with unproven new technical gizmos. Equally, don't let the old-school agencies hold you back, because it suits their bygone business model and set of competencies. If you brief a classic ad agency, guess what many will still come back with: a TV-based campaign with a 30" spot at the core.

What else explains that classic TV channels stay in business so long, even though the writing is clearly on the wall? Still to date, with C-suites stacked by people from the TV generation, nobody will be fired for a strong TV-backed marketing plan with lots of (potential) *reach*. Many companies keep allowing agencies to make 30" ads, even tough they will admit in meetings the facts show most people will actually zap away. The self-delusion is mind-boggling. *For somebody who is good with a hammer, every problem is a nail*[13]. For big brands the objective is often to give their massive distribution systems a good feeling. Sales conferences attended by 50+ years olds are TV networks' best friend.

As modern marketers have learned, social media is not free, despite what many CEOs believe. They are a copy/paste of the classic TV network pricing model, just a bit more targeted. *Reach at acceptable cost* has become a CMO's nightmare these days. The fact remains: TV and social media are indirect tools to achieve a result. They are inputs creating outputs, and possibly outcomes (brand health). They are a means to an end. Where possible, get them for free, and where possible, if you have the people capacity, invest in systems that allow you to *go direct* over time, without paying any middle man. Connect to your consumers as direct as you can. Control your connection to increase your chance to eliminate all the noise, and increase the chance of your signal to reach the consumer mind:

- Tactical insights

- Connection strategies and tactical touchpoint planning

- Visual content and creative development

- Own/paid/earned media allocation and planning

- Social-media planning and community management

- Influencer marketing

- Experiential marketing

- Agency management

- Sponsorship and asset management

- Stakeholder management

- eCRM, lead generation

- New tech experimentation

- …

3. Continuous reinvention

These tools are used continuously during the year, across your brand or portfolio, to ensure a perennial short and long term refreshment of your value propositions. To remain topical, any brand, and any company, should have full pipelines of renovation and innovation ideas to keep its portfolio fresh and vibrant. In this toolbox, your will typically encounter the following components:

- (Innovation) insights

- Renovation pipeline management

- Innovation pipeline management (growth development platforms)

- New in-house business model design, true internal disruption

- Involvement in cocreation with start-ups and targeted M&A

- Upstream collaboration with government and universities

- …

How do you organize most effectively, as a brand or company, to balance renovation, innovation and disruption? That depends a lot on the DNA of your company. An excellent book for the CEO/CMO/CFO is *Customer Innovation: Customer-centric Strategy for Enduring Growth* (2014), by Marion Debruyne, Dean of Belgium's Vlerick's Leuven Gent Management School, and former visiting professor at Wharton, Kellogg and Emory. What is clear is that, again, everything starts with the right mindset. This area of the toolbox needs to be approached with an incredible dose of humility, especially on the most complex area: developing true disruption of your business model. Somebody somewhere is always aiming to disrupt you, whether you notice it or not.

Every brand should remain paranoid. Ideally you have a few people or somebody at an agency watching out to look at what happens at the fringes, and design with you how to develop your future options. If you can think of an idea, somebody usually has already thought about it somewhere. William Gibson, an American-Canadian writer who also coined the word *cyberspace* around 1982, said it best: *The future is already here, but not evenly distributed*. Here are the basic elements of that third part of the toolbox. Alcohol should have watched out earlier for the *craft* phenomenon a decade ago. The signs were there, but ignored for the longest time. But at least it was alcohol too, and it was easier to rectify. Now many industries should better understand cannabis. The signals are louder and louder, and still many ignore to listen. In another area, IKEA should watch out for Detroit-based upstart Floyd[14].

We are increasingly ready for lift-off. Getting closer to defying gravity. The rocket engine is roaring and ready to create net forward thrust. To win, galactic marketing teams will need to be more insightful than anybody else. Having the best rocket motor is a great step forward, yet superior rocket fuel will will boost its performance.

Three power toolbox reflections for the CEO/CFO/CMO:

1. What does our company's marketing (and finance) toolbox look like?
2. How do we know both are the most updated toolboxes possible?
3. How are both functions learning from each other?

Personal Notes

An artist is like a pig snouting truffles.

Igor Stravinsky

Chapter 17
Fundamental 5 (how) – Insights

Insights are indispensable rocket fuel. The number-one tool in the galactic business marketer toolbox. No actionable insights, no real value proposition, no moves in brand health, and no sustainable pricing power. This is the one key area where marketers can still show their real human added value, both on a high conceptual level (strategic insights), as well as on a very detailed level (tactical insights).

Picture a pizza delivery guy at your door with your favorite pizza—right before you actually thought to order. How could they have known? This is the favorite cartoon used by Dr. Lisa Fortini-Campbell, Professor at Northwestern University's Medill School of Integrated Advertising/Marketing Communications. She uses it to illustrate the power of empathy. The key skill one needs to unearth insights.

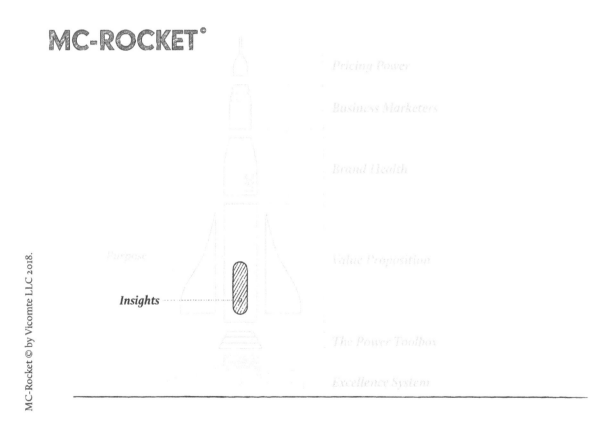

I discovered Lisa's little book *Hitting the Sweet Spot: how consumer insights can inspire better marketing and advertising* (1992) in my starting years as a marketer. There are few better and simpler fundamental works on the subject. When we started training AB InBev senior (marketing) leaders at Kellogg business school 18 years later, it was a pleasure to experience her thinking live. Her class was always one of the hits, and proved at least one key insight by itself: pizza examples work naturally best to impact the mind of hungry beer executives. Pizza and beer, a match made in heaven.

The friction in the pizza-buying funnel is systematically being addressed: from *1-click* ordering on the mobile app perfected by Amazon, to *zero-click* by Domino's pizza. Domino's worked with one of their core constituencies, hungry lazy teenagers playing video games in their smelly caves, and developed the next level of ordering. After setting up once, teens just *open* the zero-click app and their preset-choice pizza will fly in soon after automatically. Boom. And it may take a few more years, but Lisa's cartoon on predicting pizza needs will soon belong to marketing history classes. Under the AI impulse, the days of predicting your needs is already partly here. E-commerce companies like Chewy.com (now PetSmart) predict your pet food needs and test to send replenishment even before you officially press a button to refill. If you don't want it, you can send it back or just keep it.

The truth about truffles

Why do people pay so much for real truffles? Because they are adding a very unique aroma and taste to food, and are rare to find? Or because of the stories we developed around them?

Truffles are pretty much a Veblen (scarce) good. Over years of story building, they confer status on the person consuming them. The white ones even more than the black ones. The best truffles are (allegedly) harvested in traditional French *a la mouche* style (with a stick and flies), and are even more sought after than the classic ones dug up by specially trained dogs and pigs[1]. They fetch an even higher premium. Because you want to believe that story.

Finding powerful insights is akin to finding rare truffles.

One of Lisa's key points: insights start with empathy, the ability to understand and share the feelings of another. A deep curiosity and appreciation for why people do what they, and/or why they think what they think. More than ever, galactic marketers will need to be masterful observers of the human species, much like National Geographic naturalists or Pulitzer Prize winning journalists. The *aha* moment where you truly understand, is like that *Eureka* miracle moment of Archimedes we referred to in Part 2. It is the result of one of the seven key traits espoused by Leonardo Da Vinci. Everything for him started with *curiosita*, Italian for curiosity[2].

Insights, not Observations

A galactic marketer needs to reset his or her brain to a level of what is referred to as *Intelligent Ignorance*, to attack a new problem with new eyes, to eliminate the biases we referred to in the previous chapter. Algorithms will become smarter and help predict the next sale better. But how long will it take before it can unearth true insights as well as a human can?

Empathy is just the start. The process needs to lead to decision making in business. What is a definition of an actionable true insight? Let me tell you first **what it is not**. It is not a broad general statement like *Gen Z loves Electronic Dance Music*. That is not an insight. It is a very broad observation, a general statement at best. Here is the best definition I could find over time. It builds on my marketing training at P&G in the early Nineties, and combines it with the notion of brand health. For nearly three decades, each time I am in a meeting with even the most senior marketers, I check to see if there is anything better. Like with Lisa's little book, I have not found a much better definition so far.

What is *true* insight?

True insight: An accepted belief, habit or practice related to your brand or category, that, if understood, can intelligently be acted upon... to impact brand health (behavior and/or perception).

It is critical again to make the distinction between an *insight* and an *observation*, which is merely a statement of what we can see. An insight is drilling deep into the underlying *why* of what we can observe. The hidden iceberg. Drill deep and peel back layers to find the deepest causes, the most deeply held beliefs your consumers have. They may be conscious or unconscious. Observations help to make educated, logical, linear, and (likely) obvious decisions that won't drive competitive advantage. Insights will help you to make an intuitive leap and to generate ideas that will impact the business.

The best marketers will spend real time, money and energy on finding the most actionable insights relevant for a galactic age. You or your teams may not be the best at this. DIY is not necessarily the way to go, as you may be subject to bias. An insight is not a validation of your own assumptions, a trap most senior managers can easily fall into. The technique to get there is to keep asking why, again and again, until you feel you have uncovered the root cause. It therefore often makes sense to hire *neutral* specialized firms to help you unearth them, and to help you act on them. Kristof de Wulf, CEO of **InSites Consulting**, framed it simply as follows: *Insights without activation are useless.*

A quick example in the classic industry of detergents. As a young brand manager at P&G in the early Nineties, I lived the start of the historic shift from powder to liquid detergents. Back in these days, most people in the world did still use soap or powder for their classic washing needs. Today there is a mix of solutions (powder, liquid, pods, new from of dry or no cleaning).

The brand I needed to build further was called **Vizir** in Europe (and Liquid Tide in the US). I simplify a little for the sake of the example, but to convince people to try this new form factor (the first step on the behavior ladder), we needed to better understand what mothers, who mostly performed this task, believed about washing with powder related to temperature and textiles. Here is what they *believed* at that time:

Temperature

- The higher, the better a detergent can do its job
- The higher, the more risk of damage or color fading impact
- Hot water costs more money
- Typical temperature I trust most: 90 degrees Celsius

Textile

- Special clothing like silk or special woolens is most delicate to wash
- White is toughest to clean
- Cotton *sucks* dirt deep into its natural fibers and is toughest to clean

These insights served us to develop and test a first compelling value proposition to convince young moms first, expressed later on in a beautiful piece of classic TV 30" advertising (yes those were the days still).

If we can prove to you that this new Vizir Liquid detergent,
which costs X for Y size,
can actually take out all stains out of a classic white cotton T-shirt,
while washing at only 30 degrees Celsius,
would you consider trying us?

P&G and other competitors started a new chapter in the detergent landscape with that value proposition. Liquid detergents have conquered many parts of the world since, evolving to the pre-dosed pods and other form factors. Unfortunately for P&G, some teenagers seem to mistake its latest Tide pods for Domino's pizza, eating them to create some stupid *high* effects. Apart from the social drama behind that incomprehensible misuse of a detergent product, it shows you again that all marketing is done in a broader societal context, and you never know what consumers will end up doing with your brand.

Remember the effect of putting Mentos in Diet Coke bottles?[3] Whatever consumers do or don't do with your product adds to the brand health in the minds of individuals and of the collectivity. It will give rise to new strategic and tactical insights. Good strategic insights are enduring: they go to deeper reasons why. Then they will be amplified with many tactical insights, supporting topical advertising claims or social media connections. Whatever level, they are indispensable, and rare. Worth hunting for. In other words, to get back to our space theme, insights are the indispensable rocket fuel of your MC-Rocket.

Rocket Fuel

The earliest stories on rocket fuel as a combination of steam and gas used for a rocket-like device (a wooden bird) go back to early myths B.C. in Greece[4]. More verifiable evidence started to pop up during the Chinese and Mongol fights in the 13th century, where gunpowder in bamboo tubes started to create reactions and power. The epicenter of fine-tuning forward thrust to increase range of rockets move to Europe, where by the 16th century the step rocket was invented in Germany: a multi-stage contraption to send fireworks to ever higher altitudes. To escape gravity, a big first step fuels the first phase of flight until it is all consumed and detaches itself from the rocket, after which a second and a third ignites. This has been the base principle for rockets all the way to today.

The idea of liquid propellants for space exploration rockets to achieve greater range was proposed by the Russian Konstantin Tsiolkovsky in 1903, later named the *father of modern astronautics* for his great vision[5]. Innovation, spurred not in the least by the various world wars in the 20th century, continued to drive how to generate more forward thrust efficiently. After much experimentation, the American Robert Goddard successfully tested using liquid oxygen and gasoline mixes in 1926. He developed ever bigger rockets, flight control systems, the payload idea for science, parachute recovery systems and more. He, in turn, became *the father of modern rocketry*[6].

In Germany, in the meantime, on the other side of the alliance, Werner von Braun and top scientists like Hermann Oberth developed the V-2, a new type of rocket burning very fast through a mixture of liquid oxygen and alcohol to achieve a long range. After World War II, most top German scientists were lured to the two superpowers at that time, the US and the USSR (at that time), and cross-fertilized their thinking with what was there already[7]. This interaction started not only the next chapter in long-range war missiles development, leading to sophisticated rocket shield systems and nuclear warhead developments, but also threw the space race wide open. Sputnik won the first step by 1957. After some similar trials, the US formally set up NASA in October 1958, with the goal of peaceful exploration of space for the benefit of all mankind.

Rivalry between billionaires and a more open competitive playing for government contracts is credited to be the true rocket fuel of the latest progress in space. Like with anything else, rocket fuel is also again entering a new era in the 21st century. Moore's law is finally at play again, both for good and potentially less good intentions. The North Korean regime is allegedly testing very different systems in its drive to create missiles that can reach the US, and turn it into yet another formidable nuclear power to be reckoned with. Former NASA astronaut Franklin Chang-Diaz and his team have been developing a new *electric* propulsion rocket engine[8]. It leverages electric power and magnetic fields to channel superheated plasma out the back, generating a steady, efficient thrust that uses low amounts of propellant, builds up speed over time, and potentially cuts travel times for long-range missions (like to Mars) by a factor of six.

Great insights power great value propositions and other strategic and tactical decisions. Insights are the indispensable rocket fuel of your MC-Rocket. Indeed Insights are the number one tool in the toolbox. Galactic marketers need to be excellent at it. The search for excellence is in fact the hardest fundamental of all. (Lucky) Nr 8?

Three insights reflections for the CEO/CFO/CMO:

1. What current key insights actually underpin the Value Propositions of our key brands?
2. How do we action/leverage these insights into our marketing plans?
3. How do we ensure our insights stay fresh and relevant for new generations and across cultures?

Personal Notes

We are what
we repeatedly
do. Excellence,
then, is not an
act but a habit.

Aristotle

Chapter 18
Fundamental 8 (how) – Excellence

This is the final fundamental. The part of the MC-Rocket that connects all the other seven components over time to create exponential forward thrust. For big companies it could be the hardest one of all, as it requires a long-term commitment from a board and executive leadership. But it is also the one that makes the difference over time between a company with average brands versus one with galactic ones. It helps galactic marketing teams to achieve speed faster than the speed of light: *warp speed.*

You're simply the best… better then all the rest (1991). Tina Turner's song is what excellence is all about. We look for the best in everything at all times, from cars to wines, from schools to athletes to our financial advisors. There are rankings on absolutely everything and anything on this planet.

But is there a secret recipe to become the best marketer you can be? Is there really *method in the madness* behind a marketing capability model like the MC-Rocket? Or is becoming the best mostly dumb luck?

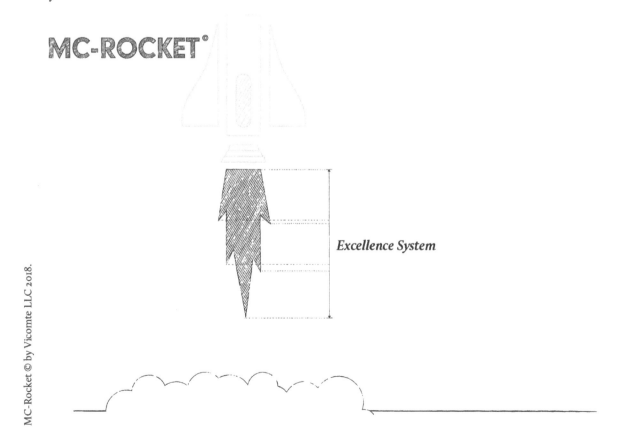

Excellence System

Freek Vermeulen is a professor at London Business School (LBS). In his own Dutch way, frank, open and entertaining, yet leveraging empirical research, he will try to convince you why he is skeptical of so-called high fliers, and of rockstar CEO cults. In *Business Exposed* (2010), he demonstrated how many proverbial emperors in business are just plain lucky, and in actual fact wear no clothes.

On the other side of the Atlantic, in the US, famed management writer Jim Collins (from *Good to Great*, 2001) often gets the question in his sessions: how much of achieving greatness is luck versus talent? Or luck versus planning? His answer was consistent with the subtitle of his later *Great by Choice: uncertainty, chaos and luck – why some thrive despite them all* (2011). Collins essentially contends that luck favors the prepared.

His point: the more you are systematically prepared, actively looking for accelerators, the better you will recognize sudden opportunities, and the more you will get additional leverage on lucky breaks. In his talks he made it very clear he did not think you can or should plan for luck, but you can *actively choose* a mindset and organization forms and systems and processes that are conducive to capitalize on luck—if and when lightning strikes.

I deeply respect both well-researched perspectives described above. I am not an LBS professor, nor a bestselling author and management guru. I am a consumer scientist, with a passion for space. But I also was, and I still am, for 30 years, a *practitioner* of marketing. I lived, and still love to live in the marketing trenches. So I will build on the perspective of the *expert observers* above, and add the viewpoint of the *participating observer*.

Perfection versus Excellence

In my professional life as a CMO, I always tried (and still try) to keep the company board and leadership focus on the eight marketing fundamentals. The CMO role needs to be focused on how to create and then to elevate marketing capability, making it the best it can be at all times. I ran the global and European marketing machines of 2 major FMCG companies for many years. And given the results I can assume there was something in it that was working. In close partnership with other functions, we never got any machine to perfection, but perfection was also never the goal. Excellence was the goal.

Excellence is an iterative process. You build, measure, learn and repeat. You get better every year, achieving milestones on a never-ending journey. Over years one learns which components of that approach are most useful for what size of company at what phase of development. Excellence systems can grow and adapt with you, from startup to scale-up to mature company.

Permanent Beta

Excellence models have everything to do with a desire to fly to infinity, and beyond. Or for finance people, to alpha and beyond. Striving for mastery is the purpose. To achieve the highest rung on the ladder, and then keep reinventing the subject again from the ground up. Achieve Six Sigma black belt status, or 7th dan levels in fighting sports. In sports, it is about raising the bar and seeking the next level of performance. It is reflective of a mindset of eternal discontent and reinvent or die.

In quality management practices, this is captured in the ideas around Total Quality Management, ISO certification mechanisms, or Kaizen. My very first experience in the US back in 1989 was actually to work in this field. I published an article about it in the Journal of European Business at that time[1]. The idea was to prepare US companies to break in what they perceived as *Fortress Europe*, the emerging European Single Market of 1992. For any US company, being able to demonstrate ISO standard quality would secure access to that new single market. Frankly, at first I perceived this field of quality consulting as rather boring. Only later did I realize how useful this thought-ware would be. It taught me all the basics of internal and external consumer-centric transversal process design, and to think in iteration loops.

In biological terms, excellence systems are all about regenerating the skin on a continuous basis. As I learned during my Seabird chapter, planes are like snakes. A plane is constantly being re-skinned. Every single component of a plane (or a rocket) is logged and has a lifetime. Each one is carefully changed at the right time, keeping the vehicle as current as can be.

Personal careers are like software too, argues Linked in founder Reid Hoffman, urging us all to be in a state of permanent reinvention, of *permanent beta*[2]. The same goes for anybody striving for excellence. Including the best marketers.

These systems should always be architected to be *means* to the *end*, not the end. It is critical to ensure everybody owns their part of it, plays their role in it, complies with it, and contributes to making it better, without taking the eyes of the purpose of the company.

At a beer company like AB InBev, one is not in the business of driving excellence. The purpose *Beer: The Original Social Network*, served to inspire us to brew and sell the best beers our consumers wanted, to create sustainable top-line growth. That remained the focus. Excellence systems were there to increase the probability of success, to eliminate repetition of previously well documented failures, to drive best practice, to share one language, etc. In short, to drive effectiveness and efficiency[3].

We therefore treated the well-documented components and processes embodied by the *AB InBev Way of Marketing* as software releases, with a 1.0 start version, all the way to N.0 with N=infinity. The idea was for the organization to always be learning during a cycle, usually a calendar year, to collect and discuss all learnings once per year, and then prepare the next aligned upgrade. All changes were packed in the new release which was then again *frozen* for some time, typically one calendar year, so people could get to work for a year with a level of certainty.

Unlike classic software though, an excellence system needs to balance continuous self-learning and an auto-renew mindset with a stable operating routine, KPIs, etc. The whole machine needs to be able to digest every major change each time. If you change too much or too fast, if the excellence process starts overpowering its intent, adoption and effectiveness suffer. You can repeat every year. Routine matters here: 1% inspiration and 99% perspiration. It helps to tune the athletic performance to ever higher levels, until your proven successful training approach hits a wall and even this good old *playbook* may need to be rewritten entirely.

Within AB InBev we started to capture and to celebrate excellence internally, contrasting and comparing results between countries and Zones to detect who was the best at improving each year. With typical AB InBev rigor and discipline, we 1) set challenging and measurable targets for capability, 2) duly tracked and monitored progress during the year, and finally 3) audited results prior to celebrating winners onstage during the yearly company jamborees the next calendar year.

Winners felt not only proud, but they felt it in their wallets and career progression too. Progress in *means* tended to also correlate with progress in the *end*, in business success. Progress on excellence was equally linked to their personal targets, and therefore to the company's bonus system. And rest assured that operating heads were always watching who were the movers and shakers that represented the spirit of excellence. A great nudge to drive desired behavior.

The hardest fundamental

The Excellence part of the MC-Rocket connects all the other 7 components *over time* to create *exponential forward thrust*. It is the most complex part of the model. Typically only the most committed companies are able to implement and sustain it to unlock its exponential benefit. This is where the difference is made between an average marketing company and a world-class, or now, galactic one. That is also why it forms the basis for the new *Alpha M* investment model I will introduce in stage 4. A proposal for a first-ever rating tool in the world that will help predict marketing excellence, a kind of *Moody's for Marketers*.

When you strive for excellence, you partly de-risk your old processes with new learning. Yet at the same time you increase the risk again, by raising the bar. Do it wrong, taking shortcuts, and your rocket might spectacularly crash. Do it right, without shortcuts, and eternal glory is yours, as you will discover alpha first.

Three excellent reflections for the CEO/CFO/CMO:

1. Do we have an excellence model in marketing and finance?
2. How do we celebrate and incentivize excellence across the company?
3. How do we create a company culture and mindset promoting continuous reinvention, raising the bar each year?

Personal Notes

I have nothing to offer but blood, toil, tears and sweat.

Winston Churchill, May 13, 1940

Chapter 19

No shortcuts to marketing miracle$

This is the official disclaimer part of the book. A modern marketing capability model built for Space 2.0 will definitely increase the probability to achieve marketing miracle$, but never guarantee it. If I learned anything at three top Consumer Packaged Goods companies (P&G, Coca-Cola and AB InBev) and in my entrepreneurship life after that, there are no shortcuts to building Galactic Brands. Ever.

Marketing miracle$ are never a given. Marketing is not rocket science, but it *does* require a *deliberate* and *continuous* effort if you want a clear ROI. Start up or scale up founders ask me regularly on how I can *quickly help build a brand*. At some point in time of their early growth they start to realize that branding matters to pricing power, and therefore to valuations.

Sorry, but there is no such thing. If you wanted the simplest possible brand building action list as a starting entrepreneur, here is what could get you going:

1. Hire a qualified brand responsible (or do it yourself as a start)

2. Define your brand position and value proposition

3. Define/register/protect your brand/trademark name (off/online)

4. Define your Visual Brand Identity (multisensory)

5. Create a long-term and short-term brand draft plan

6. Secure investment to fund these plans

7. Start implementing and learning – adjust as needed

8. Create the renovation / innovation pipeline

9. Start monitor brand health in some way – and resulting net pricing

10. Adjust/repeat/for next few years

That is just a quick hit list. It will still not get you overnight miracle$. It just won't. Branding is hard work over time. There are simply no shortcuts to creating a truly Galactic Brand business. Ever. Even if tech B2B or B2C brands *can* be built faster than nontech, especially if you have a direct-to-consumer platform (think Amazon or eBay or Google). Some of you may get lucky as well: sprinkle some pixie dust over a tech solution, dazzle investors, sell... and run. Buyer beware. Barring a few exceptions, only by really committing to the eight principles of marketing capability, as expressed in the MC-Rocket® below, can companies significantly increase the probability of creating so-called *marketing miracle$*.

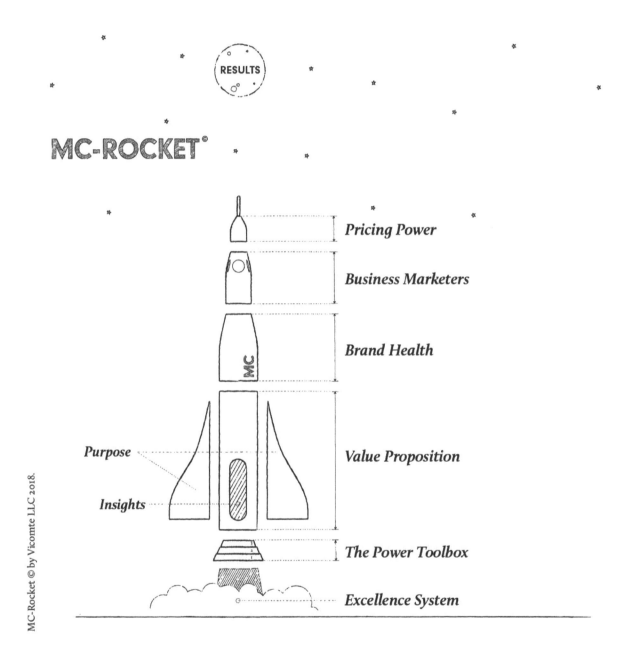

In November 2007, I became Chief Marketing Officer (CMO) of what is now Anheuser-Busch InBev, the world's largest brewer, and the most profitable CPG (Consumer Packaged Goods) or FMCG (Fast Moving Consumer Goods). The challenge given by CEO Carlos Brito and the board: to help what was then still called *InBev* evolve from a *sales-driven company* to a *consumer-centric*, *sales-driven company*. Since its creation in 2004, InBev started to be known, respected, and feared, for its core functional competence in areas like finance, brewing/operations and sales. As the owner of 250+ brands globally at that time, the byproduct of decades of M&A activity and integration of local brewers into an ever bigger holding, the company felt it needed to become equally excellent in marketing, as well as in stakeholder management fields like corporate branding and corporate affairs.

As a Belgian, naturally passionate about great beer and great beer brands, and as a marketer, infused by 17 years of brand portfolio management at global marketing schools like Procter & Gamble and The Coca-Cola Company, joining InBev as CMO felt like a miracle for my career, albeit scary at the same time. It is one thing to work *for* the CMO at the Coca-Cola Company, even when I was already leading marketing of the most profitable operating unit (Europe). *Becoming* part of a company's senior leadership *as* the CMO was a whole other ballgame altogether. In those years, the average CMO lasted at around two years. Only for kamikaze pilots. I felt the butterflies in my stomach. I told my close friends this had to be what it felt like to be asked to come play for one of these teams that were suddenly serious on winning the soccer Champions League. They looked at me in bewilderment, and actually did not empathize at all. Few people around the world had ever heard of InBev to begin with. Many of my good Coke colleagues thought I was about to make my worst-ever career decision. Condolences, and few congrats. Not what I wanted to hear, really.

In the meantime, on the InBev side, expectations were high, as they always are for somebody new joining the leadership team. My future colleagues did respect the classic schools of FMCG marketing. They were surprisingly critical of their own shortcomings in the marketing area, and ready to close any gaps fast versus whatever could be *best-in-class*. Fast also really meant fast, like private equity style fast, not Coca-Cola or P&G speed. More like warp speed for FMCG. Still, I sensed there were many doubts about this new guy coming from outside, a natural and probably healthy skepticism for a company that prides itself only on promotion from within (as P&G did too). They had mixed experiences with CPG hires from outside before.

I was super excited to help this new underdog company unleash its full potential in the marketing area. The holy fire was burning inside. To help manage expectations, with no Harry Potter magic wand in my toolbox, and with all respect for anybody of the Christian faith, I started to remind everybody in every meeting in those first months: *My name is Chris, I do marketing. My name is not Christ, I don't do miracle$ (though I deeply believe marketing is a way to create more of them).*

Our shared dream energizes everyone
to work in the same direction to be the:
Best Beer Company
Bringing People Together
For a Better World

Our greatest
strength is our
people. Great People
grow at the pace of
their talent and are
rewarded accordingly.

We recruit, develop
and retain people
who can be better
than ourselves.
We will be judged
by the quality of
our teams.

We are never
completely satisfied
with our results, which
are the fuel of our
company. Focus and
zero-complacency
guarantee lasting
competitive advantage.

The consumer is the Boss.
We serve our consumers by
offering brand experiences
that play a meaningful role
in their lives, and always in
a responsible way.

We area company
of owners.
Owners take
results personally.

We believe common
sense and simplicity
are usually better
guidelines than
unnecessary
sophistication
and complexity.

We manage our
costs tightly, to free
up resources that will
support sustainable and
profitable top line growth.

Leadership by
personal example is
at the core of our culture.
We do what we say.

We never take
shortcuts. Integrity,
hard work, quality,
and responsibility
are key to building
our company.

Dream People Culture

I had to adjust to a new culture. Not unlike P&G (where people were called *Proctoids*), or Coke (*Coke heads*), InBev had its own idiosyncratic, cult-like Manifesto on how it did business, summarized as *Dream/People/Culture (DPC): 10 Principles for High Performance* (see below: the 2018 version. DPC was the summary of guiding principles defining InBev company culture, inspired mostly by the Brazilian owners, the private equity group called 3G Capital[1]. I loved it. I still do.

As part of the leadership, one needs not only to embrace, but to role model DPC. We believed it was the true magic behind a high-performance culture. Every word truly matters in these statements, and it was our role as senior leadership to ensure it was as strongly articulated as it could be. For example, around 2009 – 2010 we evolved the Dream statement from *Best Beer Company in the World*, to *Best Beer Company in a BETTER World*. Only one word changed, but it ushered in a world of difference for the company. For the first time, InBev, and later AB InBev, deeply acknowledged it was becoming a global leader with global responsibility and multiple stakeholders. It took that one word very, very serious. In the last years the Dream got rephrased even further, resulting as well in the 2025 sustainability goals, an exponent of thinking with a mindset of doing the right thing for the next 100 years. As corporate brands go, AB InBev is actually still a very young (giant) startup. It has a lot to learn, and a lot to discover still. It has incredible built-in sources of strategic advantage that still need to play out on a global scale, while it becomes truly galactic in its thinking.

Back to the Future

I will come back to what happened at AB InBev a bit further in this chapter. Let's return to the end of the Eighties. After I started working a few years in sales and finance for a tech and a consultancy scale up, P&G became my *marketing boot camp* in the early part of the Nineties. Procter & Gamble was, along with Unilever and a few others, considered one of the best marketing schools worldwide, just like GE was a great school for general management. P&G seriously invested to teach its aspiring Brand Managers all the marketing basics, along with bunch of other useful professional life skills. I can still write *one page memo's* in my sleep if needed. I still see value in *side by side* performance visualization or in *from/to* frameworks. It was a phenomenal training school indeed, focused on fundamentals, and with application in real business. You would have to ask Gen Z and younger graduates if they still see P&G as a preferred marketing school these days. I for one am grateful for my base training there.

Moving on, from 1995 to 2007, The Coca-Cola Company (TCCC) really gave me the chance to hone and refine my marketing skills in every direction. More entrepreneurial than P&G at that time among big corporates, Coke had convinced me to come pioneer with them across both the most developed and most emerging countries of Europe and Eurasia, and across new and established brands and beverage categories. My marketing expertise increased quickly: from leading a category, to running full local portfolios, to managing the entire core soft drink portfolio across the full European Union Group (55 markets) after being 10 years in the company. From being a successful *painter*, I became the *manager of ever bigger painting ateliers*, ensuring many brilliant other team members could paint on the right canvas with the right tools at the right time, with impact.

Besides the *art* of marketing, in which Coke excelled, I gradually discovered the need to better integrate the fast evolving *science* behind marketing. Digital was in its infancy, but exponentially impacting the field. Data availability started to explode as more and more frequent and actionable data became available, the need for more discipline became apparent. Across the Europe Group we had now *captured lightning in a bottle* a few times. The launch and fast expansion of Coke Zero in 2006/2007 was an example of a big strategic move with lasting impact. So was the bold partnership between Coke and iTunes. Many older Coke managers (including me) consumed music in the ways we had grown up with, but by connecting Coke with the fast-growing new digital music wave at scale, we again regained relevancy with the new millennial drinker cohorts coming through. Coke's full trademark portfolio was going through a full renaissance in Europe, defying the business press rather gratuitous assessment in 2005 that *Coke Europe was in mortal decline*. I am not saying soft drinks did/do not have to deal with consumer shift pressures, but the words were a slight exaggeration. Today Coke is still the heart & soul of an ever-evolving portfolio. As slow as it may be perceived, The Coca-Cola Company is still proudly standing. Can it go faster? Surely it can. Many CPGs actually would, if they started too *think and act galactic* more.

Back in 2005, in Coke's senior (marketing) management circles, we started to wonder: how does one create such marketing miracles in a *scalable* and *repeatable* way? Can one capture the proverbial lightning in a bottle more frequently? Under the leadership of fellow top marketers in Atlanta (Marc Mathieu, Penny McIntyre, Esther Lee and Rebecca Messina[2]), and working with fantastic colleagues around the globe, we developed *DNA: the Coke Way of Marketing*. DNA was an attempt at coding and anchoring the universal power and long-lasting business impact of true marketing capability. Architecting and building the ecosystem that would allow our world-class TCCC brands to keep increasing willingness to pay in people's heads in a systematic way.

TCCC has been truly a wonderful place to work for. There is no better way to see a company's true set of values than when calamity or adversity hits. I had experienced it many times already, but nowhere near as viscerally as in the weeks and months following the summer 1999 earthquakes in Istanbul, Turkey, where I was marketing director at that time. An estimated 35,000 people died that night. Lucky to be alive, we immediately rallied and ensured the Coke trucks serviced all affected areas with water and material, even faster than the Red Crescent / Red Cross. An event like that makes you not only live and appreciate life to the fullest forever after, it also brings out the best of real top managers. I am deeply grateful for what I learned during those intense years from the Turkish senior people: Cem Kozlu, Ahmet Bozer and Muhtar Kent (who later would become TCCC CEO and Chairman).

Coke's new DNA Way of Marketing was a brilliant piece of work. There was only one issue with it: the company did not really enforce it. It was too optional. The complex Coke franchise system stifled speed of decision making and agility. Country operators (on company and/or on bottler side) continued to do whatever they wanted without consequences, disregarding solid learning and best practice. Even as I deeply loved Coke, I started to wonder how the board at that time (2007) would inspire and allow a true change of culture in an even faster global, digital, frugal world, where consumers and stakeholders started to call the shots like never before. Right at that time of existential questioning, I got the call to join this little known new beer company called InBev. I never thought I would leave Coke, but this call would change my life forever.

The long game

I had the pleasure and honor to be ABI's CMO for five years (07 – 12). I figured I know had a unique chance to eat my own dog food, and implement a marketing capability system I would be proud of. Together with a passionate small marketing leadership team, in close tandem with Frank Abenante (who ran the critical Global Brands group, and is one of the best classic marketers I met in my career), we put in place our own clear and measurable *InBev Way of Marketing*. In InBev style, that was accomplished much faster and much more decisively than at Coke, by a factor of at least 10. It took only 3 months to finalize a workable blueprint, completely integrated in the company's DPC performance culture (targets, incentives, reviews), and internally and externally benchmarked.

We had learned from Coke, but also benchmarked versus Unilever's Way of Brand Building and Diageo's Way (DWEEB). We learned from tech companies like Cisco and Oracle. One year later, we evolved it to become the *AB InBev Way of Marketing (ABI WOM)*, following the bold and risky 52 billion USD combination/integration between InBev and Anheuser-Busch in the midst of the financial crisis in 08. That combination is a fascinating different story altogether, and not mine to tell. Some books paint an interesting perspective, but none really has the full story yet from the AB InBev side[3]. One day, the world should hear about it, and students should learn from it.

As per the original brief from the CEO and the Board, the ABI-WOM became an excellence program nicknamed internally *the fourth muscle*, next to the other three muscles that helped InBev be a high performance athlete (Sales, Finance and Operations). It is a living muscle that essentially creates *one* language across all operating units and brands, creates *one* superior methodology and leverages *one* core set of tools. It inspires people to raise the bar each year in a disciplined way, promotes comparability and mobility, and especially helps marketers and their colleagues repeating avoidable mistakes.

Did the AB InBev Way of Marketing create miracle$? I am not sure I would go as far. But the new fourth muscle *did* made an impact. It anchored the idea that Marketing *is* Finance *is* Business. The new mix of art, science and discipline in marketing resulted in systematic progress on the critical Focus Brands portfolio, the select group of about 25 global/regional/local brands in its then about 250+ portfolio that we decided to consistently prioritize scarce resources on. You are welcome to check the investor relations reports of all those years (07-12) as proof on ab-inbev.com, and of the first years after. Strategic decisions on brands sometimes take years to show long-term impact: e.g. when the board agreed to renew a global asset like the World Cup for eight more years (two major events for Budweiser and all local football activating brands). As a CMO, you need to be aware you likely influence the company well beyond your tenure[4]. Building galactic brands is a long game.

There are no shortcuts to creating marketing miracle$. As a CEO/CFO/CMO you can *never* stop focusing the company on the 8 fundamentals. You can never stop investing in true marketing capability. Your shareholders and stakeholders (should) expect you to never relent. In stage 4 of this book we will swap perspective to this investor side of the equation. As marketing-driven companies start thinking and acting galactic, how will investors pick the winners of the new Space Age?

Stage 4
ESCAPE VELOCITY: SUCCESSFUL INVESTING IN THE GALACTIC AGE

α^M

The greatest
obstacle to
discovery is
not ignorance;
It is the
illusion of
knowledge

Daniel J. Boorstin

Chapter 20
Beyond financial ratings

Since the 19th century, financial service companies have been providing investors with insight on how to assess and to mitigate financial risk. Who are these investors, and why do they value that information so much? There is something crucially important missing in the old toolbox though. How, and why, would one assess marketing risk? Is there *a one number* rating model to better assess marketing risk?

To invest money, you either need to have it, or be able to borrow some. This book will not discuss whether wealth is fairly distributed over society. For deeper discussions on possible wealth inequality, peruse Thomas Piketty's *Capital in the 21ˢᵗ Century* (2014). Also, if you are in the money business, jump directly to the next chapter. I just want to give readers new to the world of investment a basic sense of how much investable money is out there, and who decides to invest it.

There are many reports tracking how the pool of investable assets from the wealthy grows over time. Every major global investment bank (UBS, Credit Suisse, Goldman Sachs…) has their regular tracking. Other sources are the surveys done by global or regional business magazines (like Forbes, the Huron Report…). But to keep things simple, there are basically two kinds of investors: private investors and institutional investors.

- **Private investors:** According to the 2018 edition of the Wealth-X Billionaire Census, there were a record 2,754 billionaires on the planet in 2017, representing US$ 9,205 Bn. The Cap Gemini World Wealth Report shows there are now 18.1 million so-called dollar millionaires in the world[1]. The report estimates people's investable assets of at least 1 million USD excluding the value of their first private real estate. In 2010, there were 10.9 million such high-net-worth investor. Both reports show most wealth is now to be found in Asia as a broader geography. Outside Asia, wealth remains concentrated in the US and in Germany. Cap Gemini predicts that assets held by high-net-worth investors may exceed $100 trillion by 2025, compared to $42.7 trillion in 2010.

How the average wealth is invested can swing wildly from year to year, depending on how collectively financial markets react to what happens in the world. We have seen 2018 shape up in a very different way than 2017. But as a datapoint in the recent past, here are the average allocation in Q2 2017:

- Stocks (31.1%)

- Cash and cash equivalent (27.3%)

- Real estate (14%)

- Fixed income (18%)

- Alternative investments (9.7)

- **Institutional investors:** There is much more money going around than the money from the rich and super rich individuals alone. And most of their money gets pooled and then invested via professionals, who earn a fee for their work. Welcome to the world of the so-called *institutional investors*: banks, mutual funds, hedge funds, pension funds, family funds, insurance companies, sovereign wealth management funds, venture capitalists, private equity, etc. They collectively invest in the capital markets on behalf of most of us.

Anybody with savings in the bank contributes indirectly to big pools of money the banks will carefully work with, i.e. partially invest in capital markets. Every premium paid to an insurance company gets pooled in investment. Every dollar you give to charity will be accumulated in endowments that will invest part of it. Any contribution to a pension plan aggregates to huge sums managed by professional organizations investing it. Last but not least, the government can also be a big player in the financial market. Besides directly managing nationalized companies (like in many oil- or gas-rich countries), it pools tax money in so-called *sovereign wealth funds*. They tend to become huge players in the global investment markets (like the funds from Norway, Qatar, Singapore, etc.).

Rating financial risk

When a lender provides a loan, it will always assess the ability of its customer to pay back the loan as part of its due diligence. In the US (and in many countries), as a consumer, you don't exist if you don't have an acceptable credit score. On the basis of complex algorithm testing essentially five components, your FICO score will measure your creditworthiness (risk of default) on a scale from very bad to excellent (see table below). FICO scores are an invention of and named after *Fair, Isaac and Company* created in 1958. The company rebranded itself as FICO in 2009, and became a household name.

FICO Score
Assessing individual creditworthiness (USA)

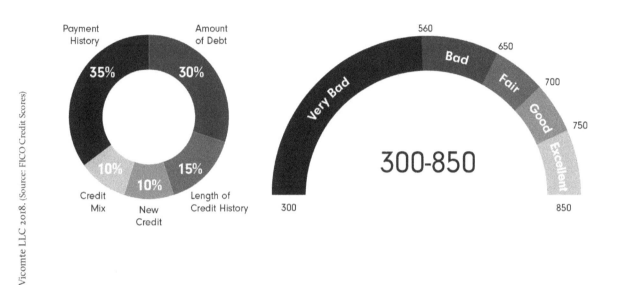

Vicomte LLC 2018. (Source: FICO Credit Scores)

The same principle applies to investors. As we saw in flight training, every investor is looking for that elusive finance miracle called *positive alpha*. Prior to finally pressing the investment button, costly due diligence may be performed to assess risk, especially negative risk. Whenever an investor can afford it, full teams may even be deployed to assess the company's relative health. Investors and the analysts who serve them have a well developed toolbox to assess and quantify a company's negative credit risk and default potential.

Since more than 150 years, professional service firms offer ever more sophisticated tools to measure and manage negative risk for funds, companies, industries, and nations. A relatively small group of companies holds the keys to this profitable rating kingdom, controlling well over 95% of the market: Standard & Poor's (1860), Moody's (1909), Fitch (1914), Kroll Associates (1972), Morningstar (1984), The Economist Intelligence Unit (2013) and a few more. This ecosystem contributes, or at least aims to contribute, to the transparency and integrity of the global financial markets.

Not unlike credit scores, financial rating agencies deploy their own rigorous methodology: a sort of a beauty contest, creating a relative ranking versus an ideal standard that reflects the theoretical highest level of excellence in managing financial risk, resulting in an ordinal, not in a cardinal ranking. Here are three well known examples:

- **Moody's** : from AAA to C, Default and no rating. Moody's also appends numerical modifiers 1, 2 and 3 to each generic rating classification from AAA through CAA

- **Standard & Poor's (S&P)**: from AAA to C, Default and no rating

- **Fitch**: from AAA to D, Default and no rating

The most used financial models date back to the Sixties. Here is another key concept born in that era. Back in 1968, NYU Stern professor Edward "Ed" Altman developed the *Z-score, the* proxy to assess risk for a firm or sector to go bankrupt within two years[2]. Over 50 years later it is still one of the most widely used metrics to predict financial distress. In a June 23, 2018, special lunch seminar for the TRIUM Global EMBA 1000 alumni anniversary, Altman shared a 50-year overview of his work. Here are a few key takeaways:

- Bloomberg terminals offer Z-scores, and are consulted between 5,000 to 10,000 times monthly, even as many small companies have still never even heard of Z-scores.

- Bankruptcy remains a real risk at all phases of a company's life. Even in the benign credit cycle of the last eight years, already over 14 USD 1+ billion dollar revenue companies defaulted from January to June 2018.

- Top-rated companies (AA or AAA) became the rarest of beasts, driven by the astronomical rise of commercial debt and companies leveraging up—while money remains cheap. The more debt, the more risk. The BBB type group of companies is growing the fastest at the moment.

Anything and everybody gets ranked and compared these days, from the day we are born to the legacies we leave behind. The ratings business reflects this desire to condense and summarize disparate data in a convenient way, turning data into insights. People panic when their Uber ratings drop below four[3]. Universities and think tanks like the Reputation Institute rank companies and countries[4]. Switzerland-based university IMD created its much-watched global competitiveness index[5].

On a regular basis new ratings see the light. Early 2018, a new fintech startup called Sigma Ratings launched the world's first *integrity ratings* on 500 companies[6]. It aims to assess compliance, conduct and regulatory risk by financial groups in certain geographies in terms of doing business with terrorists, drug dealers and organized criminals. Mid-2018, Goldman Sachs rolled out a new exchange-traded fund (ETF) based on billionaire investor Paul Tudor Jones' *Just Capital* rating model ranking companies on social metrics (including environment, social and governance issues)[7].

The role of the analyst has seen its own evolution and redesign over the years. What they can write, how they write it, and for whom they write it, has evolved. The regular financial crashes may have dented the image of invincibility of these *Masters of the Universe*, but financial markets forgive and forget quickly. All in all, the capital allocation system works reasonably well within its limitations, and financial ratings play a critical role in that ecosystem. For the time-starved analysts doing all the preparation, all these financial ratings help make their argument to assess the attractiveness of a certain investment.

Rating marketing risk

Let's flip perspective now. Analysts have a lot of tools at their disposal to assess financial risk. But they essentially have no simple measures in their toolbox to assess excellence in marketing and top-line growth capability. Companies seldom offer to talk about their proprietary *ways of doing marketing* in their investor talks. The power of marketing excellence is mostly hidden from investors eyes. In space language, marketing remains a black hole for analysts. Absent insight, what proxies *are* analysts using today to assess how good a company is at marketing?

Most analysts will start by checking *marketing investment as a percentage of net sales*, and benchmark that versus peer companies and one time. Often they will still conclude: the higher the budget, the better the company *must* be at marketing. Investors care about earnings growth and quality of earnings, and there will always be the fear that a company is cutting back on marketing related investment (like advertising). Investors often see such cuts in marketing as a short term way for management to boost earnings. Clearly a potential short-term catalyst for any public stock.

While this metric may have been a relevant proxy in the past, when TV ads truly ruled our minds, it is just a crude proxy in the much more complex digital world. The more one spends or could spend on TV ads, that can be skipped away so easily, should *not* anymore be a sign of marketing excellence. It is merely a proxy of money firepower and theoretical capacity to buy reach. Classic TV, and even social media video, should not anymore be automatically equated to marketing excellence, whatever classic or social networks want you to believe. Social media is as crowded and skippable as classic TV. They are in the business of selling ads, not your brand.

Analysts will then dig deeper and get numbers and data from all public places they can get their hands on: market volume and share, price/mix data, consumer sentiment, etc. They will spice up their reports with comments on the TV ads and past media investment, on past R&D investments and innovation pipelines, and on *impressions* achieved by social media campaigns. For B2B companies (Business to Business) or SAAS models (Software as a Service) they will track CAC (Cost of Acquisition of a customer) versus LTV (Lifetime value of the customer) or ARPU (Average Revenue per User).

The best-funded analysts can and will even run their own surveys[8]. For example, if the company does not provide Net Promotor Score (NPS) data, they may run their own survey to get a first feel for consumer's loyalty towards their target investment. They will also add people related facts to the emerging narrative, again looking for *catalysts for change*, whatever the direction. They will comment on the top team, the (lack of) charisma of the CXOs, and even on the perceived relationship between CEO and CMO to see how much support there is for certain strategic campaign choices. They will look at external recognition, like marketing awards in Cannes or New York. Ultimately they will try to access management for more commentary and numbers to corroborate their thesis: capex investment, new launches, cost savings, M&A announcements, new synergy predictions following an M&A, etc.

During and after my AB InBev career, I have had many conversations with companies and investors on how they could get more insight in that marketing black hole. I concluded it is a truly missed opportunity for any marketing-driven company investing in its marketing excellence models not to leverage that capability to the outside world, in particular to the investment world. Marketing due diligence is clearly the toughest nut to crack for analysts or due diligence teams. So far, no robot is displacing humans in the analyst area yet. However, under pressure from regulations and cost reductions, experiments are already on the way in various major banks to replace (part of) research report writing with artificial intelligence[9].

I introduced you before to Aswath Damodaran, another one of NYU Stern's esteemed faculty and a real valuation guru. In his latest book *Narrative & Numbers: the Value of Stories in Business* (2017), he shows companies how to tell their story based on where they are in their development phase. If a company does not convincingly tell its story their way, implying how much of *alpha* it possibly represents, it will de facto be written for them by analysts (or business journalists). Based on any data they can get their hands on, and on personal perception, they will boil their interpretation of the company story down to a *Buy, Hold or Sell* rating, accompanied by a target price for the stock.

AI is definitely coming to financial analysis, but the human factor will likely remain strong for a while. So I started to wonder: why are there no simple rating models or frameworks to assess the impact of excellence in marketing capability? Could there be *one number* that could serve to measure positive risk, potentially even becoming over time a proxy able to predict top-line growth? A simple datapoint- and checklist-based methodology that can easily be added next to Z-scores and other ratings on the over 325.000 Bloomberg terminals in the world?[10]

Like a *positive FICO score for Marketers...* or a *Moody's or S&P for Marketers*?

Rating models: buyer beware

Everybody in the financial world uses the services of the financial ratings services. In many instances, institutional investors can simply not even officially invest without the instrument having received an official rating. If ratings would have been completely useless, market forces would have long pushed them out. But the contrary is true. The service is still perceived to provide the markets with a purpose. Still, like with the other models we discussed in Stage 2, it is good to know the many (perceived) dark sides of any rating model, before I introduce you to a brand new marketing rating model. Again, buyer beware.

Too emotional

Financial ratings can have a quite direct effect on the cost of business or the cost of governance. When their country ratings are *upgraded*, *downgraded* or given a *stable outlook*, governments always take notice, as does the business community and the business press. Any results are welcomed or discarded the same way a student gets good or disappointing grades.

When a country stands to lose a coveted AAA or Aaa, every head of state or minister of finance fumes[1]. Not only would borrowing cost go up significantly, but the face loss is potentially a bigger political price to pay[2]. In public, they will scold the rating agencies for non relevant and non applicable research based on the wrong facts. Governments may even sue the rating agencies, related or unrelated. E.g. when S&P stripped the US government in 2011 of its coveted triple A rating, it was sued in February 2013 by the Justice Department (DOJ), with Treasury support, for US$ 5 Bn, on fraud charges for continued sunny ratings despite a looming mortgage crisis[3]. Curiously, every time the opposite happens, and a country is positively upgraded, that same government will be the first to tweet the news, albeit with the cautious disclaimer *Even though such ratings are only a partial reflection of our policies…* Because what can go up, can come down again soon.

Too slow

Timing is everything for the investor hunting for positive alpha. The easier, the more predictable, and the more transparent the business model, the better the possible decisions on investment, and the more money may flow to the sector. But also the more difficult to unlock alpha. Speed matters. In time of light speed data sharing, time is more than ever of the essence to spot opportunities for clients. Rating agencies reports are often considered too late, stating the obvious rebound after it has happened. Which means in investor speak: positive alpha is likely gone already.

For example, after rating agencies came under fire for their alleged overoptimistic outlook of the mortgage-backed securities (preceding the 2008 financial crisis), hedge fund managers dismissed them years later for calling the rebound of the housing market too late[4].

Too fast

Rankings information can move markets unfairly[5]. Two seconds or even a few nanoseconds can mean making or losing a lot of money if you can act first on information. Financial data providers of all kinds are often investigated, castigated and penalized for providing paying Wall Street customers market-sensitive data a few milliseconds ahead of the rest of the market. US attorney-generals want to keep the markets a level playing field, with fair play.

Too bold

Any ranking or rating model seems to ultimately succumb to the principle of *moral hazard*. This can be observed when a person, organization or a whole society, takes more risks than they rationally should because someone else bears the cost of their behavior. In other words: there are unintended consequences to irrational behavior. Especially in the insurance sector, people worry about the fact that because you are insured, you will act with less respect for the protected asset. The feeling of being protected leads you to bad behavior.

But moral hazard can be observed on a much more massive societal scale. The 2008 financial crisis was the result of excess mortgage lending leading people to overspend on houses, well beyond what they could pay back in an inevitable downturn. The subsequent derivates securitization crisis led to a banking and industrial crash on a global scale. A massive shakeout took place, where some banks disappeared completely (e.g. Bear Sterns), others were absorbed, and many industries were bailed out by the outgoing Bush government on October 3, 2008.

The US\$ 700 Bn Troubled Asset Relief Program (TARP) was designed to allow the Treasury to purchase toxic assets and equity from financial institutions and to allow the financial sector to regain its footing—so life would go back to normal ASAP. Congress approved US\$ 350 Bn for use in 2008, and newly elected President Obama subsequently was fortunate enough after one year to not to have to use the remaining \$350 Bn. TARP expired two years later on October 3, 2010.

Net: the excess risk taken by a select group of speculative US (and global) bankers was paid for by taxpayers in the US (and everywhere). Ten years later we still feel the effects of that crash in many countries

Too mediocre

Moral hazard is clearly one of the key drawbacks of any rating model, according to professors Heski Bar-Isaac and Steven Tadelis[7]. A rating model solidifies reputations, positively and negatively. They did a lot of research around what they call *Seller's Reputation*: the idea that buyers *choose* sellers based on reputation, and hence reputation is a real asset with value one can invest in. A summer 2017 Wall Street Journal review showed how a group of money managers and brokers systematically misrepresented mutual fund ratings from Chicago-based leading fund rating Morningstar, to convince their retail clients[7].

Rankings are usually a combination of hard and soft data, of quantitative and qualitative criteria, objective and subjective criteria. These get all mixed in a form of algorithm that spits out winners and losers. The ranking may or not accurately reflect the reality, but it does cement reputations often long beyond reality. Just think of stars for restaurants (Michelin, Best 50, Gault-Millau…), for colleges and universities, for alcohol of all kinds… any ranking really.

Rating education institutes and hospitals may hurt consumers in the long run[8]. Heski and Tadelis go on warning that given it is costly to verify all the characteristics of a good, consumers often make purchase decisions based only on partial information. In addition, firms have to decide whether and how much to invest in the quality of different dimensions. These decisions take into account consumers' search behaviour.

One of the real reasons is that everybody (not yet) on the ranking starts to game the system. That is where moral hazard happens. People want to break the code for success as per the ranking criteria, and hence invariably all converge over time to whatever the norm may be, involuntarily creating mediocrity in the industry or area being ranked. While focusing on the rankings, they often lose sight of what the end user or customer really wants, and fail to meaningfully renovate, innovate or disrupt.

Too untransparent

Who rates the raters? In finance, who controls the quality of credit agencies Moody's, Fitch and S&P? The *Big Three* have been accused of an unholy alliance with the banking system, happily providing top quality ratings to debt paper that actually contained a lot of risk. Remember the infamous subprime CDOs we discussed above? These were repackaged bad mortgages in a high yield security. But without the rating agency support, no institutional investor could have bought them. This makes the rating agencies key actors in the biggest finance crisis of the last decades*.

Who controls the Michelin Guide (restaurants), the AACSB (a leading universities accreditation body), the Diamond Control Board, the Parker Wine Guide, or the RateBeer.com site?[9] It is actually very interesting to look up who controls any certification or review and recommendation body. Reality and perception of independence of the governing bodies matters.

As an example, you would be amazed who actually *guarantees* the quality of the diamond ring you might be giving (or receiving) at some time in your life. Any MBA student who had the pleasure to study the De Beers case knows better. You think you got a real guarantee on cut, color, carat and clarity. But what if the perceived impartial guarantor (GIA…) proved in fact to be De Beers themselves? How impartial can they be? But what truly puzzles me even more is that even when smart students get unparalleled insight in how the diamond industry really works, the dream of *Diamonds are Forever* and a *Diamond Are a Girl's Best Friend* still wins later. Seller's Reputation – based marketing works.

Too immoral

People have always been ranked: at school, during sports, at work. We accept a certain sense of comparison. If you regularly take Uber, you can rank the driver, but they rate you too. If your rating drops too low, direction 4.2/5, Uber drivers may think twice to pick you up[10]. But if you thought there is an end to comparing and contrasting people, think again. Rankings may invade privacy beyond the best European GDPR protections (General Data Protection Regulation). According to a 2014 report by the State Council of China, by 2020, the Chinese government is considering the introduction of a *social credit score*[11]. Its aim is to check the *trustworthiness* of its more than 1.3 Bn citizens. A big data exercise *to build a culture of sincerity* on a scale even George Orwell did not fathom.

Without a theory, the facts' are silent.

Friedrich A. von Hayek

Chapter 21
A new galactic marketing rating

As an investor, you want to invest at the right price, maximizing your chance for positive alpha. How can data science and analytics help this business decision? How can you assess how high your target brand rocket could fly, and at what risk? How can you assess their Daedalus Paradox risk? What if you had a *Moody's or S&P for marketers* that, as imperfect as ratings may be, still better visualized the brand risk?

My active coding skills date back to university in the early Eighties. At first we used punchcards and expensive yet programmable new HP calculators. Then came the first IBM PCs, and languages like Basic, Fortran, Pascal, C, etc. In 1984, we experienced the first Apple Macintosh, and its legendary one time 1984 intro commercial. That Super Bowl ad was shipped and shared on old VHS videotapes. There was no internet yet, and no social media. The animals were still talking,.

Throughout my corporate career and afterwards, I have always made it a point to stay as current as possible on the digital tools and data science most relevant for marketers. When NYU Stern Vice Dean Eitan Zemel asked me to help him kickstart his latest brainchild end 2012, the new Master of Science in Business Analytics (MSBA), I did not hesitate. The world needed more business savvy data scientists, and NYU Stern was determined to be among the knowledge centers in the world to help deliver on that need.

Following intense iterations and great teamwork, the program became a real success, and each year the class fills up quickly. I heard it affectionately been referred to as *The Global Nerds Program*. Nerds are cool. MSBA teaches its students the pros and cons of models, as per Nate Silver's *The Signal and the Noise: Why so many predictions fail but some don't* (2012).

Moneyball

Nate Silver, a statistician and sports/political forecaster, achieved geek stardom when he correctly predicted the 2012 US Obama presidential elections in 50 out of 50 states. His blog, FiveThirtyEight.com is named after the 538 seats in the Electoral College. But did he predict a Donald Trump win? Or was that a proverbial black swan? The jury is mixed on whether he did or not, depending the time you checked the site. Let's see how he does for future elections.

> Then there is *Moneyball: the Art of Winning an Unfair Game* (2004), the Michael Lewis book about Billy Beane, the baseball general manager best known for his revolutionary thinking. Together with a nerdy sidekick, he changed the competition playbook and upset all baseball conventional wisdom in how to select players. They identified undervalued players with data-based track records, as a means to make a low-payroll baseball club competitive with the big teams. Since he took over the Oakland A's as a manager in 1998, they made the postseason eight times. But so far they have not won a World Series.
>
> I repeat: great data-driven models, built on a solid theory, can and will help. They will definitely increase the probability to succeed. But no model can guarantee miracle$.

A whole new world opened up for me in the MSBA, using a new jargon that, admittedly, more often than not went above my head. On the technical side of the big-data world, it seemed that if you did not speak *Python* or could not code in *R*, you did not exist. However, my role and added value was never to work deeply on the *A* in MSBA, but on the *B* in MSBA. The goal for NYU Stern is to ensure MSBA students earn a Masters in *Business* Analytics, not in Analytics for analytics sake. What Eitan Zemel wanted me to achieve was to ensure the A served the purpose of the B, and the A was not just self-serving the A.

In Search of a Theory

Data needs to serve a useful purpose to earn its keep i.e. helping to make business make better-informed decisions. As a CMO, you want good data scientists in your team, or access to a good agency who can provide you with the service. You need to ensure the data sets they work on are the right sets, big enough and rich enough. You ensure the team cleans the data properly, and that you have enough understanding of the possible statistical models that can be developed and run (different models for different segments or not, different distance measures…).

Most critical, however, is to ensure there is a *theory* behind all this data analysis: a set of business-relevant hypotheses that the model is trying to (dis)prove. In modeling terminology, there needs to be a clear view on the target variable and on the drivers to be tested. What could be the theory behind the predictive impact on business of a marketing excellence rating? What would be the target variable(s) and drivers?

In the previous chapter we learned what finance tools already exist to support the investors to create alpha. In 2006 – 2007, Mitchell Gooze and Ralph Mroz developed a so-called five-step maturity model applied to marketing, inspired by the Software Engineering Institute's Capability Maturity Model (SEI/CMM)[1]. Their construct developed five levels of marketing excellence: from the lowest level (ad hoc) to the highest level (fused). At this top *fused* level, one would observe organizations where all marketing systems and processes are stable and self-correcting, a structure fused with market dynamics and a close partnership with product development.

Introducing a new galactic marketing rating

The Gooze-Mroz model is a very helpful theoretical construct. For me, as a marketing finance practitioner, it is not simple and comprehensive enough. So I decided to build on it, and merge it with the metaphor of the MC-Rocket model I presented in part 3 of this book. On the next pages I will propose a simplified theory and nomenclature for a marketing excellence rating model. Upon further design, iteration, validation and wider adoption, it could over time become a new global standard. What I will share is a concept, not a final work.

At the core of the nomenclature will be the letter *M* of *Marketing*. The model is all about helping investors to unlock *alpha thru marketing excellence*. Appropriately, the new marketing capability rating model is trademarked as **Alpha M**. It is intended to measure the probability of a company's marketing capability to deliver above-market growth. It will be compounded based on a company specific Alpha M audit, and can be compared to a broader data set and a theoretical ideal standard.

α^M The New Marketing Capability Rating Model

Alpha M ™ by Vicomte LLC 2018.

	Rating	Marketing Capability
Investment Grade	MMM+	World Class
	MM+	Superior
	M+	Above Average
Development Grade	-m	Below Average
	-mm	Emerging
	-mmm	Nonexistent

I propose six rating levels at this stage: from the best (+) *Triple M+* Marketers (MMM+), down to the worst (-) ones *Triple m* (-mmm). If you want an easy and memorable logic for the three Ms: the best of the best are *M*asters in *M*odels <u>and</u> in *M*iracles. Playing on the Galactic Team competencies discussed in Chapter 15: the best of the *Mad, Math & Method* teams (with the extra + *representing the M of mr ZBB MacGyver*). Here are the two key benefits for buyers and sellers in the investment ecosystem to use Alpha M ratings:

- **Faster analysis and calibration:** Analysts save a lot of time to develop a (re)rating for any particular stock. On the flip side, IR teams, Investor Relations teams of companies, along with CEO/CFO/CMO, now also have a calibration tool to manage perceptions not only internally, but with the external finance world. No more guesswork, no more asymmetric information. The reality of marketing capability can be priced into the valuation of the stock at any time. Of course alpha can still be generated by the ones who (legally) get the right info first, and act on it first.

- **Reduced buyer and seller remorse:** The due diligence team involved in M&A, both at buyer and seller side, can use the rating to fine-tune the price ranges and multiples being considered. Buyers avoid buyer's remorse when they acquire an asset they discover later needed a lot more extra investment than they had anticipated. As marketing is often a black hole for such teams, I have seen time and again how buyers overestimate the real strength of the brand portfolio they bought, and underestimate the future investment needs to (re)build it or nurture it further. Conversely, the closer they are seen by the buyer as having MMM+ status, the higher sellers can argue the premium they deserve. They leave no money on the table.

A Galactic Marketing Finance Fusion

There is so much more you can do with Alpha M when cross-fertilized with financial ratings. When marketing analytics fuses with financial analytics. Large institutional investors (e.g. pension funds like TIAA-CREF) invest billions on behalf of their many clients to secure their livelihoods in the future. In the new example matrix below (with S&P), we can now cross Alpha M marketing ratings with financial ratings. This has not been available before, and it provides a whole new range of strategic investment opportunities for the fund. At least it helps the investor to assess their portfolio in a new light.

Portfolio Investment Strategy

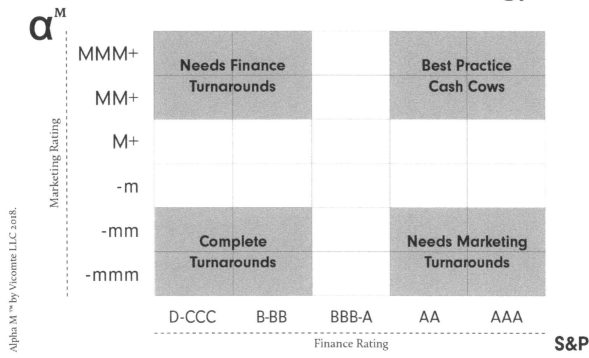

Every quadrant in the above example matrix offers a particular investment versus return potential case. Whether *alpha* will be unlocked or not in each one depends on the price the portfolio manager is able to get for pay for the asset. Let's consider three typical cases:

- **An asset in the top quadrants** will likely throw off a lot of cash for the coming years. And these companies would also be a great learning benchmark for anybody lower in the curve. But they would also likely be expensive to acquire if the seller knows what they are worth.

- **An asset in the lowest quadrants** is a red flag in terms of both marketing and finance. That does not mean the investor should shun it. It means the asset needs the right management team, and likely significant extra investment, to move to the right top corner. It is a possible turnaround case where positive alpha can be created if the asset is bought at the right low price, and changed with the right level of urgency.

- **An asset in the middle quadrants** will provide mixes of the two extremes. It is critical for the investor to delve deep in the operational details of both the financial and marketing ratings to see where the exact gaps are versus excellence, and how (fast) these drivers might by closed. Again, no risk, no reward.

A resulting typical portfolio may follow a reverse U curve, as per the table below. It would be potentially unaffordable to have only the best of the best in a portfolio (MMM+ and AAA = top earnings power), or to have a portfolio full of turnarounds. All depends on the risk/reward balance policy of the respective investor. The point of the new Alpha M tool is that investors have an important extra vector to take into account as they assess the quality of their portfolio.

Optimized Portfolio Investment

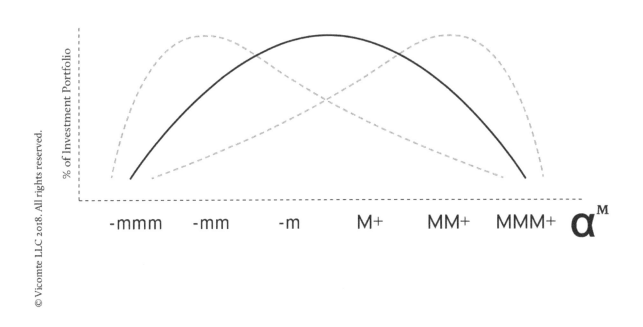

What gets measured, gets done, and may be properly invested in. Let's ensure then that we measure the right things in marketing capability, and not get obsessed only by what we can measure today. Information asymmetries are exploitable by companies if they frame their narrative right. For the decision maker, the more info you get, the more variables, the more difficult your choice may become as a consumer buying a good or service from somebody. The same goes for an analyst trying to find out how good a company is at marketing over the longer term. Or for the investor to buy its stock. Let's simplify their choice.

You start to see how the Alpha M framework might become a useful new tool in the marketing finance ecosystem. Like a FICO credit score or a classic financial rating, it is the world's first attempt to help navigate the marketing excellence landscape. It gives investors and companies just ONE number with real meaning: from a negative triple -*mmm* to a positive triple *MMM+* rating.

Now, how to turn this theory into reality? What are the biggest modeling challenges we need to overcome? Most importantly, how could you test this theory yourself?

An investment in knowledge pays the best interest.

Benjamin Franklin

Chapter 22
The new Alpha M Audit for CEOs

Here we are getting very practical: discover the new Alpha M Audit. For investors and analysts, this is the easiest and fastest way to start comparing marketing excellence between prospective assets. For CEOs and CFOs, it is the smartest way to align your expectations with a prospective CMO. Could this rating over time be built into a top line predictor?

Welcome to the **Alpha M Audit – version 1.0** (see below). As a CEO, think of it like a CMO cheat sheet in your pocket. As an investor or as an analyst, this is a list of the most important questions you should ask prospective assets. It is building on Burggraeve's 8 fundamentals and the MC-Rocket visual.

Investors should use this checklist to get a better feel for the relative marketing capability of the prospective asset. Look for clear evidence on these important questions first, before you look at anything else. Use the list to challenge the CEO and the company leadership, and to establish an aligned path to excellence and progress. Equally, it would be interesting for a CEO/CFO and their future CMO to fill this in together, if only to calibrate where they both think the company stands, and where it should go. To better connect Mars with Venus. Think of it as a job design tool as well.

The maximum numeric score on the Alpha M Audit is 100. This score then gets translated to the Alpha M rating as per the conversion model in the Audit checklist above. There are no yes/no answers. The approach is to agree with the statements on a scale from 1-6, based on as much factual evidence as you can get your hands on.

- 1   = no evidence found for the full statement
- 2-5   = partial evidence found for the full statement
- 6   = clear evidence found for the full statement.

The evidence is relatively easy to find for an internal assessment. For an outsider, it requires some more investigative skills and engagement with the company. The word *company* is used as a proxy for either the complete firm, or for the relevant scale business unit (a division, a country) being assessed on its marketing excellence level. The word *brand* is intended to cover both branded products or services (or solutions, as often referred to in B2B).

For multinational companies, it is increasingly difficult to make a claim that they are superb marketers in *all* key markets where they operate. As I have learned working for top global CPGs,

α^M Audit

The Alpha M™ Audit looks for evidence on each of the 8 fundamentals that form the MC-Rocket©

Company:

Brand:

Unit:

Period:

Conversion Table
90-100 : MMM+
70-89 : MM+
50-69 : M+
31-49 : -m
11-30 : -mm
0-10 : -mmm

Alpha M™ Rating

Total Score

/100

WHY

1. Pricing Power (25%)
Over the last three years, Company has achieved Net Revenue Growth (organic above inflation AND volume growth above industry growth).

1 = 0
2 = 5
3 = 10
4 = 15
5 = 20
6 = 25

Score

2. Purpose (15%)
Company has an official, internally and externally validated Purpose Statement, actively promoted through Company internal and external communication outlets (websites, media, senior management reputation, etc.).

1 = 0
2 = 3
3 = 6
4 = 9
5 = 12
6 = 15

Score

WHAT

3. Brand Health (10%)
Over the last three years, Company must have achieved growth in the weighted average of the relevant Brand Health KPIs for the brand representing >70% of the business.

1 = 0
2 = 2
3 = 4
4 = 6
5 = 8
6 = 10

Score

4. Value Proposition (10%)
Company X can articulate a clear and consistent value proposition for each of its top brands in each key country (and globally, for global brands).

1 = 0
2 = 2
3 = 4
4 = 6
5 = 8
6 = 10

Score

WHO

5. Business Marketers (20%)
90% of all Top marketers (direct reports to CMO and other Regional/Divisional Chiefs) AND 90% of all Top financiers (direct reports to CFO and other Regional/Divisional Chiefs) have been 1) formally trained in Burggraeve's 8 Fundamentals, 2) formally trained in their Company's Power Toolbox and 3) Have no knowledge gaps on the Company's Excellence model.

1 = 0
2 = 4
3 = 8
4 = 12
5 = 16
6 = 20

Score

HOW

6. The Power Toolbox (5%)
Company X has developed and rigorously deploys its own proprietary way of marketing: the same set of core marketing tools and language across all of its geographies, no exceptions. Noncompliance is not tolerated. There is a marketing training curriculum offered to all marketers and also mandatory for all nonmarketer country leadership.

1 = 0
2 = 1
3 = 2
4 = 3
5 = 4
6 = 5

Score

7. Insights (10%)
In each key geography, Company X can clearly articulate the key insight driving the superiority of each top local and global brand versus its most relevant local competitive set.

1 = 0
2 = 2
3 = 4
4 = 6
5 = 8
6 = 10

Score

8. Excellence (5%)
Company X has developed and rigorously deploys its own excellence model: every year it celebrates on a local and global level the best marketing results and talent, against higher expectations.

1 = 0
2 = 1
3 = 2
4 = 3
5 = 4
6 = 5

Score

they may be *MMM+* in one key country, and *-m* in another. For many external observers, especially financial analysts, a multinational is judged as the sum of its core: the sum of its key brands in its key countries. For globally diversified companies, with global brands, the final rating can be augmented by the potential to scale best practices and *ways of operating*, creating competitive advantage. If played well, the upside of global scale should offset its potential risk and complexity (see also the CAGE model of Pankaj Ghemawat we discussed in stage 2).

Applying the 80/20 Pareto rule, the best advice to determine the marketing rating of a global company is based on a weighted average ranking of its core revenue and/or Ebitda driving units. You can potentially increase or decrease the total company result with your own personal judgment factor reflecting the company's global marketing ability (scale, speed, efficiency - or global brands performance and their relative contribution to revenue/ebitda). Again, the final score will likely be a carefully weighted one, based on the evidence you could collect.

Escape Velocity

This 1.0 version of the Alpha M Audit skews the outcome 60% to *marketing outcomes/results* (the *why* and the *what*), and 40% to *marketing means* (*who*, and *how*). To measure building sustainable capability, it is important to officially recognize and honor these means. You are welcome to change these weights. But if you would be of a mind to skew the weights as extreme as 100% behind results, and 0% to the means, you are going to far. The point of investing in true capability is to recognize all its critical components. The *who* and *how* deserve to be recognized.

You are welcome to download the Alpha M Audit and make it yours. Discuss it with your colleagues. By doing so, you are de facto building your own MC-Rocket. The core purpose this book is to help you and your organization to better calibrate your respective views on marketing, and to invest smarter. The objective for your MC-Rocket is to achieve *escape velocity*, the minimum velocity it must achieve to escape the gravitational field of Earth without ever falling back.

There are many ways to go much deeper in the underlying questions and supporting evidence. You can make it as detailed as you wish. For example, check the Forbes Marketing Accountability Initiative, a combination of the Marketing Accountability Standards Board with the Forbes CMO Practice. Together they developed a framework with six questions to dive deeper in the understanding of how marketing is an asset that drives Enterprise Value[1]. It also highlights the six roles the CMO needs to have in his or her team, and dives deeper in 12 organizational capabilities[2].

Top-line predictor

Is it possible over time to make the Alpha M rating a reliable predictor of future top-line results? How could we link the rating even more to relevant sustainable business outcomes and tangible KPIs like revenue and EBITDA?

In data-science modeling terms, these KPIs would be the final target variables (Y, or the dependent variable). Once you start thinking more deeply about them, their exact definition gets tricky fast.

- Is annual revenue enough?

- What does *sustainable* really mean?

- Is the definition of *sustainable top-line revenue* growing *minimum three years in a row*, for example? Two years? Five years?

Whatever the choice, we will need datasets of companies around the world over enough time to be able to create such a target variable, and to test hypotheses. Over 2013 – 2014 I made a first attempt to crack the code to develop Alpha M into a top-line predictor, in partnership with some great marketing minds from **McKinsey**. With characteristic McKinsey rigor, Jesko Perry, Dennis Spillecke and Daniel Birke helped me bring the first rough idea behind the Alpha M model from a 'back of the envelope' sketch to the next level. I am eternally grateful for their time and pioneering contribution.

We built *MECE* (Mutually Exclusive, Comprehensively Exhaustive) lists of potential marketing and sales drivers of business KPIs. Thinking with the end in mind, we made first designs of what a dashboard could be like for a recipient of an Alpha M rating. After a series of tests, we made progress in the correlations, but did not find the holy grail yet on the full predictive power of a marketing excellence rating. Clearly, this is a big-data project, but eminently solvable with the right comprehensive approach. Every new solution innovation started somewhere. The financial rating methodology also did not develop and prove itself overnight. No one individual can develop the complete ecosystem underpinning a marketing rating model. If rocket science could overcome all the obstacles to get us as far in space as it already did, then certainly we can overcome this data challenge as a collective as well.

They say *nothing as powerful as an idea whose time has come*, and *nothing as powerful as the wisdom of the crowds*. In Linux open-source style, I am therefore offering all the thinking to date to the community that reads this book. Let's see if the time has come for this top-line predictor. Alpha M, in its current form is just the start. It is an advanced concept. In Lean Startup jargon, it is the *pretotype* before the prototype or the MVP, to get the discussion going. There is plenty to learn from the professionals in the knowledge and rating world to evolve this idea, and they will be welcome to evolve the thinking further.

Crowdsourcing

For a project of this complexity, it would be best to have *one* overall idea owner that sees long-term profit in this marketing rating idea. The Marketing 2020 model lead by Kantar Vermeer (see stage 2) was a good example of such a big marketing thinkers coalition. The ideal project leader either has the right company results databases, or the capabilities and incentives to invest in them.

For the **financial rating agencies**, this may be a natural profitable line extension of their solutions suite to their customers. Such a strategic bet could equally make sense for other companies with massive data and analytics capabilities that already serve either or both the marketing and finance community. For example: the **leading NYC/London based knowledge companies that are already close to marketers**:

- **The Nielsen Company** (1923), best known for market and viewership analytics;

- WPP Kantar unit **Millward Brown** (1973), publishing the very advanced BrandZ rankings in partnership with the Financial Times;

- Omnicom unit **Interbrand** (1979), also offering brand valuation services since decades;

- Silicon Valley data aggregators like **Google** (1998), or more recent deep data challengers like **Palantir** (2004).

- Or, why not, big banks like **Goldman Sachs** (1882)?

Under the leadership of this Alpha M project sponsor, there may be great value to tap into the collective wisdom of the global corporate marketing community. There are a whole lot of marketing expert communities out there around the world, and in each major country.

Possible global experts sources include:

- The World Federation of Advertisers (WFA);

- Global consultancies (McKinsey, BCG, Bain, Accenture, PWC, Deloitte…)

- The CMO Network on Linked In;

Major Universities with strong marketing tracks. Already there is a growing body of evidence on platforms like scholars.com and in journals like *The Journal of Marketing*, connecting certain components of the marketing mix with certain results. Unfortunately, all this wisdom is often hidden in academic journals and PhD dissertations. Based on the conversations I had for this book, I must believe there is a massive treasure trove of marketing and finance insights waiting to be finally uncovered, and to be integrated in *one* actionable model.

Expert input could be even further augmented with some sort of crowd-sourced broader public perception as well, like marketing wiki-ratings. Of course, the model builders would be well advised to take into account learnings to ensure this cannot be misused (e.g., bots, false ratings…).

Possible local experts include (US example for illustration):

- ANA (Association of Advertisers – US)

- AMA (American Marketing Association – US)

- CMO Club (Chief Marketing Officer Club – US)

- MASB (Marketing Accountability Standards Board – US)

- AAAA (American Association of Advertising Agencies – US)

There is no need to wait. The Alpha M Audit allows investors and marketers to already start a very different conversation. If the right project sponsor stands up, the Alpha M rating may further be fine-tuned to get predictive value. In the meantime, let me move to some closing thoughts, sharing a point of view as to where investors may find the most galactic marketers tomorrow?

All truths
are easy to
understand
once they are
discovered;
the point is to
discover them.

Galileo Galilei

Chapter 23
Where the galactic money will go

Where should smart money find the MMM+ marketers in a galactic age? Besides space-related companies, why would investors believe they should (still) bet on CPG, continue to bet on tech, as well as take a good look at the world of global sports and *enjoyment experiences* at large (like cannabis)?

According to Financial Times and World Bank data, there are **43.192 exchange quoted companies in the world.** This is a first massive pool of public data to apply the above models to. The real market of companies is of course much wider. Every year there are tens of thousands of start ups and scale ups under the public water line looking for your investment.

As a fun warm-up to think broader, open your browser and have a look at this infographic: the world map of languages (http://www.visualcapitalist.com/a-world-of-languages/). English continues to be by far the world's dominant language to be learned, but you will see a language rationale for looking well beyond the classic english speaking nations. Now consider the McKinsey Global Institute's analysis on the future big companies. Back in 2013, it already predicted companies based in so-called *emerging markets* will account for more than 45 percent of the Fortune Global 500 ranking by 2025, up from 26 percent currently. Given demographics, these emerging-market countries are already home to **more than 1,000 companies with annual sales above $1 billion (many not on exchanges),** and this number will only rise.

As an investor with limited visibility, would it not be great to know how many *-mmm* to *MMM+* are among these top 1000? On the flip side, as a business marketer working for these top 1000, think how much higher your company value would rise if investors understood what *alpha* you may represent? McKinsey's findings were echoed by Professors Nirmalya Kumar (London Business School) and Jan-Benedict Steenkamp (UNC Kenan-Flagler). In *Brand Breakout: How Emerging Market Brands will go Global* (2013), they researched why it was that despite the fact emerging markets accounted for 40% of global output, very few dominant global brands had emerged to date.

Most people do know Samsung and Corona now. What about Haier, Lenovo, Tata, Havaianas, Natura, ICICI, etc.? The two authors discuss 8 possible growth paths emerging brands can follow to become global brands (*before they can be galactic*), from the Asian tortoise model, to the national champions route. By the way, *emerging markets* is now an old-school concept. As we learned in Chapter 1: jargon matters. In the Hans Rosling inspired book *Factfulness* (2018), he and Bill Gates propose to drop the old nomenclature of *developed versus developing markets*, and replace it with a more fact-based different typology (*four levels*) based on much evolved GDP/capita[1]. So look for galactic marketers by each to the four levels in the future.

The future MMM+

Mapping future winners all depends on your world view, on your biases, on your expertise and on sector interest. My sector content bets are **space, tech, CPG and global sports / enjoyment solutions.** My geographic bet is to double down on the promise of the *beyond global* economy, on the sectors with *galactic mindset* potential, not on just one geographical area.

I started traveling and operating more regularly throughout a booming Asia since 1990. Ever since, I learned the key question to ask in meetings was not so much the critical *western why*, but a more provocative *eastern why not*. It is a great question to ask to discover true progress. It would be foolish to snobbishly dismiss the added value of the west/north, as there is much more fascinating stuff happening there than meets the eye. But the west/north needs to accept the cold mathematical shift in sheer population numbers as well, and look much more intensely east/south for higher alpha opportunities.

I already argued at length the case for the booming new space-related industry in stage 1 of this book. There will surely be brilliant MMM+ marketers created in that area. If somebody offered me the right Galactic fund to invest in, I would seriously consider it. New consumer categories like cannabis, cryptocurrency and consumer AI are blossoming, even though the early years will be choppy. I am placing some bets there, believing they will develop beyond what we can imagine today. They will yield new brands, and new big companies, some of which may fuse partially or completely with current mainstream CPG.

Barring black swans (or gray rhinos), the investment community may be right to keep betting that *BAT* (Baidu, Ali Baba and Tencent) will pass the current top four most valuable branded companies in the world: Amazon, Microsoft, Alphabet (Google) and Apple. On the back of its WeChat brand platform, a rather young company like Tencent (1998) already passed an even younger Facebook (2004) end November 2017 in market value. An equally young Ali Baba (1999) is right behind them. Though again, unexpected trade wars may throw black swan curve balls.

Boards of big western companies are well advised to have a detailed look at how global advertising investment has evolved over time, and how it will likely evolve further. According to Publicis Groupe's Zenith media forecast, China, already the world's second-largest ad market clocking 6-8% growth over the last years, grew to US$ 80.5 billion in 2017. In the 2018 Brand Finance Global 500 report, the growth of Chinese brands was once again the standout story. According to the report's authors, there has been a renewed emphasis on brand development by Chinese companies in all sectors since the 19th Party Congress in 2017. Brand Finance claims that *while*

China had been pursuing a dual strategy of building home-grown brands and also acquiring underperforming international brands (like Volvo and Pirelli), the emphasis is now firmly on home-grown brands.

So expect to see more from brands like Huawei, Ping An, State Grid, Evergrande, ICBC, Yili, Haval and many others. In drinks, rice wine *baijiu* Moutai was once again the most valuable alcoholic drinks brand of the world, with a total brand value of US$ 21.2 Bn, up from US$ 12.3 Bn last year. A climb from the 108th most valuable global brand in 2017, to 56th in 2018. The fastest-growing brand of 2018 also comes from China, and is also a spirit: Wuliangye grew +161% to US$ 14.6 Bn year on year, rising 184 ranks to 100th. One can observe similar significant shifts in the InterBrand and BrandZ brand ranking trends. (Tech) Companies in Asian markets will have claimed most top slots in brand value over the coming decades—again lead by China.

However, it is **not all doom and gloom for the classic nontech CPG leaders of yesterday/today**. They have one major advantage, at least if they recognize it and leverage it in time. They already learned how to carry the responsibility of greatness. Their leadership and employees have the battle scars and wisdom of some defeats. For the tech ones leading the pack now, growing at breakneck speed, that challenge is still to come. They are still subject to both the Daedalus and Icarus Paradox. Every young and seemingly invincible growth company faces major challenges at some point in its development: the law of big numbers, changing consumer tastes, hungrier investor expectations, and most importantly, changing societal expectations. The recent changes in global public opinion and regulator perspective towards *Big Tech* (arrogance, hubris, sexist, irrelevant, cheating...) is a clear Icarus-like warning that for any top marketer, the first order of business is always to earn and nurture the social license to operate, before worrying about marketing effectiveness and efficiency.

Non tech companies will indeed need all the rocket science in the world to stay *renaissance* brands, to stay relevant in the galactic age. I am confident most incumbents somehow will remain top ranked and build on some of their incredible competitive advantages. Only time will tell if the western based global leader brands of today will retain their historic excellence leadership.

Galactic Sports

Last, you may wonder why I also added *enjoyment experiences, especially global sports*. Not only will we live longer, maybe even to 150 soon, but if part of our old jobs are taking over by robots, *what are we going to do with ourselves*? That is the existential question pondered by Yuval Noah Harari[2]. Having solved many issues on the planet, his thesis is humankind risks entering an equally unprecedented age of boredom. It will have to look for new issues to solve in order to stay happy. If happiness is essentially linked to human biochemical reactions, we need to continuously find new natural equilibriums between stress/excitement and calm/tranquility. Just like in old Rome, we need *panem et circenses* (bread and games) to keep the masses entertained during their increased free time. New enjoyment products, like cannabis, may see more demand (see Sin & Soul in stage 3). Governments will always need new gladiators to entertain the masses.

Not unlike cannabis, big money starts to make galactic bets on sports and entertainment. Amazon is accelerating its foray in entertainment as a lure for its core Amazon Prime service[3]. By entering the Premier League, it starts to compete with classic networks, pay TV and lately social media to attract users. But there are much bigger plays going on already. With US$ 82 Bn in revenue, Softbank (1981) is now the 72nd largest company in the world, and number seven in Japan[4]. In May 2017, its galactic thinking founder and CEO, Masayoshi Son, also created the world's largest investment fund, the US$ 100 Bn Vision Fund, to invest in technology companies. Early in April 2018, Softbank shocked the global sports world with a bold offer to the world governing body of the biggest sport, FIFA: US$ 25 Bn for the rights to organize, amongst others, a new global super-competition between the best global 24 clubs as of 2021[5]. Their intention is to unlock the full power of a globally connected TV/video/telco market of 3 Bn soccer fans. Son already invested in the new Miami-based soccer club owned by global soccer and fashion icon David Beckham, essentially a play on Latin America and the fast-growing hispanic-American generation. But he clearly thinks much bigger than that.

Making abstraction of all regrettable scandals and intrigue that seem to inevitably surround their decisions, the global sports governing bodies do have a nose for the future centers of economic gravity (and therefore of sponsors). Russia hosted the FIFA World Cup 2018. The next one in 2022 will take place in Qatar, in the Middle East. To keep geopolitical balance while optimizing revenue, FIFA allocated the 2026 edition back to the West (US/Canada/Mexico). I would not be surprised at all to see the 2030 FIFA World Cup awarded to China. Under the inspiration of an ever more powerful and soccer-crazy president Xi Jinping, China is aiming for world dominance in socio-economic terms.

The London-based Centre for Economics and Business Research predicts China to pass the US by 2032 in GDP[6]. However, China wants to dominate in many more aspects of life, including in the world's number-one sport: soccer. China is a nation dominating or competing on top level in many world sports, including the Olympic Games. A number-one role in the world's number-one sport has so far eluded it. But now China has adopted a long term Soccer Dream with three components[7]:

- **To qualify** for another World Cup. That will have to be 2022 or 2026, as the Chinese squad did not make it to Russia.

- **To host** a World Cup. This would be a good economic driver, but it may also have less honor as it means automatic qualification. China ideally wants to earn the right to play. Still, it could be the host for 2030.

- **To actually** *win* a World Cup, putting it in the pantheon of the likes of Brazil, Germany and Italy. Note that neither USA or Russia ever got close despite being a host or participant. USA did progress well in Confederation Cups, the four yearly warm-up tournament before a World Cup. Let's see what 2026 brings.

For its third ambition, China targets 2050. As always, it plays a long game. Building brand China, to help deliver on its China Dream. The investment in soccer and the world cup is part of Marketing China. Marketing is Finance is Business, also for countries. Its *long soccer march* has started, and the strategy starts to be translated. Soccer academies are mushrooming. New soccer pitches are appearing all over China. Chinese were allowed to own foreign teams to bring back knowledge, but the practice was restricted to avoid money-laundering out of China. Still, of the top 100 most valuable soccer teams in the world, nine are already Chinese-owned[8]. Top foreign players are coming in, be it only to a certain degree, as the strategic focus is clearly to build local talent over time.

With a clear soccer Dream, the law of big numbers in their favor, and an agile learning mindset, it is only a question of time before the paradigm shift that already happened in business, from *Made in China* to *Invented in China*, also happens in soccer. Galactic Soccer, *Played by China*. Any *America or Europe First* policies may slow this overarching Asian evolution, but it is hard to beat population mathematics.

Marketing is Finance is Business was designed to provide both inspiration and practical help to CMOs, CFOs, CEOs, their boards, and their top teams to build successful brands in this new galactic age. The ambition was to let light escape from the black hole of marketing.

By now I trust you have a much better understanding of why and how **a new Think and Act Galactic mindset** and increased partnership between marketing and finance leaders can create more sustainable branded business models for any type organization in the Space Age ahead of us. You earned your **business marketing astronaut wings**, and you discovered 2 new blueprints: the **MC-Rocket©** marketing capability model, the new **Alpha M™** marketing excellence rating model, and its practical **Alpha M™ Audit**. I hope you find them memorable, simple, and useful. May you feel inspired to actively start experimenting with them, especially if you are among the key protagonists in the business of building brands today *and* tomorrow.

To the Hitchhiker's fans among you: *so long, and thanks for all the fish*. To all, I wish you a thrilling *BFG* ride, triple MMM+ status, and many marketing miracle$.

VICOMTE

vicomte.com/galactic

I don't think humans even have to be biological. I think humans are the species that changes who we are.

Ray Kurzweil

Marketing in the Cyborg Age

If we believe the media, it feels as if any business that does not offer an Artificial Intelligence (AI) – based algorithm solution is unlikely to survive much longer[1]. I did propose some rocket science to deliver more marketing miracle$, but I have not yet been able to crack the code to a cloud- and AI-based marketing excellence score. It may be coming soon to a device near you though, even if strangely enough, we may not need it anymore soon after. Why not? Because we all may become an algorithm ourselves.

AI vs. Big Data in earning calls

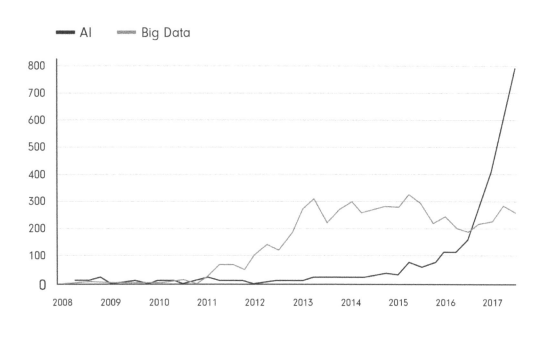

Like other key concepts in marketing, finance and space, the term *Artificial Intelligence* was also already coined back in 1956 by John McCarthy. AI's moment of truth is about to happen only 75 years later. It may become the next Space Race. The US and China are battling for first, though Europe is not ready to yield[2]. Projections from the consultants PwC and Accenture regarding AI's economic impact predict a US$ 15.7 trillion boost to the global economy by 2030 as a result of labor productivity improvements and increased consumer demand. They predict four sectors in particular will benefit from AI: manufacturing, financial services, professional services, and wholesale and retail. In all of these, branding and marketing will continue to play a big role.

When we become some form of cyborg, even the longtime immutable fundamentals of marketing may finally shift. All marketing and advertising rules may be rewritten completely when that happens, even the most fundamental ones. Dear Sergio, this time, that would really be *The End of Marketing as We Know It*. And possibly the subject of a whole new galactic 2.0 book: *Marketing in The Cyborg Age*.

I do believe in Amara's Law. Ray Amara was a past president of the Palo Alto – based Institute of the Future (IFTF)[3]. He suggests people always overestimate the short-term impact of technology, yet underestimate its long-term impact. While at AB InBev, we held more than a few key top management strategy sessions in Stanford, including a healthy dose of future-gazing with the help of IFTF and others. For years we trained all our top 300 operating managers and senior marketers in the new ABI Way of Marketing. We organized courses both in Kellogg (about fundamentals – Kotler's marketing legacy), as in Palo Alto (about change – marketing's future?). The entire AB InBev board and top management went through these courses. They actually went first.

We also opened a *Beer Garage* in Palo Alto, to get a finger on the pulse of all forms of tech that could help us brew better, market and brand differently, and ultimately sell more beer at higher prices in the future. Growth hacking with beer? Startups loved it. During those years the powerful category concept of *Beer, the Original Social Network* was hatched as well. The idea connected 9000 years of beer history with the coming galactic age. It became the language that summarized all that we stood for as the global market leader in beer. The concept is still used by AB InBev, though maybe it needs to be upgraded to *Beer, the Original Messaging App*, now that messaging apps have eclipsed social networks. Global cannabis legalization and regulation may also be forcing beer to again update and modernize its purpose. In beer, consistency and longevity matter, while you renovate and innovate slowly to ensure consumers follow along. In tech, it is upgrade fast or die. In Palo Alto, we learned both worlds can actually be symbiotic. Yin and Yang. Left and right brain coming together.

Sorry Dave, I am afraid I can't do that
(HAL 9000, in 2001: A Space Odyssey)

I also do believe in the concept of singularity, that scary point where artificial intelligence may/will pass human intelligence. So just as classic finance is being massively reinvented and challenged by fintech, or just as graphene may increase the speed of the next level internet by 100x, so the many components of the marketing toolbox may get completely disrupted and upended. All marketing capability may have to be holistically reinvented—well beyond where the field of neuromarketing is today.

As an example: in 2013, people predicted the job skills in 2020 in the US[4]. Twenty percent of these still had to do with *empathy*: sports coaches, massage therapists, school psychologists, personal planners of all kind, music tutors… The assumption was that empathy indeed remained the lasting competitive advantage of humans versus robots. But the man-machine discussion is advancing much faster than we imagine. It will fast transcend injecting sensors in our body, or wearing Google earbuds that instantly translate 40+ languages[5]. Commenting on AI at the 2018 World Economic Forum in Davos, Ali Baba founder Jack Ma urged education systems to *teach everything than what a machine can do better*: values, teamwork, etc[6].

Ray Kurzweil is the co-founder of Singularity University, and also Google's current pope of engineering. He has a rather incredible 86% track record on correct bold predictions[7]. He already provoked that the line where humans stop and cyborgs start will continue to blur. Eventually, it will upend many paradigms we hold dear today, also in marketing and advertising. The market for humanoid robots is already expected to grow an exponential 10x by 2023, from US\$ 320.3 million to \$3.9 billion, according to research company ReportsnReports[8]. Industrial robotics may account for US\$ 72 Bn by that date. But we are fast moving beyond simple robots. In past centuries, science fiction writers like Jules Verne and Isaac Asimov made us enter new and very uncomfortable worlds. In the last years, suspenseful techno paranoia Netflix TV shows like *Altered Carbon* or *Black Mirror* tap into our collective unease with how technology has, and will, transform all aspects of life.

These shows literally hold up a black mirror, reflecting existential questions. Andrew Murray is a professor of Law at London School of Economics, specializing in media and technology. He, and many with him, are pondering the very deep questions about our identity and what it means to be human in times of human-level artificial intelligence. What will be our relationship with sentient life forms different than our own?[9] Any fans of the Blade Runner movies will know the faith of *replicants*. Especially when, against all expectations, even replicants find ways to procreate.

We may soon need to ask how we will live with humanized robots. But going one step further: what happens if we gradually (can) become cyborgs ourselves? If we chose to augment our human brains somehow, with an ability to instantly access all possible factors for choice, how would brands be built and chosen? If we *become*, if we finally *are* the algorithm, is the idea of choice still relevant at that time? How would mankind still enjoy emotions if we are all too smart? Or will some be augmented so much more than others that today's inequality not only continues, but even amplifies in a galactic way? At the start of part 3 we looked at what (never) changed in marketing. But maybe, just maybe, this time, marketing itself will be forever changed from its core - as a result of how humans change in the most profound way in history.

Einstein University

I am a so-called INTJ in Myers Briggs terms. I find pleasure in thinking in terms of past, present and future, like the famous 1897 oil-on-canvas work by French painter Paul Gauguin. It makes you sit back and reflect on the big questions of life: *where do we come from, what are we, where are we going* (D'ou venons nous; Que sommes-nous; Ou allons-nous). Gauguin loved Tahiti, and the island clearly was a great inspiration for existential musings. I am equally fascinated by the Greek pre-Socratic frameworks depicting different fluidities of time: *Chronos*, the very planned and chronological time for work; *Kairos*, the right, critical or opportune moment, more linked to planned enjoyment; or the magnificent concept of *Aion*, losing yourself in an activity or an event, unbounded, when you ask yourself: *where did time go?*

So, as a future-oriented student and marketer, I have always followed people who are good at helping us understand and imagine tomorrow. From the grandfather of predictions, Nostradamus (early 1500) to Stephen Hawking; from my forward-looking fellow Belgian countrymen Peter Hinssen and Steven van Bellegem, to Futuro Gurus Joeri Van den Bergh, Herman Konings and Tom Palmaerts, to futurists like Alvin Toffler and new sci-fi authors like Charles Stross and longevity gurus like Aubrey de Grey; from the IFTF to the various Singularity University thinkers I mentioned before. There are a few others even more *out there*, like the geniuses at MIT's Future Lab, or the minds at the magistral Institute for Advanced Studies[10].

IAS is aptly located at Einstein Drive nr 1, in Princeton, New Jersey. Its purpose is to promote *The Usefulness of Useless Knowledge*. Scholarship and deep thinking in its purest form, across the fields of mathematics, natural sciences, historical studies and social sciences. Albert Einstein joined its first school, the school of Mathematics, in 1932. Among its faculty and members are 33 Nobel Laureates, 41 of the 56 Fields Medalists, and 16 of the 18 Abel Prize Laureates, as well as many MacArthur Fellows and Wolf Prize winners. In the words of the IAS Founding Director (1930 – 1939): *I am not unaware of the fact that I have sketched an educational Utopia. I have deliberately hitched the Institute to a star; it would be wrong to begin with any other ambition or aspiration.*

If there was any place in the world a consumer scientist would want to get feedback on existential questions related to marketing and humanity, by real rocket scientists from various disciplines, this had to be it. Janine Purcaro, IAS COO, gracefully showed me around the grounds. The campus is perfectly designed to facilitate *out there* thinking and the most fundamental of fundamental research. Small groups of academics argue math and social theories on blackboards placed all over the grounds, both inside and outside.

She later introduced me to some key faculty during the iconic 3 pm tea time. Since 1932, every day, like clockwork, all scholars congregate in the commons room of Fuld Hall to share their latest thoughts and findings over *high tea*. It gave me the chance to discuss with former IAS Director Peter Goddard (Mathematical Physics), Prof. Avi Wigderson (Computer Science and Discrete

Mathematics), and with Prof. Emeritus Freeman Dyson (Physics)[11]. Well into his nineties, Prof Dyson never missed an opportunity to argue with scholars and visitors over a hot cup of tea.

The Certainty of Surprise

It was rather fitting to discuss the future of humankind and computing in a place like IAS. After all, this was the place where supercomputers were born. From 1946 to 1951, mathematics professor John Von Neumann created the very first functioning electronic super computer on the planet here. As could be expected from scholars at this level, they did not agree on anything related to my provocation, albeit in the most charming intellectual way. After warm up and exploration, two schools of thought emerged.

One line of thinking was that we already were cyborgs anyway, simpletons determined by our brain. By extension via an ever more brainy smartphone, we increasingly and willingly outsource our real thinking to AI. This is the school that also found questions like *Does God exist?* irrelevant, as it can neither be proven or disproven. Believing in God is that, a belief, not a fact. This school prefers to only deal with theories that can actually somehow be verified[12]. They then started to discuss the hereto unsolved computer science problem *P versus NP*, which asks whether any problem whose solution can technically be verified easily and quickly, can also be solved quickly[13]. My head started to spin.

The other end of the spectrum remained convinced the most plausible future scenario would be for humans to (be able to) maintain control over their free will. People would fight to somehow consciously keep determining their own future. We would keep choosing our paths, and control our destiny, even if most of our brains would now have the equivalent of a *Google Inside*. By the way, they mused, who would sell the implants and make money off that? What types of implants? Why don't you ask Jeff Bezos, they suggested. Could Amazon sell augmentation? Bezos happens to be a Princeton graduate too.

Signaling we came to the end of tea time, slowly putting down his cup, Prof Dyson, a contemporary of Von Neumann, eventually reminded us all how wrong we can be about the future:

John thought the whole US would need only 18
supercomputers to serve all its future needs.

He never even fathomed the idea of a PC,
let alone what we see today in mobile and AI.

I am excited about how we will continue to be surprised,
because that is the only certainty I have.

And that is how it should be.

Acknowledgements

This book is not just my work of passion. It is the result of thousands of planned and serendipitous interactions with many people over 30+ years. More experienced writers know *it often takes a village* to complete a book in style, and to unleash its full potential afterwards. From the very first outline to the never-ending (and often painful) editing, you slowly craft what hopefully becomes an interesting and useful story. And I intend to actively build on reader and presentation feedback afterwards. So, a big thank you, to all the people below: from the rocket scientists to the marketers to the many *Hidden Figures*, you are all *galactic*, in your own ways…

Iterating the Thinking and Narrative

- Frank Abenante and Jorn Socquet (great marketers that pushed the base thinking)

- Robert Ottenstein (for the analyst view – Evercore)

- Christian Loos (KitchenNYC – see About the Designer)

- Rudy Moenaert (TIAS-NIMBAS, pushing to just start writing, and for links to journals)

- Peter Vanham (WEF, for reverse mentoring on writing and publishing)

- Peter De Keyzer (Growth-Inc, for great structure advice)

- Magali Geens (Insites Consulting, for very detailed feedback)

- David Moran (you are a pricing guru)

- David Moritz (Toast cofounder and fellow space enthusiast)

- Mark Gompertz (demystifying publishing)

- Paul Seroka (TRIUM colleague)

Iterating the Design, Prototyping, Visualization…

- Christian Loos from Kitchen NYC (again)
- Little Fury (Tina and Wendy – the original Vicomte designers)
- Digiti (working with Kitchen NYC on Vicomte 2.0)

Providing Insights and Inspiration

- P&G, Coke and AB InBev colleagues, alums and friends – thanks for all the experience and for the great times
- Vicomte clients, partners, and the founders and funders I had (and still have) the pleasure to work with
- (Trium and MSBA) Students and faculty colleagues
- The colleagues and friends at nonprofits and associations (WFA, BelCham, Prince Albert Fund, BeCentral)
- The rocket scientists, fellow future astronauts and the magnificent Astronaut Relations team at Virgin Galactic
- The other rock(et) star companies leading Space Race 2.0

Notes

Preface: how to best navigate this book?
1. One of the most famous flight-related quotes, attributed to Leonardo Da Vinci, but never proven to be from him. As mysterious as the maestro himself.

Stage 1
Look Up: Adopt a New Galactic Mindset

Chapter 1 – Look Up: Adopt a New Galactic Mindset
1. Look up any academic evidence or post-mortem analysis over time by leading investment bankers or consultancies (the same ones who often recommended the move to the CEO in the first place).
2. Finish Big: How Great Entrepreneurs Exit Their Companies on Top (2014), Bo Burlingham
3. engage.kornferry.com/2018-cmo-pulse-survey?mkt_tok=eyJpIjoiTnpsaE16Qm1NVE13Tm1ZNSIsInQiOiJVNUU3VUhZXC9EVH-FEXC9jVVl4RTNJeVY5V0t1c1c3aEw2aDNpRlBDa3dTUGpkTFFKMmZlQ3VZbWJTTjBObkE1aTg5MUZGdGpKcWMwYzVNclBuM2Z2V29Ec-DlDeHdlS2RTV2c5OEhkUXZSWmlYRFRkZ0p5eFplQlRVYU5KTnpzV1luIn0%3D
4. www.spencerstuart.com/research-and-insight/cmo-tenure-2017
5. hbr.org/2017/07/the-trouble-with-cmos
6. www.fournaisegroup.com/ceos-do-not-trust-marketers/
7. the-evolution-of-the-cmo
8. www.linkedin.com/pulse/cmo-mess-how-we-can-clean-up-jenifer-kern
9. We are both longtime fans of our home team FC Bruges.
10. Marketing met Ballen, Rudy Moenaert (2016),
11. www.ft.com/content/0583d78c-019b-11e8-9650-9c0ad2d7c5b5
12. the-left-brain-vs-right-brain-myth-elizabeth-waters
13. www.forbes.com/sites/kimberlywhitler/2015/02/05/why-todays-marketers-are-tomorrows-ceos/#6fb6d3063126

Chapter 2 – Mars is the new Moon
1. Wikipedia
2. Marketing the Moon (2014), David Meerman Scott & Richard Jurek, p 111.
3. For more information about NASA's plan for the future, visit:
   https://www.nasa.gov/feature/nasas-exploration-campaign-back-to-the-moon-and-on-to-mars
4. "Who Needs Nasa?" Wired, 1/1/2000 www.wired.com/2000/01/schmoes/
5. www.nasa.gov/news/media/trans/obama_ksc_trans.html
6. www.mckinsey.com/.../McKinsey/Global%20Themes/.../Urban%20world/MGI_ur...
7. www1.nyc.gov/nyc-resources/service/2220/planyc-2030
8. Think of Persepolis, Babylon, Rome, Florence, Athens, Constantinople, Jerusalem. People today may say I love New York with deeper passion than they may say I love the US. Cities are again starting to challenge the old order of nation states. Some are even calling for a new global legislative body comprising the world's biggest cities: the Global Parliament of Mayors, the brainchild of acclaimed NY based scholar Benjamin Barber in his provocative book If Mayors Ruled the World: Dysfunctional Nations, Rising Cities (2014)
9. Societal experiments with new towns has happened before, e.g. Milton Keynes, close to London, a new town created in the Sixties. or in our recent decades: Dubai. The jury is out on how easy it is to manufacture cities.
10. fortune.com/2017/11/13/bill-gates-arizona-smart-city-cascade-belmont/
11. Factfulness: Ten Reasons We're Wrong About the World, and Why Things Are Better Than You Think (2018), Hans Rosling.
12. Abundance (2012), Peter Diamandis.
13. www.aerofarms.com
14. www.kateraworth.com/doughnut/
15. The whole era has been exquisitely documented in Marketing the Moon: The Selling off the Apollo Lunar Program (2014), David Meerman Scott & Richard Jurek
16. for the fans of the Hitchhiker's Guide to the Galaxy. Also used on Elon Musk's red Tesla sent in space on February 18.
17. Homo Deus (2018), Yuval Noah Harari.
18. www.cnet.com/news/elon-musk-at-sxsw-id-like-to-die-on-mars-just-not-on-impact/
19. www.washingtonpost.com/news/wonk/wp/2014/01/09/nasa-plans-to-keep-the-international-space-station-going-until-2024-is-that-a-good-idea/?noredirect=on&utm_term=.82b648ef1e9f
20. www.nasa.gov/content/preparing-for-mars
21. www.nasa.gov/press-release/nasa-s-newest-astronaut-recruits-to-conduct-research-off-the-earth-for-the-earth-and
22. www.outerplaces.com/science/item/18175-investigation-mars-one-project-scam
23. There is no evidence of any decent partnership with a company that can give it a Mars spaceship, like Lockheed Martin or SpaceX. Mars One has been trying since a long time to get a Frankfurt listing for its Ventures arm. In theory this company should be worth around US$ 400 Mn. It also wants to hire a CEO with relevant global storytelling and monetization experience to help get to its long

long-standing goal goal of raising USD 6 billion, a goal that is far away.
www.inverse.com/article/42965-mars-one-is-a-money-grab-where-everyone-loses

24. www.nydailynews.com/entertainment/tv/mars-chooses-100-applicants-reality-tv-show-mars-article-1.2118081
25. community.mars-one.com/last_activity/ALL/18/82/ALL/ALL/5/3
26. www.nasa.gov/press-release/nasa-confirms-evidence-that-liquid-water-flows-on-today-s-mars

Chapter 3 – The new Galactic Age: open for business

1. www.dailymail.co.uk/sciencetech/article-3765291/Mark-Zuckerberg-Yuri-Milner-Stephen-Hawking-begin-100-million-search-alien-life-nearby-Earth-like-planet.html
2. www.cnn.com/2017/03/13/world/trappist-exoplanet-belgian-researchers/index.html
3. www.singularityhub.com/2017/11/27/how-will-humans-colonize-space-in-the-years-ahead/
4. Lee Morin, interviewed for his NYUAA E.J Keogh Award for Distinguished Public Service in April 2018
www.alumni.nyu.edu/s/1068/alumni/interior_3col.aspx?sid=1068&gid=1&pgid=17712&cid=30910&ecid=30910&crid=0&calp-gid=17706&calcid=30898&utm_source=sidebar&utm_medium=web&utm_campaign=2018_awards
5. www.bloomberg.com/news/articles/2017-12-13/space-startup-raises-90-million-to-bring-ads-to-moon-by-2020
6. stories.ehf.org/emeline-paat-dahlstrom-building-a-spacebase-in-new-zealand-88e88c5
7. www.commercialspaceflight.org
8. venturepulse.cmail19.com/t/d-l-bgjktt-ctttuuuo-e/
9. news.crunchbase.com/news/rockets-deliver-satellite-startups-see-explosion-interest-vcs/
10. www.cbinsights.com/research/space-tech-startups-market-map/?utm_source=CB+Insights+Newsletter&utm_campaign=7c43d32e4d-
11. https://www.fastcompany.com/40507858/space-startups-record-investment-rocket-labs-interorbital-phase-four
12. www.cnbc.com/2017/10/12/morgan-stanley-how-to-invest-in-1-trillion-space-industry.html
13. The Entrepreneurial State: Debunking Public vs Private Sector Myths (2013), Mariana Mazzucato.
14. en.wikipedia.org/wiki/United_Nations_Committee_on_the_Peaceful_Uses_of_Outer_Space
15. www.space.com/40471-trump-teases-military-space-force-again.html
16. www.theoceancleanup.com
17. blogs.esa.int/cleanspace/
18. www.theverge.com/2018/2/17/17019796/where-is-roadster-website-tesla-spacex-elon-musk-falcon-heavy
19. www.virgin.com
20. heleo.com/conversation-how-to-have-fun-while-earning-a-billion-dollars/17144/
21. www.dailystar.co.uk/news/latest-news/707045/Concorde-Boom-Supersonic-British-Airways-Air-France-US-UK-New-York-London-pictures
22. eng.ctaweb.org
23. www.blueorigin.com
24. The Space Barons: Elon Musk, Jeff Bezos, and the Quest to Colonize the Cosmos (2018), Christian Davenport.
25. www.wsj.com/articles/amazon-ceo-jeff-bezos-pledges-to-expand-his-space-ventures-1527349075?emailToken=a09f9f-8b1e3187afab4f409156ddf26dmkOyEKhbfwtjv8cqtuTfM5TE+inTrAWbs1I21Fr1R91mWAdgoal3/0M11xmCqbrIixUKZuI0zF1gRYzKec7Fzj-CeA/pLExn+sm6XekfMGskHe+z7xisuV0g9n3URKB/7&reflink=article_email_share
26. www.spacex.com
27. www.independent.co.uk/life-style/gadgets-and-tech/news/elon-musk-spacex-passengers-japan-billioniare-yusaku-maeza-wa-space-moon-a8542416.html
28. futurism.com/spacex-launched-device-change-interact-space/
29. www.fcc.gov/document/fcc-authorizes-spacex-provide-broadband-satellite-services
30. www.cbinsights.com/research/report/elon-musk-companies-disruption/?utm_source=CB+Insights+Newsletter&utm_campaign=4e69c97fdf-ThursNL_01_18_2018&utm_medium=email&utm_term=0_9dc0513989-4e69c97fdf-87833113
31. Finding My Virginity (2017), Richard Branson, p 340. More on this chapter in Virgin Galactic's story in Chapter 5.
32. www.thesmokinggun.com/documents/crime/amazons-jeff-bezos-helicopter-crash
33. spacenews.com/xcor-aerospace-files-for-bankruptcy/
34. www.bloomberg.com/news/articles/2017-12-06/nissan-plans-to-introduce-fully-autonomous-driving-cars-in-2022
35. dubaiofw.com/dubai-flying-taxis-2020/
36. www.airbus.com/newsroom/press-releases/en/2017/11/airbus–rolls-royce–and-siemens-team-up-for-electric-future-par.html
37. www.emiratesmarsmission.ae
38. www.theguardian.com/business/2017/sep/27/easyjet-electric-planes-wright-electric-flights
39. www.ft.com/content/d117c978-31c8-11e8-b5bf-23cb17fd1498
40. lunar.xprize.org/news/blog/important-update-google-lunar-xprize
41. en.wikipedia.org/wiki/Breakthrough_Starshot

Chapter 4 – Think Galactic, Act Galactic

1. www.wsj.com/articles/if-we-can-put-a-man-on-the-moon-why-cant-we-put-a-man-on-the-moon-1514833480
2. www.washingtonpost.com/archive/business/1989/07/22/pan-am-still-plans-moon-flight-and-93000-are-on-waiting-list/3a14e8c7-e2f8-4e23-870e-e40ff850e0f9/?noredirect=on&utm_term=.9b8bd17550df
3. One off their remarkable last ones was on 15 February 2017, when ISRO launched an unprecedented 104 satellites in a single rocket.
www.isro.gov.in/pslv-c37-successfully-launches-104-satellites-single-flight
4. www.ft.com/content/fc1467b8-c601-11e7-b2bb-322b2cb39656

Notes

5. www.cnbc.com/2018/06/19/walgreens-replacing-ge-on-the-dow.html
6. www.nytimes.com/2017/11/10/business/alibaba-singles-day.html
7. amp-businessinsider-com.cdn.ampproject.org/c/s/amp.businessinsider.com/walmart-named-retailer-of-the-year-2017-12
8. Expert Market report, 2016
9. medium.com/@ankurjain2/silicon-valley-is-under-attack-heres-why-we-deserve-it-79b047ace230
10. www.youtube.com/watch?v=wK_hxXAYVzA
11. Jorge Paulo Lemann Says Era Of Disruption In Consumer Brands Caught 3G Capital By Surprise
12. www-forbes-com.cdn.ampproject.org/c/s/www.forbes.com/sites/kimberlywhitler/2018/04/26/why-unilever-general-mills-and-procter-and-gamble-arent-good-at-marketing-in-the-modern-economy/amp/
13. www.ft.com/content/194cd1c8-6583-11e8-a39d-4df188287fff
14. www.forbes.com/sites/quora/2017/04/21/what-is-jeff-bezos-day-1-philosophy/#2e86c1ff1052
15. www.ft.com/content/a2ad6d78-a43c-11e7-8d56-98a09be71849
16. www.ft.com/content/fc090e84-c9ff-11e7-ab18-7a9fb7d6163e
    https://business.linkedin.com/marketing-solutions/blog/content-marketing-thought-leaders/2016/marketing-book-worth-a-look--its-not-rocket-science--by-mary-spi
17. www.coca-colacompany.com/stories/coke-in-space-2
18. www.forbes.com/sites/taranurin/2017/11/21/beers-in-space-why-the-next-budweiser-you-drink-could-be-on-mars/#7c639255aaf7
19. www.indiegogo.com/projects/vostok-space-beer#/
20. www.washingtonpost.com/technology/2018/09/10/why-nasas-next-rockers-might-say-budweiser-side/?noredirect=on&utm_term=.6f259418952f
21. singularityhub.com/2017/07/02/forget-flying-cars-the-future-is-driving-drones/

Stage 2
Prepare for Launch: Basics Before You Fly

Chapter 5 – The Daedalus Paradox: why preparation matters
1. www.history.com/topics/challenger-disaster
2. www.history.com/topics/columbia-disaster
3. www.wired.co.uk/article/elon-musk-bfr-big-rocket-earth-mars-spacex
4. www.sbs.com.au/news/elon-musk-completes-south-australia-s-battery-ahead-of-100-day-deadline
5. The Icarus Paradox,, Danny Miller (1990)
6. We owe that radicalism to Charles Darwin, the illustrious English biologist and explorer best known for his On the Origin of Species (1859). You can appreciate his work best while admiring the stunning fauna and flora on the Galapagos islands. The core of his evolution theory is that it is all based on natural selection. In short: on survival of the fittest.
7. www.space.com/26204-chuck-yeager.html
8. http://www.redbullstratos.com/about-felix/pilot-training/.

Chapter 6 – Key marketing models the CEO/CFO should know
1. www.insidermonkey.com/blog/11-countries-that-consume-the-most-mayonnaise-349914/
2. sirkensingtons.com
3. Mid 2018, Miracle Whip is being refreshed by Vayner Media
   www.linkedin.com/company/miracle-whip?trk=public-post_share-update_update-text
4. archive.org/details/miraclesofmarket00levy
5. www.smartinsights.com/traffic-building-strategy/offer-and-message-development/aida-model/
6. https://slooowdown.wordpress.com/2016/04/07/how-brands-grow-what-marketers-dont-know-by-byron-sharp-summarised-by-paul-arnold-facilitator-trainer-and-strategic-planner/
7. Jobs to be done: Theory to Practice, Anthony Ulwick (1991)
8. www.digitaltrends.com/cars/care-by-volvo-subscription-program-explained/

Chapter 7 – The one finance model the CMO should know
1. For more color on the asymmetries in decision making in daily life, read Skin in the Game, Nassim Nicholas Taleb (2018)
2. www.omegawatches.com/planet-omega/space/
3. Along with Merton Miller, Markowitz and Sharpe were awarded the 1990 Nobel Prize in Economics for their contributions to financial economics and to theory of corporate finance
4. pages.stern.nyu.edu/~adamodar/

Chapter 8 – Models work, but buyer beware
1. www.eisenhower.me/eisenhower-matrix
2. www.bcg.com/en-us/publications/2014/growth-share-matrix-bcg-classics-revisited.aspx
3. www.ghemawat.com/globe-course/readings/195/Differences+and+the+CAGE+Distance+Framework
4. strategyzer.com/canvas/business-model-canvas
5. en.wikipedia.org/wiki/OGSM
6. Measure What Matters: OKRs: The Simple Idea that Drives 10x Growth (2017). John Doerr

7. www.bbc.com/sport/football/28102403
8. www.bbc.com/sport/football/44637063
9. www.vox.com/culture/2018/4/20/17261614/black-panther-box-office-records-gross-iron-man-thor-captain-america-avengers
10. The Grey Rhino: How to Recognize and Act on the Obvious Dangers We Ignore (2016), Michele Wucker
11. www.bloomberg.com/view/articles/2016-09-14/how-superforecasters-think-about-the-future
12. www.gjopen.com
13. Today, Kahneman is a Senior Scholar and Professor of Psychology and Public Affairs Emeritus at the Woodrow Wilson School of Public and International Affairs. He is also the Eugene Higgins Professor of Psychology Emeritus at Princeton University, and a fellow of the Center for Rationality at the Hebrew University in Jerusalem.
14. 5' shower challenge in hotels
15. www.ft.com/content/218afad2-c54b-11e7-a1d2-6786f39ef675
16. www.cnbc.com/2017/10/09/the-nobel-prize-winner-for-economics-had-the-perfect-response-to-the-win.html

Chapter 9 – From Marketing Dreams to Miracle$

1. fortune.com/2017/06/27/startup-advice-data-failure/
2. For more popular songs in this spirit, from Luis Armstrong to Myra, surf to https://www.thoughtco.com/popular-songs-about-miracles-124504. Sing along and dream away.
3. The Space Barons; Christian Davenport (2018)
4. www.ft.com/cms/s/0/b7a58650-ab2d-11e2-8c63-00144feabdc0.html
5. www.andreabalt.com/leonardo-davinci-coverletter/
6. www.forbes.com/sites/trevornace/2018/03/27/flat-earth-rocket-man-finally-blasts-off-in-homemade-rocket-to-prove-earth-is-flat/#1649b0aa9b6f
7. darksky.org

– Certification: Congrats, business marketing wings

1. Around 2005 at Coke, I helped set up Coca-Cola University, to teach the new Coke Way of Marketing (DNA) to thousands of marketers each year. I had limited experience as an educator at the time. I discovered Kolb's model while doing the AACSB Bridge program, which was specifically designed to help people with a business background to move to academia. https://www.aacsb.edu/events/bridgeprogram

Stage 3
Lift-off: Successful Marketing In The Galactic Age

Chapter 10 – A new galactic marketing model

1. www.litcharts.com/lit/the-little-prince/symbols/stars

– Marketing is not rocket science

1. For inspiring aviation quotes capturing the magic and wonder of flight, surf to skygod.com
2. For any fans of rockets, take this masterclass of Astronaut and former ISS Commander Chris Hadfield www.masterclass.com/classes/chris-hadfield-teaches-space-exploration
3. blogs.oracle.com/marketingcloud/marketing-rocket-science www.bandt.com.au/marketing/marketers-warned-internet-things-will-change-everything blog.hubspot.com/marketing/the-rocket-science-of-social-media-marketing
4. business.linkedin.com/marketing-solutions/blog/content-marketing-thought-leaders/2016/marketing-book-worth-a-look–its-not-rocket-science–by-mary-spi
5. Except this gentleman: Marketing Miracles (2012), Dan Kennedy.
6. We successfully fused insights from top restaurateurs like Danny Mayer with the brand building skills of Coke. Starting in 2003 on a boat, Soul Group now runs multiple unique restaurant properties right on the stunning European Bosphorus side of Istanbul.

Chapter 11 – Fundamental 1 (why) - Pricing Power

1. www.wsj.com/article_email/p-gs-price-cuts-ripple-through-consumer-products-1516724949-lMyQjAxMTI4MTIzMzMyMzM4Wj/
2. www.ft.com/content/c3ebb978-0052-11e8-9650-9c0ad2d7c5b5
3. organicbasics.com
4. www.businessinsider.com/-underwear-you-can-wear-for-weeks-without-washing-2018-5
5. www.usatoday.com/story/tech/news/2018/01/19/amazon-raises-monthly-prime-rate-annual-rate-stays-99/1046646001/
6. www.usatoday.com/story/tech/talkingtech/2017/10/05/netflix-raising-price-its-most-popular-plan/734837001/
7. www.usatoday.com/story/tech/news/2017/01/18/netflix-shares-up-q4-subscriber-additions/96710172/
8. www.cnbc.com/2018/06/13/goldman-sachs-raises-its-netflix-price-target-by-100-to-street-high.html
9. www.reuters.com/article/us-apple-stock-trillion-race/apple-is-almost-a-1-trillion-company-but-watch-out-for-amazon-idUSKBN1IC257
10. www.wsj.com/article_email/how-apples-pricey-new-iphone-x-tests-economic-theory-1505660400-lMyQjAxMTE3OTE0ODcxNDgzWj/
11. www.artnews.com/2017/12/06/leonardo-da-vincis-salvator-mundi-coming-louvre-abu-dhabi/
12. www.soccernews.com/soccer-transfers/
13. www.soccerex.com/insight/articles/2017/manchester-city-pack-most-financial-punch-on-planet

Notes

14. www.ft.com/content/7e47b3fa-802b-11e8-bc55-50daf11b720d
15. www.wsj.com/article_email/why-streetwear-brand-supreme-is-worth-1-billion-and-abercrombie-isnt-1508331601-lMyQjAxMTA3MjEwO-DlxOTgyWj/
16. www.6sqft.com/crown-building-penthouse-may-be-in-contract-for-180m-beating-nyc-record-by-80m/
17. screenrant.com/avengers-infinity-war-records/
18. www.vinexpo-newsroom.com/alejandro-santo-domingo-bought-20-of-petrus/
19. www.ft.com/content/cde6163c-7f4a-11e2-97f6-00144feabdc0
20. www.businessinsider.com/impact-of-teachers-on-lifetime-earnings-2013-9
21. http://www.rajchetty.com/chettyfiles/taxsalience_nberwp_15246.pdf
22. solutions.mckinsey.com/periscope/

Chapter 12 – Fundamental 2 (why) - Purpose

1. www.ft.com/content/8a8bb9a0-0613-11e8-9650-9c0ad2d7c5b5
2. hbr.org/2011/01/the-big-idea-creating-shared-value
3. hbr.org/2014/07/the-ultimate-marketing-machine
4. consulting.kantar.com/wp-content/uploads/2018/07/Real-Initiative-for-Growth-Purpose-2020.pdf
5. www.jimstengel.com/grow/overview/
6. www.sustainablebrands.com/news_and_views/walking_talk/libby_maccarthy/practicing_purpose_how_turn_social_purpose_growth
7. www.adweek.com/brand-marketing/infographic-what-consumers-expect-of-brands-when-it-comes-to-issues-they-care-about/?utm_source=AMA+New+York&utm_campaign=8577291f55-EMAIL_CAMPAIGN_2018_04_18&utm_medium=email&utm_term=0_10dd4dd87a-8577291f55-61108237&mc_cid=8577291f55&mc_eid=becc2b12be
8. www.reuters.com/article/us-nike-kaepernick/nikes-kaepernick-ad-spurs-spike-in-sold-out-items-idUSKCN1LZ2G4
9. www.wsj.com/article_email/outfoxed-by-small-batch-upstarts-unilever-decides-to-imitate-them-1514910342-lMyQjAxMTI4NTAwMjEwNTIx-Wj/
10. http://www.ab-inbev.com/news/company/faq/what-is-ab-inbevs-dream.html
11. www.ab-inbev.com/news/our-stories/better-world/king-of-beers-reveals-renewable-electricity-symbol.html
12. www.fastcompany.com/3069080/how-loreal-is-turning-itself-into-a-sustainability-leader
13. Comments made at a Trium Alumni presentation at NYU STern on July 22, 2018.
14. www.nytimes.com/2018/01/15/business/dealbook/blackrock-laurence-fink-letter.html
15. www.blackrock.com/corporate/en-us/investor-relations/larry-fink-ceo-letter
16. www.bloomberg.com/news/articles/2017-10-03/tpg-seals-record-2-billion-for-rise-impact-fund-co-led-by-bono
17. cbey.yale.edu/node/3441
18. www.timewellspent.io
19. www.ft.com/content/a4a0d8d0-f3fc-11e7-8715-e94187b3017e
    www.wsj.com/article_email/what-if-children-should-be-spending-more-time-with-screens-1516539618-lMyQjAxMTE4MDIwMTkyMjE4Wj/
20. www.drinksbulletin.com.au/
21. Ikigai : the Japanese Secret to a Long and Happy Life; Hector Garcia (2017)

– Balancing Sin & Soul

1. Homo – Deus, Yuval Noah Harari (2018), p 382.
2. www.marketplace.org/2018/04/12/business/facebook-fallout/woman-going-after-worlds-biggest-tech-companies
3. www.cowen.com/reports/cannabis-75b-opportunity-category-cross-currents-keep-us-cautious-on-booze/
4. www.thecannabist.co/2018/01/08/pew-poll-marijuana-adults/96217/
5. eu.usatoday.com/story/tech/news/2017/11/15/zuckerberg-surprised-extent-opioid-problem-but-facebook-full-illegal-opioid-ads/865879001/
6. money.cnn.com/2018/06/07/news/economy/canada-marijuana-legalization-pot/index.html
7. www.who.int/substance_abuse/publications/cannabis_report/en/
8. www.theguardian.com/environment/2017/nov/18/uk-considers-tax-on-single-use-plastics-to-tackle-ocean-pollution
9. business.financialpost.com/commodities/agriculture/constellation-brands-to-acquire-9-9-per-cent-stake-in-canopy-growth-for-245m
10. www.cnbc.com/video/2018/08/15/constellation-makes-new-4-billion-bet-on-cannabis-industry.html
11. seekingalpha.com/article/4207395-coca-cola-cannabis-expansion-means-coke
12. www.cnbc.com/2018/09/20/this-chart-shows-whats-really-behind-the-crazy-rally-in-pot-stock-tilray.html
13. www.bloomberg.com/news/articles/2017-11-13/budweiser-s-ex-marketing-chief-sees-weed-as-the-new-craft-beer
14. www.wetoast.com
15. www.forbes.com/sites/johnmccarthy12/2018/06/13/how-toast-aims-to-build-the-moet-hennessy-of-cannabis-colorado-edition/#44d-3c55f3fd2
16. www.greenrush.com

Chapter 13 – Fundamental 3 (what) – Brand Health

1. uk.businessinsider.com/silicon-valley-insiders-tell-bbc-how-tech-firms-turn-users-into-addicts-2018-7?r=US&IR=T

Chapter 14 – Fundamental 4 (what) – Value Proposition

1. www.wsj.com/article_email/things-go-better-with-coke-laxative-edition-1515354223-lMyQjAxMTI4NzA4NzUwNDcxWj/

2. www.ft.com/content/ef2be1bc-809f-11e8-bc55-50daf11b720d
3. www.independent.co.uk/news/business/news/is-spotify-worth-more-than-the-entire-music-industry-10195439.html]
4. fortune.com/2017/09/28/spotify-ipo-valuation/

Chapter 15 – Fundamental 5 (who) - Brand Business Leaders

1. www.spencerstuart.com/research-and-insight/the-anatomy-of-a-disruptor?utm_source=Elevate&utm_medium=social&_lrsc=a71dbc9f-72e9-4406-a5c9-31650d2d4ed0
2. www.cnbc.com/2018/08/07/tesla-says-no-final-decision-has-been-made-to-take-company-private.html
3. www.ted.com/talks/angela_lee_duckworth_grit_the_power_of_passion_and_perseverance?language=en
4. www.forbes.com/forbes/welcome/?toURL=https://www.forbes.com/sites/startswithabang/2015/12/15/the-astronaut-hopefuls-manifes-to-an-insiders-guide-to-nasa-astronaut-selection/&refURL=https://www.google.com/&referrer=https://www.google.com/
5. The Space Barons; Christopher Davenport (2018)
6. navyseals.com/3877/sealfit-slow-smooth-smooth-fast/
7. Lifehacker.com/5480477/the-man-behind-macgyver-swiss-army-knife-or-duct-tape
8. streetsmartbrazil.com/brazilian-culture-got-ginga/
9. en.wikipedia.org/wiki/Zero-based_budgeting
10. educationtechnologysolutions.com.au/2016/06/impact-of-a-in-steam/

– Let Earth go

1. www.princealberfund.org
2. news.delta.com/runways-campaign-celebrates-how-good-things-come-those-who-go
3. usat.ly/2hPTVpH

Chapter 16 – Fundamental 6 (how) - The Power Toolbox

1. The biggest strategic challenges faced by CMOs; OC&C; Campaign March 27, 2017
2. www.briansolis.com/2013/06/disruptive-selection-natures-way-of-weeding-out-the-average-business/
3. www.bloomberg.com/news/articles/2018-08-20/gen-z-to-outnumber-millennials-within-a-year-demographic-trends
4. Verlinvest CEO conference, Brussels, November 2017
5. Verlinvest CEO conference, Brussels, November 2017
6. www.wsj.com/article_email/data-revolution-upends-madison-avenue-1516383643-lMyQjAxMTA4MjExOTExNTk4Wj/
7. www.ft.com/cms/s/0/9ecf5a64-d8cf-11e2-a6cf-00144feab7de.html
8. www.gartner.com/smarterwithgartner/top-trends-in-the-gartner-hype-cycle-for-emerging-technologies-2017/
9. Silicon Snake Oil: second thoughts on the information highway, Clifford Stoll (1996)
10. www.nytimes.com/interactive/2018/01/27/technology/social-media-bots.html
11. www.thedrum.com/news/2018/09/24/wfa-chief-stephan-loerke-brand-safety-gdpr-and-what-makes-top-marketer-today
12. medium.com/@obtaineudaimonia/the-medium-is-the-message-by-marshall-mcluhan-8b5d0a9d426b
13. en.wikipedia.org/wiki/Law_of_the_instrument
14. www.fastcodesign.com/90151390/this-detroit-furniture-startup-wants-to-dethrone-ikea

Chapter 17 – Fundamental 7 (how) - Insights

1. thefrenchmuse.com/how-to-find-truffles-in-provence-an-insiders-guide/
2. How to think like Leonardo Da Vinci, Michael J. Gelb (1998)
3. www.eepybird.com/featured-video/coke-and-mentos-featured-video/science-of-coke-mentos/
4. www.grc.nasa.gov/www/k-12/TRC/Rockets/history_of_rockets.html
5. www.space.com/19994-konstantin-tsiolkovsky.html
6. www.space.com/19944-robert-goddard.html
7. allthatsinteresting.com/wernher-von-braun
8. arstechnica.com/science/2017/02/nasas-longshot-bet-on-a-revolutionary-rocket-may-be-about-to-pay-off/

Chapter 18 – Fundamental 8 (how)- Excellence

1. Frost & Sullivan, Journal of European Business, ISO 9000 series: New Standards to keep the Quality Edge, Chris Burggraeve, May 1990
2. The Start-up of You: Adapt to the Future, Invest in Yourself, and Transform your Career, Reid Hoffman (2012)
3. www.wfanet.org/news-centre/a-b-inbev-cmo-on-global-marketing/

Chapter 19 – No shortcuts to marketing miracle$

1. If you want to start to understand how 3G thinks, read Christiane Correa's Dream Big: How the Brazilian Trio behind 3G Capital - Jorge Paulo Lemann, Marcel Telles and Beto Sicupira - acquired Anheuser-Busch, Burger King and Heinz (2013)
2. This entire group all became CMO or CEO of top companies afterwards (Samsung, Senior Living, MetLife and Uber)
3. Dethroning the King: The Hostile Takeover of Anheuser-Busch, an American Icon (2010), Julie Macintosh
4. Your successors now have assets they can/must leverage. I inherited the rights to activate South Africa (2010) and Brazil (2014). We optimized and leveraged those deals substantially - based on my deep prior Coke experience with global assets. I then convinced the CEO and the board it made strategic sense to extend the deal (which turned out to be Russia and Qatar).

Notes

Stage 4
Escape Velocity: Successful investing in a galactic age

Chapter 20 – Beyond financial ratings
1. www.capgemini.com/news/capgeminis-world-wealth-report-2018-global-high-net-worth-individual-wealth-surpasses-us70-trillion-for-the-first-time/
2. www.accountingtools.com/articles/the-altman-z-score-formula.html
3. www.wsj.com/articles/stuck-with-an-uber-rating-under-four-better-hit-the-bricks-1536141080
4. www.reputationinstitute.com
5. www.imd.org/wcc/world-competitiveness-center-rankings/world-competitiveness-ranking-2018/
6. www.ft.com/content/f4cfde28-7bab-11e8-bc55-50daf11b720d
7. amp-businessinsider-com.cdn.ampproject.org/c/s/amp.businessinsider.com/goldman-sachs-etf-paul-tudor-jones-just-capital-2018-6
8. www.netpromotersystem.com/about/measuring-your-net-promoter-score.aspx
9. uk.businessinsider.com/commerzbank-ai-artificial-intelligence-research-reports-2018-6?r=US&IR=T
10. www.bloomberg.com/professional/solution/bloomberg-terminal/

– Rating models: buyer beware
1. www.ft.com/cms/s/0/9fcd5f10-9635-11e2-9ab2-00144feabdc0.html
2. www.ft.com/cms/s/0/118ddd14-7db3-11e2-aff5-00144feabdc0.html
3. www.ft.com/cms/s/3/b9bee224-720c-11e2-896a-00144feab49a.html
4. en.wikipedia.org/wiki/Credit_rating_agencies_and_the_subprime_crisis
5. on.ft.com/182U0tO
6. Heski et all, Information-Gathering Externalities for a Multi-Attribute Good, Journal of Economics, 2012
7. www.wsj.com/article_email/many-fund-ads-misrepresent-morningstar-ratings-1510958391-lMyQjAxMTE3NjIzMzQyNDM4Wj/
8. "NYU Stern Magazine Nov 2012 - "The "Best" Lists: Not all that good - why rating schools and hospitals may hurt consumers in the long run" pp. 25-26
9. goodbeerhunting.com/sightlines/2017/6/2/ratebeer-zx-ventures-acquisition-minority-stake-anheuser-busch-inbev
10. www.ft.com/content/05df5746-7e56-11e8-8e67-1e1a0846c475
11. www.wired.co.uk/article/chinese-government-social-credit-score-privacy-invasion

Chapter 21 – A new galactic marketing rating
1. www.valueacceleration.com/bonuschapter.pdf

Chapter 22 – The new Alpha M Audit for CEOs
1. www.forbes.com/sites/brucerogers/2017/11/17/six-questions-every-ceo-needs-to-ask-their-cmo/#38fb5d8e6900
2. Marketing Accountability: A CEO Blueprint for Driving Enterprise Values

Chapter 23 – Where the galactic money will go
1. www.gatesnotes.com/Books/Factfulness
2. Homo Deus, Yuval Noah Harari (2018).
3. www.bloomberg.com/news/articles/2018-06-07/amazon-makes-u-k-soccer-foray-in-premier-league-streaming-push
4. www.softbank.jp/en/
5. www.ft.com/content/3a9acf48-3dc3-11e8-b7e0-52972418fec4
6. www.bloomberg.com/news/articles/2017-12-26/china-to-overtake-u-s-economy-by-2032-as-asian-might-builds
7. www.nytimes.com/2017/01/04/world/asia/china-soccer-xi-jinping.html
8. www.soccernomics-agency.com/?p=995

Epilogue: Marketing in the Cyborg Age
1. www.visualcapitalist.com/economic-impact-artificial-intelligence-ai/
2. qz.com/1264673/ai-is-the-new-space-race-heres-what-the-biggest-countries-are-doing/
3. www.iftf.org/home/
4. www.businessinsider.com/10-skills-employers-will-want-the-most-in-2020-2018-1
5. qz.com/1094638/google-goog-built-earbuds-that-translate-40-languages-in-real-time-like-the-hitchhikers-guides-babel-fish/
6. www.facebook.com/worldeconomicforum/videos/10155081394521479/
7. bigthink.com/endless-innovation/why-ray-kurzweils-predictions-are-right-86-of-the-time
8. futurism-com.cdn.ampproject.org/c/s/futurism.com/market-humanoid-robots-grow-ten-times-2023/amp/
9. LSE Connect autumn 17, Rise of the Machines, pp10-11
10. www.ias.edu
11. www.ias.edu/scholars/goddard
    www.math.ias.edu/avi/home
    www.sns.ias.edu/dyson
12. www.math.ias.edu/avi/book
13. en.wikipedia.org/wiki/P_versus_NP_problem

About the Author

Astronaut training for Virgin Galactic: testing zero gravity flight – May 3, 2014

Chris R. Burggraeve is a passionate and award winning global business marketer turned investor, entrepreneur, advisor, board member and adjunct faculty. Chris has nearly 30 years of deep *Sin & Soul* expertise merging brand management, societal context, and P&L's across the following 5 areas:

- **Corporate marketing:** CMO Anheuser-Busch InBev (07-12), Group Marketing Director Europe for The Coca-Cola Company (95-07), Brand Management at P&G (90-95); Prince Albert Fund Laureate (89-90); Tech scale up (88-89).

- **Entrepreneurship and board governance:** Created a select global portfolio of disruptive yet responsible micro ventures. Investing and advisory/board roles. Noteworthy exits to date: Sir Kensington's, sold to Unilever (4/17), and FlashStock, sold to Shutterstock (7/17). He is one of the first classic global CPG leaders to have actively recognized the importance and potential of the cannabis industry. He co-founded Toast Holdings (2016) and became an early investor/advisor in, and now chairman of, greenrush.com. He is an active speaker and evangelist on the creation of a sustainable cannabis eco-system: one that balances societal responsibility with capitalism and enjoyment.

- **Marketing capability and strategy advisory:** Vicomte LLC - *Creating Renaissance Brands™*. Since end 2012, serving corporates, new tech and non tech ventures, private equity, and family funds (like Verlinvest, owned by AB InBev families, operating advisor 12-)

- **Teaching and keynotes:** Since 2012, adjunct faculty and executive-in-residence at NYU Stern (TRIUM Global EMBA; MS of Business Analytics); Regular speaker at companies and other top universities worldwide;

- **Non profits and industry association leadership:** Executive committee member and president of the Brussels based World Federation of Advertisers (08-13); Board member and president of the NYC based Belgian-American Chamber of Commerce (10-18); Advisor in Economic Diplomacy for Belgium (13-). Chairman of the Prince Albert Fund, part of Belgium's largest foundation (the King Baudouin Foundation, 14-)

A multilingual Belgian-American based in NYC, he constantly strives for the elusive balance between endurance sports and the joys of pure gastronomy. A consumer scientist with a passion for space, he can't wait *to get up there*, having secured his Virgin Galactic suborbital flight ticket back in 2011. He may become the first CMO in the world getting his basic astronaut wings.

For more details and free model downloads:
vicomte.com/galactic

About the Designer

Christian Loos is a passtionate, awarded designer. After studying Graphic Design at Ensav La-Cambre in Brussels, he started his career as an art director for advertising firms such as Ogilvy, Duval Guillaume and Happiness Brussels. In 2008, he was awarded Best Belgian Art Director. Other advertising awards include NY Festivals, Eurobest and several Lions at Cannes' International Festival of Creativity. In 2014, his work ranked among the *World's Twenty Most Genius Print Ads Ever* by the leading Italian newspaper *La Repubblica*.

In 2014, Christian moved to New York City where, after four years with TBWA/Chiat Day NY, he founded his very own branding studio: KitchenNY. Kitchen creates a brand's unique fingerprint, as the starting point for all brand challenges, from packaging to strategy, identity and communication. His work keeps getting recognized. In 2016, he won the Best Packaging Award at NAMTA.

Christian admires how the best kitchens and chefs operate. He can see the big difference between cooking for the sake of eating, versus cooking as the art of creating an unforgettable meal. The exact same goes for crafting a truly memorable brand identity. Memorable brand cuisine is impossible to attain without adding ingredients like passion, intuition, craftsmanship, integrity and commitment. The work in Kitchen NY typically follows 6 stages:

1-Analyze   2-Simplify   3-Create   4-Taste   5-Refine   6-Deliver

The six-step process was applied to find the fitting visual language for Chris Burggraeve's gravity-defying book on marketing fundamentals. Continuous iteration between Christian and Chris resulted in a unique design fingerprint reflective of the galactic mindset the author intended to evoke.

The book's cover isn't defining the future, as much as contemplating it. Part mysterious, part threat, part inspiration. Who is this astronaut?

The MC-Rocket© rocket-shaped structure brings Burggraeve's 8 fundamental drivers of world-class marketing alive in a (galactic) visually consistent and memorable way.

Each element in the book and model design added its own flavor. Together, all elements work together in harmony, like the multiple cross-fertilizing tastes in an excellent recipe. They are also in sync with the Visual Brand Identity of Chris' company Vicomte LLC (which Christian helped refresh before).

KitchenNY and Vicomte LLC have worked together on a number of projects. The last one was the complete redesign of the newly created Singapore-based A-Star Education Holding and its many global sub-brands. And they are just getting started…

Christian Loos and Chris Burggraeve at the 2018 Belcham Gala at Guastavino's.
(Belcham's redesign of its Brand Identity being their first collaboration ever).

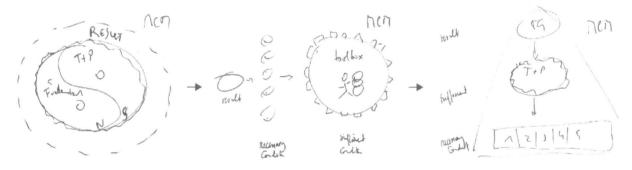

Examples 1: *Various concepts showing fundamentals versus tools versus results*

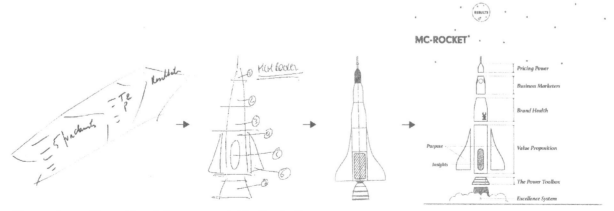

Examples 2: *From Final Concept to MC–Rocket©*

Index

Index

CPSIA information can be obtained
at www.ICGtesting.com
Printed in the USA
LVHW070715090922
727943LV00008B/95